THE PAPER WALL

Ian Kenneally, from County Limerick, studied history at University College Cork. He has completed his MPhil in History and is currently self-employed. *The Paper Wall* is his first book.

THE PAPER WALL

Newspapers and Propaganda
in Ireland 1919–1921

IAN KENNEALLY

The Collins Press

First published 2008 by
The Collins Press,
West Link Park,
Doughcloyne,
Wilton,
Cork

British Library Cataloguing in Publication Data

Kenneally, Ian
    The paper wall : newspapers and propaganda in
    Ireland 1919-1921
    1. Newspapers - Ireland - History - 20th century
    2. Ireland - History - War of Independence, 1919-
    1921 - Mass media and the war 3. Ireland History - War
    of Independence, 1919-1921 Propaganda
    I. Title
    941.5'0821

ISBN-13: 9781905172580

Typesetting: The Collins Press
Font: Bembo
Printed by ScandBook AB, Sweden

For My Parents

Contents

Acknowledgements

I would like to take this opportunity to express my appreciation to all of the many people who helped in the writing and research of this book. Firstly, I would like to thank the people at The Collins Press and my editors Paula Elmore and Winifred Power, whose advice greatly improved the book. This book is based to a large extent on a thesis I completed for the History Department in University College Cork and I would like to thank the staff of the Department, especially Gabriel Doherty who acted as the supervisor for that thesis. A debt of gratitude is owed by me to staff in many archives and libraries. Special mention must be given to the staff in the Special Collections of the Boole Library in UCC where so much of the research for this book was undertaken. They were helpful and efficient at all times. I would also like to thank the staff of the Military Archives in Cathal Brugha Barracks, the National Library of Ireland, the National Archives of Ireland, Cork City Public Library and Archives, Cork County Public Library, University College Dublin Archives, Trinity College Dublin Archives as well as Goldsmiths College Library and the National Archives in the United Kingdom.

I would like to thank my parents, Joe and Mary, for all their love and support. The same goes to my brother and sister, Enda and Aoife, although it must be said that they are very lucky to have such a wonderful brother. My Grandmother and my family in Cork, Billy, Mary and Seán also receive my heartfelt gratitude for their unceasing care through my college years. Speaking of my college years, Mick Lennon, Paul Meskell, Ger Naughton, Kieran Leonard, Gavan Boyle and Brendan Mullan – all of whom I shared a house with – deserve a mention. Sincere thanks are also offered to my partner's family, especially Ignatius and Laura.

Finally, I would like to thank Fiona, whose love lights my life.

Notes on the Text

The terms 'Nationalist' and 'Unionist' beginning with capital letters refer to the two political parties while the lower case 'nationalists' and 'unionists' refer to the two communities or traditions. Irish names and institutions such as Sinn Féin and Dáil Éireann are spelt with the fada or accent except when they are cited in direct quotations by sources that did not use the fada. For example, many newspapers used the spelling 'Sinn Fein' without the fada.

Abbreviations

CS	Chief Secretary
DMP	Dublin Metropolitan Police
DORA	Defence of the Realm Act
GHQ	General Headquarters
GOC	General Officer Commanding
IPP	Irish Parliamentary Party
IRA	Irish Republican Army
ITGWU	Irish Transport and General Workers' Union
MLA	Martial Law Area
O/C	Officer Commanding
PIB	Public Information Branch
PR	Proportional Representation
RIC	Royal Irish Constabulary
ROIA	Restoration of Order in Ireland Act

Chronology of Events

1919

21 January:	Dáil Éireann opened. Soloheadbeg Ambush: Two RIC men killed.
24 January:	Irish Unionist Alliance splits. Unionist Anti-Partition League formed.
31 January:	*An t-Óglach* states Volunteers are entitled 'morally and legally to slay British police and soldiers'.
03 February:	De Valera escapes from Lincoln prison.
22 February:	Irish Race Convention meets and drafts a resolution calling on President Wilson to give his support to Ireland's claims for international recognition.
02 March:	Irish bishops criticise the 'drastic military law' in Ireland.
04 March:	US House of Representatives and Senate pass motions that the Versailles Peace Conference should favourably consider Ireland's claims to self-determination.
26 March:	Planned march by de Valera prohibited by General Shaw, CinC Ireland, under DORA regulations.
01 April:	Second session of Dáil Éireann: Ministers elected with de Valera as President.
04 April:	Beginning of Dáil Loan to raise funds for the new Dáil.
08 April:	De Valera re-elected as President of Sinn Féin.
14 April:	Limerick 'Soviet' begins in protest against Martial Law.
29 April:	Bryan Cooper succeeds Lord Decies as the Irish press censor.
11 June:	President Wilson divulges that there is a British veto on discussion of Ireland's claim to nationhood. De Valera leaves Ireland for New York.

18 June:	Dáil Éireann establishes arbitration courts to deal with land disputes.
19 June:	Dáil approves National Loan prospectus.
22 June:	Statement of Ireland's claim to independence given to M. Clemenceau, President of the Peace Conference.
23 June:	De Valera tells a press conference that he is in the USA 'as the official head of the Republic established by the will of the Irish people'.
25 June:	William Martin Murphy dies aged 75. He was the owner of Independent Newspapers.
28 June:	*The Times* begins a special series of articles dealing with the Irish question.
02 July:	Dr William Lombard Murphy, son of W.M. Murphy, becomes chairman of Independent Newspapers.
12 July:	Edward Carson calls for a repeal of the Home Rule Act.
16 July:	Attorney General announces that Edward Carson will not be prosecuted for his threat to mobilise the Ulster Volunteers.
21 July:	During the second reading of the Peace Treaty Bill, Lloyd George tells Parliament that self-determination is not for Ireland.
24 July:	*The Times* proposes two state legislatures for Ireland under an all-Ireland parliament.
30 July:	G. Division detective Patrick Smith shot dead by IRA in Dublin.
20 August:	Dáil Éireann passes Cathal Brugha's motion that the Irish Volunteers swear allegiance to the Dáil and the Irish Republic. They thereby become the IRA.
30 August:	Censorship of newspapers ends.
07 September:	Liam Lynch's North Cork Brigade attack military personnel near Fermoy and kill one soldier. British soldiers wreck town during the first reprisal of the War of Independence.
12 September:	Dáil Éireann suppressed for being a dangerous organisation. G. Division detective Daniel Hoey shot dead outside police headquarters.
17 September:	*Cork Examiner* and allied newspapers suppressed for carrying a prospectus for the Dáil Loan. Liquidator appointed to *Freeman's Journal*.

20 September:	All republican newspapers suppressed. Suppression of *Cork Examiner* ends.
07 October:	Cabinet committee formed to consider Irish Government.
12 October:	Curfew law revived with application to Ireland only.
15 October:	Sinn Féin and IRA outlawed by proclamation. Cabinet Committee on Ireland holds its first meeting in private session.
25 October:	Piaras Béaslaí and Austin Stack are among a group of six prisoners to escape from Lincoln Jail.
11 November:	Publication of the first issue of the *Irish Bulletin*. Dáil headquarters raided by Crown forces.
15 November:	Over 10,000 people assemble in the Albert Hall in London in support of Irish self-determination.
26 November:	Sinn Féin, Gaelic League, Cumann na mBan and the Volunteers are suppressed throughout whole country.
09 December:	Sinn Féin headquarters at No. 6 Harcourt Street permanently closed under DORA regulations.
12 December:	Massive raids by military and police in Dublin
15 December:	The *Freeman's Journal* is suppressed by military authorities for criticising the police.
16 December:	Owners of *Freeman's Journal* replace the paper with an 'early morning edition' of its sister paper, the *Evening Telegraph*.
18 December:	Winston Churchill tells the House of Commons that there are 43,000 troops in Ireland.
19 December:	An IRA attempt on the life of the Lord Lieutenant, French, narrowly fails.
21 December:	IRA raid the offices of the *Irish Independent* in retaliation for that paper's reporting of the recent attack against the Lord Lieutenant

1920

03 January:	Recruitment to the RIC under General H.H.Tudor begins. These recruits become the 'Black and Tans'.
08 January:	General Sir Joseph Byrne resigns as head of the RIC.
15 January:	Using PR for the first time, local government

	elections give Sinn Féin, other nationalists and Labour control of 172 out of 206 boroughs and urban district councils.
21 January:	Assistant Commissioner of the DMP, William Redmond, shot dead by the IRA.
27 January:	Bishops condemn the military rule in Ireland.
28 January:	*Freeman's Journal* begins publishing again.
11 February:	Arthur Griffith addresses a mass meeting in London in support of Home Rule.
14 February:	IRA units commanded by Ernie O'Malley capture RIC barracks in Ballytrain, Co. Monaghan.
23 February:	Curfew from midnight to 5am becomes effective in Dublin Metropolitan District.
25 February:	Text of Government of Ireland Bill introduced into House of Commons.
19 March:	Tomás MacCurtain, Sinn Féin Lord Mayor of Cork, shot dead at his home by members of the RIC.
25 March:	First 'Black and Tans' arrive in Ireland.
26 March:	Magistrate Alan Bell shot dead by IRA in Dublin. He had been investigating funding of the republican movement.
April:	Nevil Macready arrives as GOC of British army in Ireland in mid-April.
03 April:	Around 100 RIC barracks destroyed by the IRA.
05 April:	IRA hunger strikers begin a mass hunger strike in Mountjoy Jail.
12 April:	Sir Hamar Greenwood appointed Chief Secretary of Ireland.
14 April:	Hunger strike ends with freeing of prisoners.
28 April:	Black and Tan reprisal in Limerick city for attack on Ballylanders barracks.
May:	John Anderson arrives as Under Secretary for Ireland heralding a mass change in the higher levels of Dublin Castle administrative staff.
10 May:	Three police officers shot dead near Timoleague, County Cork. Government of Ireland Bill enters the Committee stage.
12 May:	Over 50 RIC barracks destroyed by the IRA. Many tax offices also destroyed.
19 May:	On the orders of the ITGWU workers refuse to

	unload military equipment from the vessel, the *Anna Dorette Boog*. This is the beginning of a bitter munitions strike.
28 May:	IRA attacks and destroys Kilmallock RIC barracks in County Limerick.
30 May:	Hamar Greenwood and General Macready leave for special Cabinet meeting on Ireland in Downing Street.
12 June:	PR elections to rural districts throughout Ireland result in extensive successes for Sinn Féin. In Ulster Sinn Féin gain control of 36 out of 55 rural district councils.
16 June:	RIC at Listowel 'mutiny' in protest at military activities.
19 June:	Beginning of intense rioting in Derry.
26 June:	IRA captures General Lucas near Fermoy. Rioting in Derry ends with around 30 dead.
28 June:	'B' and 'C' companies of the Connaught Ranger mutiny in the Punjab after receiving news from Ireland.
29 June:	Dáil assembles for the first time since October 1919.
12 July:	Carson warns that if Britain cannot protect unionists from Sinn Féin then 'we will reorganise'.
17 July:	DC Smyth from Listowel shot dead by IRA in Cork.
19 July:	Further sectarian violence in Derry.
21 July:	Rioting in Belfast.
22 July:	Violence in Derry ends with 19 dead.
27 July:	British army ex-officers formed into the Auxiliary Division of the RIC.
August:	Public Information Branch created with Basil Clarke as its head.
02 August:	Bill for the Restoration and Maintenance of Order in Ireland brought before the House of Commons.
06 August:	Dáil sanctions boycott of goods emanating from Belfast.
09 August:	Restoration of Order in Ireland Bill passed.
12 August:	Terence MacSwiney arrested in Cork.
13 August:	Dublin Castle begins issue of the *Weekly Summary*.
22 August:	DI Swanzy shot dead in Lisburn. He had been

implicated by the jury in the shooting of Tomás MacCurtain. This sparks off riots in Lisburn and Belfast directed against nationalists.

02 September: British Government concedes to Sir James Craig's demand for a force of full-time constabulary for the six-county State.

09 September: Secret military courts of inquiry replace coroner's inquests in ten counties.

20 September: Black and Tans cause massive damage in Balbriggan, Co. Dublin.

28 September: Military barracks in Mallow captured by IRA. Large-scale military reprisal in the town on the following day.

14 October: Seán Treacy killed on Talbot Street.

17 October: IRA hunger striker Michael Fitzgerald dies in Cork Jail.

20 October: Directors of *Freeman's Journal* summoned to appear before a military tribunal.

25 October: Terence MacSwiney dies after 74 days in Brixton Prison. Joseph Murphy dies in Cork Jail after 76 days.

01 November: Kevin Barry executed in Dublin. Ulster Constabulary enrolled: 'A', full-time, 'B', temporary, 'C', emergency reserves.

02 November: Ellen Quinn shot dead by Crown forces in Gort. Highly publicised in the press.

21 November: Bloody Sunday: IRA squad organised by Michael Collins kills 14 British officers. In retaliation Auxiliaries kill three of their prisoners in Dublin Castle. Twelve people killed in Croke Park by Crown forces.

24 November: Trial of *Freeman's Journal* opens in Dublin.

28 November: Cork No. 3 Brigade under Tom Barry wipes out a squad of Auxiliaries at Kilmichael.

29 November: *Freeman's Journal* offices attacked by Auxiliaries. Very badly damaged.

10 December: Proprietors of *Freeman's Journal* sentenced to six months in prison. Martial Law is proclaimed in Cork, Kerry, Limerick and Tipperary.

11 December: IRA ambush RIC near Victoria Barracks in Cork

	city. Later Auxiliaries and Black and Tans set fire to parts of the city destroying large sections of Patrick Street, City Hall and all of Winthrop Street.
12 December:	Bishop Cohalan of Cork issues a decree excommunicating all those engaged in 'ambush, murder and kidnapping'.
14 December:	Irish Trade Union Congress and Labour Party announce end of seven-month munitions strike.
15 December:	Canon Magner of Dunmanway and Timothy Crowley shot dead by an Auxiliary Officer.
23 December:	Government of Ireland Bill becomes law. The new Act for the Better Government of Ireland creates states of Northern Ireland and Southern Ireland. De Valera arrives secretly in Dublin from USA.
24 December:	Editor and owners of *Freeman's Journal* sentenced to twelve month's imprisonment. Offices of *Cork Examiner* attacked by IRA.
25 December:	Attempt made by Auxiliaries to burn the Commercial offices of the *Freeman's Journal*.
26 December:	Five people shot dead by RIC in Ballingarry, County Limerick.

1921

01 January:	Beginning of official reprisals. Destruction of seven houses by order of military in Midleton.
04 January:	Martial Law extended to Clare, Kilkenny, Waterford and Wexford.
06 January:	Directors and editor of *Freeman's Journal* released from Mountjoy Jail on 'medical grounds'.
01 February:	White Cross organisation founded by Sinn Féin to distribute US-raised White Cross funds.
03 February:	Eleven Black and Tans shot dead in ambush near Pallasgreen, County Limerick. Three Auxiliaries shot dead near Ballinalee and six seriously wounded.
04 February:	James Craig succeeds Edward Carson as leader of the Ulster Unionists.
14 February:	Frank Teeling escapes from Kilmainham Jail.
15 February:	Strickland Report into the burning of Cork suppressed.

19 February:	Brigadier General Frank Crozier resigns his command of the Auxiliaries after being unable to control the excesses of his command.
28 February:	Six IRA prisoners are executed in Cork. In retaliation the IRA shoot dead six British soldiers in the city.
07 March:	George Clancy, Mayor of Limerick, along with former Mayor Michael O' Callaghan and Joseph O' Donoghue shot dead by Crown forces. Unionist Anti-Partition League tries to bring Sinn Féin and British Government together to discuss a more broadly based settlement.
14 March:	Six IRA prisoners executed in Dublin.
17 March:	Bonar Law resigns from House of Commons due to ill health.
19 March:	Day of Crossbarry Ambush.
24 March:	*Freeman's Journal* reports 470 dead since 01 January 1921.
26 March:	Offices of *Irish Bulletin* raided by a party of Auxiliaries. Dublin Castle quickly begins the issue of false editions of the bulletin. *Irish Independent* reports massive capture of IRA arms in Dublin.
30 March:	De Valera tells an American correspondent that 'the Government is therefore responsible for the actions of this army (IRA)'. This is the first time the Dáil assumed responsibility for the actions of the IRA.
14 April:	Ex-Ulster King of Arms, Arthur Vicars, shot dead by the IRA as a spy in Listowel. His house is also burned. Death is highly publicised.
21 April:	Lord Derby has secret meeting with Eamon de Valera.
28 April:	Four IRA men executed by military in Cork.
29 April:	Party of Auxiliaries enters offices of *Freeman's Journal* and forces all the staff on to the street for searching.
02 May:	Viscount Fitzalan, first Catholic to hold the post of Lord Lieutenant since the reign of James II, is sworn in.
05 May:	Meeting between Craig and de Valera in Dublin.
08 May:	John Dillon says the National Party will not contest the Southern elections with Sinn Féin.
13 May:	Nominations close for general elections to

parliaments of Northern Ireland and Southern Ireland. There are 128 candidates nominated for 128 seats in Southern Ireland (124 Sinn Féin; 4 Dublin University) all of whom are deemed elected.

22 May: Pope Benedict XV in a letter to Cardinal Logue appeals for peace in Ireland. Calls on both English and Irish forces to 'treat of some terms of mutual agreement'.

23 May: *Cork Examiner* employee killed in Cork by an IRA bomb. The bomb had been thrown into a group of four employees while walking on a street.

24 May: General election to the parliament of Northern Ireland. Unionists win 40 seats, Sinn Féin, 6 and Nationalists, 6.

25 May: Custom House attacked and burned by the IRA. Great destruction of Government records.

30 May: *Irish Independent* reports 806 dead and 1,001 wounded since 01 January.

31 May: Seven soldiers killed and 21 wounded by a mine in Youghal. Three are band boys.

03 June: Seven RIC men killed in ambush near Westport.

07 June: Parliament of Northern Ireland meets and is attended by Unionists only. Two IRA men executed in Dublin.

22 June: George V makes a speech in Belfast calling for reconciliation between the communities. De Valera arrested in Blackrock but he is released a few hours later on the intervention of the Assistant Under Secretary, Cope.

24 June: IRA mine derails train between Newry and Dundalk. Four soldiers, three civilians and dozens of horses killed. Incident is highly publicised in Britain.

28 June: Parliament of Southern Ireland meets. Only 4 Dublin University MPs and 15 Senators attend.

30 June: Arthur Griffith released from prison after almost eight months. Part of a series of releases over this period.

04 July: Beginning of a series of meetings involving de Valera and Lord Midleton, a southern Unionist, who becomes an intermediary between Sinn Féin and

the British Government.

09 July: Truce signed between Dáil Éireann and the British Government. Serious rioting begins in Belfast after the publication of the terms of the truce.

11 July: Truce comes into effect. At least 16 people killed in the hours before the truce. *Irish Independent* gives a casualty list of 1,082 dead and 1,516 wounded from January to July 1921. 377 of the dead are members of Crown forces. The rest are civilians and members of the IRA. *Freeman's Journal* gives a death total of 1,086 and a list of wounded reaching 1,311.

INTRODUCTION

In the decades after the Irish War of Independence (1919–1921) many books on the period were published. These works usually followed a similar pattern, being mainly general narratives of the years between 1916 and 1923 or memoirs of the fighting men and women. Many of these books made for great reading but there remained a number of gaps in our knowledge of the time. Since the 1980s more specialised studies have made exciting progress in our understanding of these dramatic years. There have been works on specific counties, studies of the Dáil courts, the role of women, public opinion in Britain, the IRA and its volunteers, the role of trade unions and much more on politics, Sinn Féin, Unionism and the role of the British Government. As such, what we now know about the War of Independence has grown dramatically and many more paths of research have been opened by these studies. This book follows one of these – as yet largely unexplored – paths. It examines the relationship between the competing protagonists and the newspaper press during that time. The war is often referred to as a 'propaganda war' or a war 'in which newspaper ink was spilled more freely than blood' but very little has been written on the spilling of this ink. Yet at that time in Ireland daily newspapers sold a combined total of around 500,000 copies every day, in an era when the newspaper press was at its zenith and unhindered by competition from radio or television.

While newspapers are often used as a source for the period, practically nothing has been written about the producers of this source. Republican memoirs make passing comment on the bravery of the *Manchester Guardian* and other English papers in exposing the campaign of reprisals but the Irish newspapers are mentioned rarely. What little commentary exists on the republican side is nearly always critical of the Irish newspapers. Even the few scholarly works on the subject that have been written, such as D. George Boyce's superb *Englishmen and Irish Troubles*, concentrate on the English press. Many

1

works concentrate solely on propaganda and ascribe awesome powers of persuasion to either the Dáil or British propaganda departments, depending on taste. This book examines what attempts were made to control, influence or intimidate the press. Although propaganda is an important part of this story, it is only one part. The book also shows how the press in Ireland and England was not an impartial observer of events but a distiller of news and opinion of a certain bias. This bias may have been because of political, religious or financial reasons. I hope to explain the reasons why each paper followed the course that it did and what outside or hidden influences existed.

Historians have often been somewhat disdainful of newspapers as a historical source. After all, newspapers are merely 'the first draft of history', a draft that is irredeemably tainted by the bias and prejudices contained within their columns. Historians, on the other hand, are supposed to calmly and objectively sift away these biases to arrive at the truth. This condescension is not held by all historians, by any means, but it remains a palpable presence within the profession. While the press may be used as a source in historical work, frequently the creators of that source – the journalists – can be seen as mere hacks. As a source the newspapers are tainted but no more than any other tool that must be used in the reconstruction of the past. Even when they do not tell us the whole story about the events they are covering they still provide us with evidence of the influences, prejudices, assumed beliefs and the attention to detail (or lack of) that went into each report. This provides another window into history. What is more, the reports within their pages bring a thrilling immediacy to the study of the past.

What was a newspaper in 1919 like? Firstly, it was usually thin, comprising around eight to twelve pages. All the newspapers were constrained by a world-wide shortage of paper in the years after the First World War. Unlike their gargantuan modern equivalents there were no special pull-out supplements on gardening, lifestyle or property. Another difference that would strike the modern reader was the absence of the reporter's names (similar to an edition of today's *Economist*). While there were some celebrity journalists such as Hugh Martin in the *Daily News*, these were very much the exception. This has the drawback of often making it impossible to know which journalists wrote specific articles. But the journalistic modesty does have a refreshing silver lining. That species of celebrity journalist and controversialist who pontificates with equal knowledge on an endless array of topics had yet to come into existence. Opinion pieces in the newspapers of the time were confined to the editorial page. Two to three pages of news, letters, financial listings, some sports, reviews and advertisements filled the rest of the paper.

To establish the context within which the newspapers operated, the opening chapters deal with the British Government and Dáil Éireann. Chapter 1 deals with the relationship between the British Government, its administration in Ireland and the press. It casts new light on the attitude of the British in Ireland at this time by examining not only propaganda but also looking at how the Irish Administration and the Crown forces sought to influence, utilise and control the press. Newspapers were initially subject to censorship through the Defence of the Realm Act (DORA), then suppression and prosecution: they constantly risked intimidation and violent attack. The chapter also examines Colonial Office files that have been open for over twenty years but which had not been fully employed in a study of this kind. Chapter 2 deals with Sinn Féin and Dáil Éireann, their use of the *Irish Bulletin* and the relationship of republicans with the press in Ireland and foreign correspondents working in the country. Although Dáil and Sinn Féin propaganda was directed almost entirely abroad, Dáil members such as Michael Collins, Eamon de Valera and Arthur Griffith were fully aware of the need to maintain a strong relationship with the Irish press. Other republicans were not so worried by this consideration. As Chapter 2 discusses, there were a number of violent attacks on newspapers.

Chapters 3 and 4 provide a case study of the nationalist press and its reactions to Dáil policies, IRA violence, Crown violence and British rule in Ireland during this time. They entail an examination of the two Irish nationalist national dailies – the *Freeman's Journal* and the *Irish Independent* – chosen because of their substantial readerships, being the most widely read papers in the country at the time. They were not only nationalist but national papers. In the ensuing chapters I concentrate on three newspapers, the *Cork Examiner, The Irish Times* and the *The Times* of London. Chapter 5 discusses how the *Cork Examiner* (the most widely read regional newspaper) provides an excellent example of how both the British and republicans tried to control the news. Suppressed by the military, the paper later suffered the constrictions of Martial Law. While a nationalist paper, it was a constant critic of IRA violence. *The Irish Times*, the most famous and widely read Unionist newspaper, provides a window into the minds of the contemporary southern unionist establishment. A detailed study of the paper's editorials and reports in Chapter 6 reveals how – while the paper was completely opposed to the aims of Dáil Éireann – by 1920 the paper carried an editorial line that was strongly critical of the Irish Administration and the British Government. The four Irish papers studied in this book constituted around half of the daily readership of newspapers in Ireland.

Chapter 7 looks at *The Times* for a number of reasons: it gives the book a wider dimension in that English newspapers played a vitally important role during these years in showing the English public what was happening in Ireland. The hostility of English papers such as the *Daily Mail*, *Daily News* and *Manchester Guardian* towards British actions in Ireland is well known but *The Times* was one of the first English papers to grasp the importance of events in Ireland. From early 1919 the paper consistently put forward detailed proposals for a settlement in Ireland. Indeed, the paper was heavily involved in the manoeuvrings leading to the Truce in 1921. What is also interesting in the context of this book is that while it was a historic opponent of self-government for Ireland, *The Times* completely reversed this policy during the War of Independence. As Chapter 7 shows, its reasons were not initially any new-found sense of affiliation with Ireland but a fear that Britain's standing would be damaged on the world stage, among the Dominions and especially in the United States.

The newspapers in 1919 were working in an Ireland where Sinn Féin was in the ascendancy following its overwhelming success in the 1918 General Election. Sinn Féin was quick to take advantage of the election results by inaugurating the first Dáil Éireann in 1919. This body they now claimed as the only legitimate Government of Ireland. The rise of Sinn Féin and the emergence of the Dáil left the British Government and its Irish Administration struggling for a coherent response. The competing forces of republicanism and the British Government were to intensify their struggle over the subsequent years. We shall see in the following chapters how the newspapers were constrained by the Irish Administration as 1918 ended and the new year began. We shall see how the newspapers, although covering the same events, had very different stories to tell throughout these years and we shall see, also, how individual newspapers often came to be at the centre of the story.

1

DUBLIN CASTLE AND THE CROWN FORCES

At the beginning of 1919 the press in Ireland was under the control of the Defence of the Realm Act (DORA). This legislation dated from the outbreak of the First World War in 1914 and was intended to provide wartime control of all aspects of society throughout the Union. Press censorship under DORA began in Ireland and Britain during August of that year but was tightened significantly in Ireland after the 1916 Rising. Although the war was now over, censorship continued in Ireland into 1919 with Lord Decies in the position of Censor of newspapers. Under this system editors had (technically of their own volition) to submit proofs of their print copy to the Censor. A member of the newspaper staff would bring the proofs to the Censor who would then judge what could and could not be printed.

Censorship

The DORA press regulations 'forbade printing of seditious speeches, articles or other matters which might cause disaffection' and Decies'[1] work consisted mainly of checking letters and reports in newspapers for material in these categories. He had little trust in the Irish press, especially republican newspapers, as can be seen from his report on censorship for January 1919:

> On the whole the tone of the mosquito press[2] has been more moderate than usual. This may be explained by a desire on their part to show that the censorship is unnecessary and shall be discontinued. If this were done it is possible they would quickly assume their usual violent nature.[3]

He also suggested that this was one reason for the condemnatory reports on the first Dáil Éireann that marked the editorials of the more moderate and widely read Irish newspapers, commenting that: 'it would not suit them at this juncture to provoke the interference of

5

the Government by inflammatory articles'.[4]

Examples of censorship for the early part of 1919 make it clear that the reason for its continuation in Ireland was to combat the rise of radical nationalism, specifically Sinn Féin. There were to be no mentions of a republic in the Irish press. Consequently, the coverage of the opening session of Dáil Éireann was heavily censored. The Declaration of Independence, the oath to the Dáil that 'I do hereby pledge myself to work for the establishment of an independent Irish Republic', the Democratic Programme and the speeches of Cathal Brugha and Piaras Béaslaí were prevented from being published in Irish newspapers. Reports of speeches were the most common items subjected to the marking pencil of the Censor and some of the following examples should suffice to clarify the general trend. A speech by Edward Donnelly of the Armagh Sinn Féin club encouraging the people to boycott the Royal Irish Constabulary (RIC) 'in the church, in the street' and to 'make life so unpleasant for these people that they recognise that they are up against a determined people' had fully three quarters of its length deleted from the *Armagh Guardian* (see Appendix 1).[5] Similarly, any speech criticising DORA, threatening violence against the Crown forces or claiming ill-treatment of prisoners was – if not totally censored – then heavily cut. In many instances the original text was so heavily cut that the whole report was reduced to a few scattered and unrelated sentences that could not be published. The *Freeman's Journal* had the following extract deleted from the speech by Michael Kennedy in the dock at Castlepollard Courthouse. Kennedy voiced his contempt for DORA saying: 'We have broken DORA. No matter how many of us you imprison there are others to take our place. Our movement is not a movement of individuals, it is a national movement.'[6]

The censorship was bitterly resented by the Irish newspapers. The *Freeman's Journal* expressed its anger in sentiments echoed across the press. In April the paper argued: 'The Irish indictment of the censorship is not on the grounds that it keeps Englishmen in the dark, but that it denies to Irishmen elementary rights, which is the very badge of serfdom.'[7]

Some commentary like the above slipped past the Censor's gaze. Decies had wanted to resign in January, owing to the 'arduous' nature of the previous two years but the Lord Lieutenant, John French, had refused the resignation.[8] Perhaps, by now, Decies had simply lost interest in the job. The role required constant attention to detail and it is unsurprising that some material went unnoticed. Frank Gallagher, a Sinn Féin journalist, who later worked on the *Irish Bulletin* (see Chapter 2) detailed in his memoirs how republicans attempted to slip proofs of articles and reports past Decies by distracting him with discussions of horse racing and the excessive levels of income tax, topics in which Decies had an obsessive interest.[9] Another tactic was to overwhelm Decies with unacceptable proofs in the hope that some would go unnoticed.[10] While Gallagher wrote of the 'great game' the reality was that most newspapers could not afford to risk the wrath of the Censor and the Administration. Suppression was a costly business.

The censorship continued to operate until 30 August 1919 when Ireland was brought into line with the rest of the Union. It had followed the pattern examined above and that had endured for five years, with severe restrictions imposed on news reporting. The only change that occurred in the preceding months was when Decies was granted his wish and allowed to resign at the end of April. He was replaced by Major Bryan Cooper. Despite bringing an end to the censorship, the decision of the Irish Administration was greeted with an outpouring of cynicism from the Irish press. The papers were furious that while the censorship may have ended DORA remained. The newspapers were no freer to publish than before, and a wave of newspaper suppressions quickly swept the country.

Suppression

As the papers had predicted, this was because the Irish press had now to implement the DORA regulations themselves with no Censor to guide them as to what would contravene the Act or be deemed unacceptable to the Administration. In September 1919 the *Cork Examiner* and all its allied newspapers were suppressed for three days after printing a copy of the prospectus for the Dáil Éireann loan fund. Sylvain Briollay, a French journalist residing in Ireland, wrote that this was the forty-second paper to be suppressed for publishing the same material.[11]

Within a week Arthur Griffith's *Nationality*, *The Voice of Labour*, *New Ireland*, *The Republic*, *The Irish World* and *Fianne an Lae* followed the Cork newspaper.[12] On these occasions newspaper offices and print machinery were destroyed by the military and at least two newspaper editors were taken to Cork Jail for committing offences against DORA.[13] The suppressions aroused a hostile reaction from sections of the press. The *Irish Independent* termed the move against the

Cork Examiner 'a drastic military action'.[14] Criticism from *The Times* was particularly strong and held a warning for the Government as to opinions within certain influential sections of English society. The editorial expressed anxiety at the temptation to misuse power 'inherent in this autocratic control (DORA)'. The editorial also warned that there are limits to the lengths the Irish Administration could go in tampering with the free expression of news and public opinion 'to which prima facie Nationalists and Sinn Féiners are as fully entitled as any other citizen': 'A right of interference would be fully sustainable if the press were used as an instrument of crime but not otherwise. We do not regard the advocacy of any political opinion as within this definition'.[15]

This editorial was reprinted in the following day's *Irish Independent*, which reported that the *Dublin Leader* and *Midland Tribune* were now also suppressed.[16] The list continued with the *Kerry News*, *Kerry Weekly Reporter*, *Killarney Echo* and the *Dundalk Examiner* suppressed for carrying the Dáil Loan Prospectus. The same day the *Irish Independent* reported that in Limerick city the only paper left to city readers was the *Weekly Unionist Journal*.[17]

The use of regulations under DORA against newspapers provoked both confusion and anger from the press. The *Cork Examiner*'s editor, George Crosbie, signed an article on the paper's return from suppression which stated that if the Government had directed the paper not to print the advertisement, they would not have done so. Crosbie added that while the censorship was 'in vogue' innumerable paragraphs appeared without any comment in Irish and English newspapers. As this was so, he argued 'it did not seem to us that we were acting very recklessly in publishing matter that had already appeared in substance in our news columns'.[18] The *Manchester Guardian* special correspondent, after attacking Lord French, the Lord Lieutenant, for 'his policy of repression', displayed similar sentiments:

> A few weeks ago a paper like the *Cork Examiner* would have submitted the tainted matter to the censor and would have abided by his decision. There is no oracle to consult now, but DORA is still in full operation, and DORA represents the censorship in its crudest and stiffest form.[19]

The recently deposed Censor, Major Bryan Cooper, in a letter to *The Times*, joined in the chorus of condemnation. While he had no sympathy for the 'Sinn Fein Press', which had 'declared war on the

Government' he thought the policy was flawed. The Prospectus, he surmised, would continue to be printed secretly and passed from hand to hand and so it was futile to punish newspapers, especially what he believed to be 'moderate' newspapers. This move would only serve to 'inflame and exasperate moderate opinion in Ireland'.[20]

An outraged press did not cause the Government to abandon its policy of newspaper suppression and in December 1919, a leading national newspaper, the *Freeman's Journal* suffered this fate. Under the new ownership of Hamilton Edwards and Martin Fitzgerald the paper had called for the resignation of all senior staff in the Irish Administration including Ian Macpherson (Chief Secretary), John Taylor (Under Secretary) and Lord French (Lord Lieutenant). The paper was also a persistent critic of the Administration's policies, including the decision to abolish political status for Irish prisoners (see Chapter 3). This increasingly sympathetic reporting of Dáil activities from a leading national daily evidently caused much dismay in Government circles. In late November the *Freeman's Journal* reported that a plain-clothed Dublin Metropolitan Police (DMP) official had visited its offices. The officer verbally warned the manager, J. Cunningham, about the nature of its coverage of events in Ireland and its criticisms of the Administration. The *Freeman's Journal* dispatched a series of letters to DMP Headquarters seeking clarification of the order, but the only reply was a warning that the paper could be prosecuted under the Criminal Law and Procedures Act of 1887 or under DORA for publishing any matter that would constitute an offence under either regulation. The paper dealt a public and embarrassing snub to the Irish Administration by publishing the details of the affair, including correspondence, and continued with its criticisms of the Government.

As the Administration's threats had been made public, an action against the paper was inevitable.[21] On 15 December 1919 the *Freeman's Journal* was suppressed for publishing offensive articles about the military, RIC and the proposed recruitment of a new auxiliary force. Its Townsend Street office was isolated by the military while an army technician removed vital operating parts of the printing machinery. Superintendent Willoughby read a warrant signed by Brigadier General T.S. Lambert, the Competent Military Authority, charging the paper with 'offences against the Defence of the Realm Regulations', namely 'to prejudice the recruiting of persons to serve in a police force' (these new recruits would later became known as the

'Black and Tans').[22] The army departed the offices after 90 minutes 'amid the boos and ironical cheers of a crowd that had assembled in the locality'.[23]

The owners of the *Freeman's Journal* decided to replace it with an 'early morning edition' of its sister paper, the *Evening Telegraph*. This acted as a surrogate *Freeman's Journal* throughout the period of suppression. Eight days after the suppression a legal action taken by the proprietors of the *Freeman's Journal* in the Court of Chancery was dismissed by Justice Powell. Powell judged the suppression 'was justified in law and fact'.[24] Others did not see the matter so clearly especially as the ban ran its eventual 44-day course. Practically all sections of the British press attacked the suppression. Indeed, the editor of the *Daily News* offered two daily columns to the *Freeman's Journal* throughout its ban, an offer gratefully accepted by the paper.[25] T.P. O' Connor, one of the few Irish Parliamentary Party members in the House of Commons, expressed the view that the articles in the *Freeman's Journal* were paralleled by similar articles in *The Times* and that the *Freeman's Journal* was being made a scapegoat for the increasing unrest in Ireland.[26] The *Westminster Gazette* commented that it had also discouraged the raising of a special constabulary yet no action was taken against that paper.[27]

Many others mentioned this dichotomy between the freedom of the press in Ireland and England, both, ultimately, being parts of the same jurisdiction.[28] The *Evening Telegraph* commented on the case of the English editor of the British *Catholic Herald*. He had composed an editorial stating that the shooting of policemen by Irish republicans was not necessarily murder. In that case the editor was currently being tried through normal law and the paper continued to print.[29] This hostile press reaction helped to finally end the suppression which at 44 days was, perhaps, more than a mere attempt by the administration to punish the *Freeman's Journal* for contravening DORA.[30] The paper's financial problems were well known and the lengthy suppression undoubtedly deepened these difficulties. Undeniably, the suppression was a warning to all newspapers in Ireland, especially the increasingly critical nationalist papers of what could happen to any of them. For a newspaper to criticise the Administration was to risk suppression 'therefore destroying for the time-being its whole circulation and advertisement revenues'.[31]

Relations between the press and the Irish Administration continued to be strained during the following months.[32] In April, Lord French complained to a journalist of 'a certain section of the

Irish press and also of the London press … which is wilfully exaggerating matters'.[33] That same month and shortly after his arrival as the new General Officer Commanding (GOC) of the British army in Ireland, General Sir Nevil Macready criticised the *Freeman's Journal* reportage publicly. Macready also met with 'representatives of the Dublin daily newspapers and representatives of the English press' in Dublin and informed them that they would now be supplied by the military 'the facts in possession of headquarters regarding occurrences'.[34] Macready was particularly apprehensive of the negative effects of press reports on the morale of ordinary soldiers, especially after 'seeing himself and his comrades vilified and abused by the press and the Kenworthy's of Parliament, and no effort made to place the real facts before the public'.[35]

On taking up his post as GOC, Macready immediately 'arranged for an officer of the Staff at headquarters to be available to supply newspaper representatives with official reports, which they could use or not if they liked'.[36] This was based on the model Macready had previously established in Scotland Yard, while Commissioner of the London Metropolitan Police. It was run by a Major Reginald Marians, who was assisted by a Captain Charles Tower.[37] These two, with the aim of neutralising the effects of critical press reports, began to issue a 'daily report of outrages' to the press.

The reaction to these 'daily reports' showed clearly the limits of 'official news' at this time. The unionist *Irish Times* started publication of these reports immediately and was warm in its praise, arguing that if the lists were mere propaganda they would have 'been exposed within twenty-four hours'.[38] Nationalist papers saw it differently. The *Irish Independent* claimed that the reports were designed 'to poison English minds against Ireland' and as a means of preparing the British public for 'more coercion' in Ireland.[39] The *Freeman's Journal*, calling the policy of the Irish Administration 'a new regime of bayonets plus bulletins', refused to carry the lists and attacked them as a 'propagandist method of vilifying and blackening the character of the Irish people'.[40] The *Freeman's Journal* also reported that the reports had been disseminated 'in the columns of the Orange press in Ireland and the Anti-Irish press in England'. Indeed, the reports were carried in the pages of the *Morning Post*, the most hawkish press supporter of the Irish Administration (a paper the *Cork Examiner* accused of 'Jackboot Journalism').[41] As such, the 'daily reports' were in a sense preaching to the converted. They were clearly a counterpoint to the republican

11

Irish Bulletin and the news reports issued by Dáil Éireann and its representatives. Despite the mixed reception to the new publicity initiative of the Irish Administration, the creation of these 'daily reports of outrages' signified that it was now aware that it needed to make a more concerted effort to counter negative press coverage and to combat republican propaganda.[42] It is to these new attempts at influencing and controlling the news that we now turn.

July 1920 – A new approach or 'bayonets plus bulletins'?

This move to create a press bureau was symptomatic of the new vigour introduced into Castle Affairs, firstly with the arrival of General Macready, to be followed soon after by the new Under Secretary, John Anderson, supported by more efficient civil servants such as Andy Cope and Mark Sturgis. Ian Macpherson, a long-time target of the Irish press was replaced by Hamar Greenwood as Chief Secretary. They had much work to do after the moribund regime of John Taylor.[43] On arrival in May 1920 Anderson was shocked at the administrative mess that was Dublin Castle, especially the Chief Secretary's Office:

> No business that was not urgent was being attended to and business that had become urgent was disposed of in very many cases without proper consideration. The general state of this office, on which the whole civil administration of the country should pivot, was really incredible.[44]

Even with these personnel changes at Dublin Castle, the Administration and military were determined to maintain the previous Administration's tough line with the Irish press. In an attempt to deal with the increased disorder in the country, the Restoration of Order in Ireland Act (ROIA) replaced DORA in August 1920. Regulation 27 dealt with the press:

> No person shall, by word of mouth or in writing, or in any newspaper, periodical, book, circular, or other printed publication –
> • spread false reports or make false statements; or
> • spread reports or make statements intended or likely to cause disaffection to His Majesty or to interfere with the success of His Majesty's forces or the forces of any of His Majesty's allies by land or sea or to prejudice His Majesty's relations with foreign powers.[45]

It was left to the Irish Administration to dictate what constituted a false report or statement. Moreover, even if a report were completely true and verifiable, if it was judged by the Administration to be intended, even indirectly, to cause 'disaffection' then a newspaper could be prosecuted under the provisions of the Act. This signalled the end of what remained of free speech for Irish newspapers. British newspapers and papers from other countries could not be prosecuted under the terms of the ROIA.[46]

In the previous six months a confrontation between the Irish papers and the Government had become inevitable. In late August the Under Secretary, John Anderson, wrote individually to the newspaper editors in Ireland bemoaning the: 'increasing frequency with which misleading statements, often untrue and in any case calculated to cause disorder and disaffection, have appeared in the columns of certain newspapers'.[47] He cautioned that the managers and editor would be held responsible for a 'breach' by any Irish newspaper. As a final warning he wrote that any 'breach of the law' (in this instance the ROIA) would force the Administration to 'deal with Newspaper companies and individuals concerned as drastically as the circumstances warrant'.[48] Mark Sturgis noted in his diary that it was agreed between Anderson and Macready that the Administration would prosecute newspapers in 'every case for incitement to murder, disaffection etc' from the date of this letter.[49]

In October, it seemed that the Administration's chance had come as both the *Freeman's Journal* and *Irish Independent* gave prominence to claims by Arthur Griffith that there 'existed a plot to assassinate Sinn Fein leaders'.[50] Reprisals by the Crown forces against Irish towns and civilians were becoming more common. Griffith now also claimed that these reprisals were a calculated campaign to antagonise the Irish people and not the reactions of a few hot-headed soldiers or police. Anderson and Macready were both in agreement on the need to prosecute the newspapers involved. However, a prosecution of the newspapers would have meant that Arthur Griffith would also have to be charged for playing a part in spreading the 'false report'. This would have been a move that would undoubtedly have aroused fierce opposition not only in Ireland but also in England – Griffith was the face of Irish nationalism and also perceived as a moderate. Furthermore, it is known that the Prime Minister, David Lloyd George, did not want Griffith arrested, as he was a potential route through which a possible truce could be reached. Indeed, tentative secret negotiations were already under way.[51] Proceedings were begun by Dublin Castle against the two newspapers but were then stopped. Macready informed Sturgis of the decision: 'As for the Griffith interview I have been told not to go on – haute politique – and if I may not go for the man I suppose there's no sense in going for the papers.'[52]

As Anderson would undoubtedly have known of the Prime Minister's wishes, his only option on this occasion was to halt the proceedings. The Administration's sole response to Griffith's claims was a statement issued through the Chief Secretary's Office to the press stating that Griffith's comments were 'untrue in all respects'.[53] It was to be a brief respite for the press.

Weeks later, a newspaper prosecution was undertaken and again it was the *Freeman's Journal* that had invoked the ire of the Administration. Macready made it clear in his memoirs that he was the initiator of the prosecutions and that they were the culmination of many previous demands for similar action.[54] On 20 October 1920 a summons was issued to the *Freeman's Journal* under both sections of Regulation 27 (see above) of the ROIA. The offensive report concerned both a reprisal in Tullow and also the deaths of two policemen for which the newspaper blamed the Black and Tans.[55] Six days later the paper received a second summons for once more contravening the provisions contained in Regulation 27. This concerned a case involving the shooting of Patrick Nunan near Buttevant, Co. Cork. The paper published a short report stating that the young man had been taken by British soldiers from his home. In the belief that he was someone else, presumably a republican, he was summarily shot by the soldiers and left in a critical condition.[56]

A third summons under Regulation 27 was issued on 5 November 1920 for a report on the alleged flogging of an unnamed man (later named as Arthur Quirke) in Portobello Barracks, Dublin. The paper reported that Quirke was tied face down to a bed and beaten with rifle-butts and belts until his back was a 'mass of broken flesh'.[57] Soon after this report the paper printed a photograph of Quirke showing his back, which was clearly scarred and bandaged.[58] Greenwood declared to the House of Commons that this photograph was a fake and as such another prosecution was inevitable. The trial by military court martial of the proprietors and directors, Martin Fitzgerald and Hamilton Edwards and the editor, Patrick Hooper, began in late November (see Chapter 3 for an account of the trial).

Significantly, the Nunan charge had been dropped by this time after an investigation that seemed to prove the substance of the *Freeman's Journal* report.

On 24 December 1920 – in a move that astounded the British press – Fitzgerald, Edwards and Hooper were sentenced to twelve months' imprisonment. The sentences aroused almost universal condemnation with the *Daily Express, Daily Mirror, Daily News, Manchester Guardian*, the *Star, The Times* and the *Westminster Gazette* being particularly critical. The *Manchester Guardian* special correspondent wrote that the sentences 'discredit any belief in the impartiality of British justice that may still linger in Ireland'.[59] Both the Newspaper Proprietors' Association and the Newspaper Society passed resolutions condemning the sentences and calling for their reversal. The three men were well known among English journalists and were described across many of the newspapers as 'men of moderate views'. The *Freeman's Journal* also printed many supporting comments from the British and Irish provincial papers.[60] The *Cork Examiner* wrote that, despite operating in an area under Martial Law, they had to register their protest at the 'savage sentences'.[61] The *Freeman's Journal* itself wrote that the sentences had awakened a 'slumbering English conscience'.[62] This was no mere rhetorical flourish: the pressure mounted by the British press was so severe and apparently unforeseen by the Government that on 6 January 1921 the editor and two directors were released 'on medical grounds', an apparent show of sympathy that did nothing to lessen the opprobrium piled on the Irish Administration and the British Government. The decision to release the three men had come directly from Lloyd George who had taken fright at the intense press reaction. He forwarded a telegram to Anderson on 23 December asking that the men be released. Unhappy at this decision, Anderson delayed the release of the men for a fortnight. Finally, Greenwood instructed him that the Prime Minister's decision to release the three men was irrevocable and immediate.[63] Macready characteristically expressed his contempt for the decision: 'Orders were received from Downing Street that the sentences should be remitted, a decision which aroused disgust and contempt in the hearts of those who were risking their lives for the Government.'[64]

The Times may have been more correct than it realised when it called the sentences 'vindictive'. Macready was not impressed with arguments for the freedom of the press and he had a direct and powerful grudge against the *Freeman's Journal*. He blamed the paper for the IRA shootings of D.C. Smyth in Cork and Resident Magistrate Alan Bell in Dublin (see Chapter 3).[65] This seemingly blinded him to other considerations for in March 1921 he again wanted to begin prosecutions against the paper (and the *Irish Independent*). This time, Anderson, having learnt the lesson of December 1920, refused arguing that the British press would make such a move, if not impossible, highly undesirable.[66] The frustration evidenced by Macready at the inability of the Administration to silence critical elements in the press was clearly also felt by the common soldier and policeman and may have been the cause of many of the Crown attacks on newspapers.

'Unfortunate incidents'

Attacks on newspaper offices and printing presses became more regular from the middle of 1920 – over the following year the Crown forces attacked the offices of many provincial newspapers. These included: the *Enniscorthy Echo*, the *Galway Express*, the *Kerryman*, the *Kerry Sentinel*, the *Kerry Weekly Reporter*, the *Leitrim Observer*, the *Munster News*, the *Nenagh Guardian*, the *Newcastle West Weekly Observer*, the *Offaly Independent*, the *Tipperary Star*, the *Tralee Liberator* and the *Westmeath Independent*.[67] A Lieutenant Colonel Evelyn Lindsay Young stationed in the midlands during 1920 left an account of how the soldiers responded to criticism from a local paper. This paper had apparently published a series of critical articles on the conduct of the RIC and British army (Young did not name the paper but termed it the 'Yellow Express'). The editor promised that the criticisms would continue in the next editions but as Young boasted:

> Unfortunately for him there was no next edition – for the next morning the street outside the Yellow Express office was a mass of coloured papers, inside the printing and linotype machines were wrecked, the safe cracked and all was a shambles.[68]

Young's account details clearly that the attack was carried out by the army. In the weeks following the attack on the paper, he describes how the Crown forces in the area basked in the 'comparative peace which had reigned since the Yellow Express had succumbed'.[69]

Various printing works, such as those in Athlone and Nenagh were also destroyed at this time while journalists and newspaper employees suffered intimidation and threats.[70] The *Kerry Weekly*

Reporter, edited by John Moynihan, was attacked by Auxiliaries in April 1921. The paper's premises was so badly damaged that the paper did not re-emerge until the summer of 1923.[71] A printer from the *Tralee Liberator* was shot dead by Crown forces during a raid on the town.[72] The paper went unpublished as staff and journalists were too frightened to remain at work.[73] Notices distributed throughout Kerry and Cork by the so called 'Anti-Sinn Fein Society' (a cover name used by some members of the Crown forces involved in reprisals and intimidation) not only threatened the local population but 'every newspaper in the county, not forgetting the staff by any means'.[74] In Dublin, when the *Irish Independent* printed a letter from Michael Collins dismissing rumours of peace negotiations, Auxiliaries raided the paper's offices. One of the subeditors had a revolver held to his head while Auxiliaries warned the staff of the consequences of any more such publications. The paper felt unable to publish a second letter from Collins which arrived a few days later.[75] *Daily News* journalist Hugh Martin had to conduct his investigations under a false name. While in Tralee he heard Black and Tans threaten to kill 'that bastard Martin' if they ever encountered him in person.[76] Martin's account of events was corroborated by other English journalists working in the town. In December 1920 J. Denvir, B. Kelleher and J. M'Nerney (House of Commons correspondents for the *Cork Examiner, Freeman's Journal* and *Irish Independent*) wrote to the editor of the *Daily News*. The letter, which had been agreed upon by a meeting of the Irish Journalists Association, Institute of Journalists and foreign correspondents in Ireland, appealed to the National Union of Journalists to safeguard the lives of journalists working in the country.[77] Hugh Martin had by this stage made public the threats he had received and *The Times* had reported that 'the Police in Ireland have apparently decided to forbid investigation of the true conditions of affairs by the Press'.[78] Even with the outcry, attacks on newspapers continued and the *Freeman's Journal* which had suffered intense political intimidation now became a target for the violent variety.

This occurred during the same period that the paper, its editor and proprietors were being court-martialled. The paper had been in regular receipt of threatening letters from the Crown forces over the preceding months. The paper published one from the RIC camp at Gormanstown. Handwritten, the letter, 'from the leader of the secret society in the RIC' warned the editor of the *Freeman's Journal* to apologise for its coverage of the Balbriggan reprisal (see Chapter 3) or

'The premises and your life won't be worth tuppence'.[79] The editor, Patrick Hooper, forwarded the letter to the Chief Secretary, Greenwood, General Macready, Police Adviser Hugh Tudor, and Chief Inspector Smith of the RIC. Macready replied to the editor that he was not responsible for the discipline of the police. He concluded his letter with what could be considered a veiled threat. At the very least the paper was not going to receive any protection from Macready:

> In the meantime, it may be interesting to you to learn that I constantly receive letters of a very similar purport from members of associations which receive encouragement and apparent support from your paper in the campaign of lawlessness which is devastating this country.[80]

Unsubtly, Macready was telling Hooper that such threats were what could be expected when a newspaper criticised the Crown forces. Indeed, he told Anderson in a letter three days later that the policy of papers critical of the Government had the effect of 'goading both the police and the troops into a sense of exasperation against the papers'.[81] Threats turned to action in November 1920. Masked men entered the offices of *The Irish Times* on Westmoreland Street, apparently to keep journalists away from the nearby commercial offices of the *Freeman's Journal*. Another party attacked and set fire to these offices, which were so badly damaged that 'the entire of the ground floor with the exception of the counter was burnt out'.[82] Documents relating to the court martial of the newspaper were also destroyed. The *Freeman's Journal* thanked the members of the DMP and military who had helped the fire brigade quench the flames but left its readership in no doubt that it was a party of Auxiliaries that were responsible for the attack. Despite the intimidation, the paper had been consistently critical of the Auxiliaries and Black and Tans, even more so after 'Bloody Sunday' (21 November 1920). That day saw the Dublin IRA, under Michael Collins' orders, shoot fourteen British agents and Auxiliaries throughout the city. In the afternoon the Auxiliaries responded with an attack on the crowd attending a match at Croke Park. Twelve people were killed in the stadium. The *Freeman's Journal* had been particularly critical of the conduct of the Auxiliaries on that day (see Chapter 3). Two more attacks were made that December including a failed incendiary bomb attack during a busy working afternoon. These attacks, the paper admitted, were 'further severe blows at the *Freeman's Journal*'.

While there are no doubts that the higher echelons of the Dublin Castle administration and the military wished to silence the *Freeman's Journal*, there can only be speculation as to who sanctioned the violent attacks on that paper and others. What is certain is that the press criticism was bitterly resented by the military and police chiefs and that the general policy of unofficial as well as official reprisals was approved by the highest levels of the Government, including Lloyd George. Excuses were persistently made for these reprisals. Macready urged Anderson on many occasions to ensure that the civil authorities had to prosecute 'that portion of the press which is hostile to the Government' and which was also so critical of the RIC and the Army. In October 1920, he had advised that this was vital:

> ... not only to vindicate the good name of the police and military but also to avoid possible unfortunate incidents which may suddenly arise owing to the supposition that there is no legal remedy to the present press campaign of abuse and misstatement of facts.[83]

The Public Information Branch (PIB)

The mass introduction of new officials allied to Anderson's determination to energise Dublin Castle operations prompted the creation of the Public Information Branch (PIB - see Appendix II). Its genesis came in July 1920 while Macready and Anderson were part of a delegation to Downing Street to discuss the Irish situation. During this meeting Macready advised the Prime Minister that 'measures were required to deal with the Irish press'.[84] On the one hand, these measures involved control of the press, through prosecution, via the provisions of the ROIA. The other measure was the PIB. The new department was a direct attempt to counter the increasing success of republican propaganda, best personified by the wide circulation of the *Irish Bulletin*. This publication was already being extensively quoted in Irish and English newspapers by the latter half of 1920, a fact that infuriated Macready.

Basil Clarke, who had worked as a journalist for the *Daily Mail* during the First World War, was chosen to head the new department. He was to have a number of staff under his control in Dublin Castle, while Major Charles Street would work for the PIB from the Irish Office in London. Clarke's expertise could potentially be of great benefit to the new department. He was a very experienced journalist.

During the initial phase of the First World War, in order to bypass Government restrictions, he had reported from the Western Front without a Government pass for five months. He did this even with the knowledge that he would be arrested and sent from the front, if discovered, as the British Government was determined to control the war news available to reporters. Later in the war he had worked in the army GHQ on the Western Front and gained direct experience of the official provision of news and of the immense Allied propaganda operation. He knew that many journalists would dismiss official accounts, such as the Macready-inspired 'daily report of outrages', unless they could be seen to be based on relatively accurate reporting of the facts.[85]

Clarke urged a system of propaganda he termed 'propaganda by news'. This involved reporting news in a 'matter of fact' manner and in a style similar to that of the *Irish Bulletin*. He argued that it 'is upon news that press opinion is formed' rather than views and from this followed public opinion. Propaganda, he believed, 'should contain concentration of facts. Nor should one exclude even the unfavourable fact'.[86] This type of propaganda, he claimed, gained the approval and trust of the press. In this theory he may well have been correct but Clarke and his new department did not have an easy beginning. Circumstances outside of his control created a rush of 'unfavourable facts'. It is necessary to examine these now in order to witness the problems Clarke and the PIB faced.

Unfavourable facts – The *Weekly Summary* and reprisals

The circumstances which greeted the formation of the PIB were the arrival of a new police newspaper, an upsurge in reprisals, including a large and highly publicised reprisal in Balbriggan, as well as a series of controversial press interviews from General Macready. In August 1920 the RIC began publishing a new weekly police journal, the *Weekly Summary*. The paper's instigator was probably Hugh Tudor, who had been appointed by Winston Churchill as a police 'adviser' in May (he effectively was the new RIC chief of police and became officially installed in this position during November 1920). Tudor was one of the figures most responsible for the policy of police reprisals, which were now becoming more regular. He saw it as the only means by which the police force could retain any morale and effectiveness. In this belief and in this policy he was fully supported by Lloyd George. Indeed, the two men had had a private meeting in June 1920 in which the Prime Minister assured Tudor of his full support for the policy of unofficial reprisals.[87] The editorial and content of the *Weekly Summary* was composed by Tudor's appointees Captain Hugh B.C. Pollard and William Darling. Tudor had brought these two men onto his staff soon after his arrival in Ireland. Pollard's title was 'Press Officer of the Information Section of the Police Authority' while Darling was secretary of the same section. Basil Thompson, the Director of Home Office Intelligence, also had an involvement from his offices in Scotland Yard.[88] The PIB, as far as can be ascertained, had no involvement in this new police paper but its arrival was to have a significant impact on Clarke and the PIB.

In line with Tudor's attempts to revitalise the RIC the *Weekly Summary* was designed as a morale-boosting supplement for a force that was under a social boycott and constant attack from the IRA. It was this journal that lauded the Black and Tans who were engaged in the job of 'making Ireland an appropriate hell for those whose trade is agitation and whose method is murder'.[89] Printed out of Dublin Castle the paper was comprised of articles ranging from the mawkish to the inflammatory and filled with cuttings from English newspapers such as the ultra-conservative, at times racist, *Morning Post*.[90] In the early months of the paper articles with titles such as 'The Murder-Gang on the Run', 'The Policy of Hitting Back – An Inevitable Development' and 'The First Reprisal' were common.[91] Inevitably, copies fell into the hands of IRA commandants and thus the *Irish Bulletin* who described it as a tool designed with the 'intention of inciting the English armed forces in Ireland to acts of outrage and violence against the Irish people'.[92] From here, the *Weekly Summary* became a propaganda disaster for the Irish Administration as many of the articles could be (and were by both the newspapers and the police) construed as an incitement to reprisal. The paper became seen as the true gauge of British Government policy in Ireland. Nationalist papers across Ireland had no doubts that the *Weekly Summary* was designed to encourage reprisals. Many English newspapers were also very uncomfortable about the new paper. Hugh Martin who criticised the paper in the *Daily News* later wrote that any Government which supported such a paper also clearly supported 'unlawful reprisals, both in the form of murder and the destruction of property'.[93] Widespread condemnatory coverage was given to the contents of the paper in the newspapers of Ireland and England forcing Greenwood to publicly defend the *Weekly Summary* in the

House of Commons. He declared that he fully supported the new police paper. That was merely the first of many occasions on which Greenwood was forced to defend the paper in the British Parliament.[94]

The *Weekly Summary*'s inflammatory articles were soon compounded by what came to be called the 'sack of Balbriggan'. On the 20 September 1920 the RIC stationed at Gormanstown attacked the residents and premises of the town, following an earlier fatal ambush on an RIC patrol. Two unarmed men, 'reputed Sinn Feiners' were taken from their homes and killed, reportedly with bayonets. Many buildings were burned to the ground including a factory which gave employment to many in the locality. The reaction of the British Government was unsure. There was no official response bar Greenwood's denials of the event in the House of Commons and behind the scenes there was division. Field Marshal Sir Henry Wilson, the overall commander of British land forces, noted in his diary:

> At Balbriggan, Thurles and Galway yesterday the local police marked down certain SFs as in their opinion the actual murderers or instigators [of ambushes] and then coolly went and shot them without question or trial. Winston [Churchill] saw very little harm in this but it horrifies me.[95]

This is not to say that Wilson was against the principle of shooting 'Sinn Feiners'. He just wanted it all done while maintaining the discipline of the Crown forces and with the open support of the Government. English newspapers had, over the past year, become more cognisant of the increasing violence in Ireland but the Balbriggan reprisal in the words of D.G. Boyce was 'the single dramatic incident' that completely focused the attention of English papers on the issue of reprisals in Ireland.[96] Balbriggan was only a few miles north of Dublin, on the doorstep of the increasing number of foreign journalists now working in the country. There could be no hiding the destruction or deaths of two civilians from those journalists willing to look and the reaction from English newspapers was one of shock. All sections of the press joined in condemning the reprisal. For example, the *Manchester Guardian* gave a graphic account of uncontrollable policemen firing wildly and burning indiscriminately while *The Times* described refugees fleeing the town to the relative safety of Dublin.[97]

Macready, aware of the sentiments of Churchill and Greenwood and eager to defend the Crown forces from the barrage of press criticism gave an interview to the representative of the Associated Press. During this interview he defended reprisals, specifically Balbriggan: 'But now the machinery of the law having broken down they [Crown forces] feel that there is no certain means of redress and punishment, and it is only human that they should act on their own initiative.'[98]

Punishment for such reprisals was 'a delicate matter' which he implied may turn the men against their officers. This interview, which the *Freeman's Journal* claimed received wide and unfavourable coverage in the United States, was submitted by the American journalist to Macready before publication. Macready had made some changes and passed the interview for publication. There could be no doubt, then, that it accurately reflected Macready's comments (Macready, also, made no denial of the interview's accuracy).[99] The GOC of the army in Ireland had stated that the country was in anarchy, that reprisals were understandable, that human nature superseded military discipline and that the members of the Crown forces involved in reprisals would probably escape punishment for their actions. His comments were derided in the Irish and English press. The *Irish Independent* quoted the *Birmingham Post* as saying that 'either General Macready's interview or General Macready himself must be repudiated'.[100] The *Irish Independent* had an ample supply of critical commentary from which to choose. In widely expressed sentiments, *The Times* attacked Macready personally for his ambivalence surrounding the punishment of Crown forces involved in reprisals. His use of the phrase 'a delicate matter' was condemned. The paper made two points in response to Macready's comments. The Government had to maintain 'a responsible control over all their agents in Ireland' and that there should 'be no secret adoption of the barbarous methods of vicarious punishment'.[101] His comments were compared by many of the English papers with those of the German commanders in Belgium during the First World War.[102] Slow to learn the lesson (or perhaps just stubborn), Macready gave a similar interview to French newspapers a few weeks later. This time, the General was not only condemned by the press but was severely upbraided ('properly wigged' in the words of Sturgis) by Lloyd George and Churchill for the negative impact of his interviews.[103]

Regaining trust? – The PIB and the press

The arrival of the *Weekly Summary*, the reprisal at Balbriggan and the publication of Macready's ill-advised interviews had severely damaged the reputation of the Crown forces in Ireland and created a climate of mistrust of the Crown forces which the PIB had now to try and dispel. As the relationship between the press and the Crown forces foundered on the rock of reprisals Clarke was understandably doubly anxious to improve the working relations between his new department and the press. To help in this aim he began a number of initiatives. In August the PIB began to issue statements to the press that gave news of events 'of public interest' in addition to the news of ambushes and violence. Clarke also tried to establish a more personal relationship with the representatives of the Irish and foreign press. His personal history as a journalist was of use here. Although generally suspicious of the PIB's work, the *Manchester Guardian* correspondents felt that Clarke 'did a difficult and distasteful job honourably and well'.[104] His attempts at forming friendly relationships with journalists were not always successful, however. In early September 1920 the London correspondent of the *Freeman's Journal* attacked Dublin Castle, writing that 'In Fleet Street it is understood that Dublin Castle has recently recruited journalists in its service as well as "Black and Tan" police'.[105] Later that month the paper began its new policy by which statements from Dublin Castle would be inserted in the paper only if they were paid for at ordinary advertising rates and double this rate 'if it is desired that these statements appear as reading matter'.[106]

To counter some of this hostility Clarke established a 'bureau' in Dublin Castle during early 1921. In this office: 'any press man can come and I put before him any information that may be available and suitable for publication. No news is sent out to the papers now and papers at a distance act in this matter through their Dublin Correspondents'.[107] A month later he told the Assistant Under Secretary, Andy Cope, that:

> About 20 Pressmen, Irish, British and foreign, visit the Castle daily, and take our version of the facts – which I take care are as favourable to us as may be, in accordance with truth and verisimilitude – and they believe all I tell them. And they can't afford to stay away. That is an advantage which no system of press propaganda other than the news propaganda system, could win.[108]

This was an overstatement of the success of the Dublin Castle PIB.

While no newspaper could afford to ignore the potential news-worthiness of the official reports (even the *Freeman's Journal* quickly abandoned its policy of not publishing official statements), what counted was the papers' reaction to the reports and what they did with them. The Irish nationalist papers often printed the statements but reported on them which such extreme suspicion that they were useless as propaganda. The *Manchester Guardian* had commented in December 1920 that it considered Government-supplied news as 'unscrupulous propaganda'.[109] The *Daily Mail, Daily News* and *The Times* similarly complained about 'doped news'. The irreconcilably hostile *Freeman's Journal* often prefixed official accounts as having come from that 'specially organised department at the Castle' and in his history of Irish newspapers Hugh Oram notes that the Dublin and foreign pressmen knew Clarke as 'the Black and Tan publicity man'.[110]

The Government reaction to major events validated the newspapers' suspicions. When there was a huge reprisal in Cork city during the night of 11 December 1920 the British Government responded to the claims that the attack was committed by Crown forces in the time-honoured fashion of Governments everywhere when dealing with unwelcome news – they ordered that a report on the event be compiled. General Peter Strickland, the O/C (Officer Commanding) of forces in Cork, was given the awkward task of making this report (known to the newspapers as the 'Strickland Report') on the reprisal which was known to all to have been carried out by the Auxiliaries in Cork. His report duly blamed local Auxiliaries for the events of that night and the British Cabinet refused to release the findings. Practically the whole press in Ireland and England made negative comparisons between the amount of effort put into Government press releases versus their refusal to release a report, judged by all observers, to be condemnatory of Crown forces (see Chapter 5).[111] The general mood of the press was summed up by *The Times* in an editorial composed a mere eleven days after Clarke had written to Cope, lauding the success of the PIB. The paper dealt directly with the PIB and began by stating that the provision of official Government news to the press and public was vitally important but added a proviso which completely undermined the work of Basil Clarke and the PIB:

> There is no reason why skilled journalists should be employed for the purpose of communicating news to the Press. Plain statements of fact would suffice, and ordinary officials are surely competent

to make them. No skilled preparation of news can atone for the suppression of the Strickland Report ... nor will the confidence of independent organs in the Government's news be restored by the knowledge that such news reaches them only after passing through a professionally staffed propaganda department.[112]

The continued divergence between the PIB and the military press office exacerbated the problem. This resulted in Clarke sometimes being seen as inept and even untruthful. According to Sturgis, Clarke had considered resigning following a particularly large military reprisal in Mallow in which a number of houses and businesses on the main street were destroyed. Only days before he had told the *Daily Mail* that, on the authority of Greenwood, the policy of reprisals had ended.[113]

The PIB and the Crown forces

The PIB's problems were not only with journalists. Clarke and his department were often not fully supported in their work by other sections of Irish Administration and Crown forces. In practice, this was just another symptom of the divisions that dominated the relationship between the military and the civil administration of Dublin Castle and a lack of unity of command between the police and military.[114] These divisions plagued many operations and the creation of news and propaganda was not to remain uninvolved from such debilitating problems. Indeed, many of the problems between the PIB and the military remained throughout the conflict. To examine the operation of the PIB and its relations with the Crown forces it is best to begin with a series of memos written by Clarke from March to May 1921. These clearly show the faults in the Branch as perceived by Clarke to have existed during the time of the PIB's operation. Clarke had a clear view of how he wanted to run the press bureau and his ideas for improvement show the limitations of the extant structure. He believed that there were 'three main sources of news supply': civil government, police, and military.

Civil Government

According to Clarke the contact between the PIB and the heads of the Government stood 'in no need for improvement'. Within those departments, however, there were issues. Problems arose because in no department was anybody employed with the task of forwarding information on activities or items of public concern. Clarke had maintained strong informal links with each department but, as he wrote, 'the contact is too personal to be secure in the event of my absence'.[115] To combat this, he urged that the head of each division should be asked to call the attention of the PIB to matters of public concern or interest. He also asked that any periodical progress reports or special reports be passed on to the PIB for perusal and on the sanction of the head of the division be used for the preparation of 'Public Information'. This testifies to the fact that Clarke's office was understaffed, not having enough assistants to liaise with each department and more importantly even by April 1921 he was not receiving the relevant information from his colleagues.

Police

The relationship between the police and the PIB was close to Clarke's ideal working relationship and one he tried in vain to impose on the military. The PIB had access to 'all reports of day to day events' and by April 1921 access to all Chief Inspector and Detective Constable monthly reports. The police were far more liberal with the transmission of information than the military and the PIB had the services of two Cadets (Ernest Dowdall and a Cadet Vignoles) who were employed in writing special articles and paragraphs on the Auxiliaries. Auxiliary Cadets were encouraged to send articles, photos and general impressions of their time in Ireland to the PIB. Many of them did, but the results were generally not of a standard suitable for publication.[116] In stark contrast to the attitude of the military, the police were quite open to arranging tours for journalists of differing areas of the country. The potential propaganda opportunities of these tours were obvious, giving the police the chance to present their policies and actions in a positive light.

Military

The PIB's greatest difficulties lay with the military and especially General Macready. Major Reginald Marians, whom Macready had set up as the military liaison with the press, operated outside the structure of the PIB and his position was seemingly very similar to that occupied by Captain C.P. Brown (the PIB official dealing with military news). Clarke noted that the military had the right to hold up and examine all the official publication of news emanating from the Martial Law Area (MLA) (from December 1920 in effect in eight southern counties) and news from all sources concerning the military. This included news concerning joint actions between the military and the RIC. This was a large proportion of the official news of Irish affairs and Clarke was anxious that the military machinery should prove no impediment 'to free and rapid circulation'. Unfortunately for him, their 'machinery for checking news is slower than our machinery for collecting it from other channels'.[117] By 1921 the PIB had stationed a journalist, Percy J. Russell, in Major Marian's press office at military GHQ but this had not improved relations. The main problem Clarke faced was that those involved at the military side were soldiers who were totally inexperienced with dealing with the press. While this was issue could have been resolved, the second problem was more intractable: it was a question of mindsets and an: 'inability on our part and the part of our outposts to impose our propaganda policy on men of a different service and different outlook who admitted quite frankly that they did not believe in that policy.'[118]

Why were the military so loath to cooperate with the PIB? Part of the answer was that no army divulges information freely (at that time fearful of leaks to the press or even the IRA). More important was the difference in outlook that Clarke had complained of. Macready held an extremely poor view of Clarke's abilities. In early 1921 he complained to Anderson that Clarke 'has not the foggiest idea of how to set about propaganda from the point of view of a military operation'.[119] The Under Secretary John Anderson defended Clarke, saying that in regard to news of military operations 'I think we must rely on the military authorities'. Anderson continued more strongly:

> This is the basis on which we began, you will remember, some months ago though somehow or other the material did not seem to come forward very freely. Clarke's function would then be to maintain proper relations with the press and to see that the stuff was placed in the right quarter and given a good show. He would also, of course act as News Editor and criticise anything which from the press or public point of view seemed to him wrong, but I do not think he or anyone ought to create propaganda out of his own consciousness. Another point arises in regard to statements of fact. Here we are all greatly hampered by the difficulty of getting reliable information promptly and I cannot help thinking that this is a matter in which the military machine is capable of considerable improvement.[120]

Macready had many misgivings about PIB accounts of military

actions and he was obsessed, to the exclusion of all other considerations, with the reactions of the troops. In one instance he quoted a despairing letter from General Strickland, based in Cork:

> There is one thing that every soldier talks to me about, and that is while nearly every paper at home is full of the atrocities committed against the patriotic I.R.A., yet the Government avail themselves of no propaganda on the other side. The accounts are so colourless. The shooting of a murderer is as it were a 'major operation' but the murder of unarmed officers and men is just mentioned in one obscure corner of the paper as an interesting fact. The troops feel it a lot, and tell me so plainly, and I agree with them.[121]

Macready also complained on other occasions to Anderson about exaggerated reports of arms finds and military operations. On 28 March 1921 he complained that a Castle communiqué that appeared in that day's *The Irish Times* to the effect that 'information was coming forward in the Limerick area' which was under Martial Law. Macready fumed that this information was made public, as 'the IRA will take steps to see that everything is done to stop it'.[122]

What we have, in effect, are two opposing views of propaganda – that of the civil mind and that of the military mind. Clarke believed that his function was to make sure that events in Ireland were presented to the press, especially in England and abroad, in a manner beneficial to the Irish Administration and the Crown forces. Macready cared primarily about the reaction of his soldiers to adverse press-reporting and any report that could potentially prejudice military actions. There was also the mistrust of handing military news and information to a civilian. This is one reason why Macready favoured Marians over Clarke. Ego may have also played a part. In his memoirs, Macready praised the work of Marians and the military press office that Macready had created but made only an oblique reference to Clarke and his work.[123] Regardless of this prejudice, Clarke certainly seems to have been more suited to propaganda work than Marians, being both a journalist and having extensive experience as a war correspondent. Marians, on the other hand, was a soldier dealing with propaganda and as Clarke complained about the GHQ press office, 'journalistic values and word values, which count for so much in ultimate propaganda values, are not expertly weighed'.[124] Correspondence between Marians and Clarke in the Colonial Office files gives some pointers to Marian's lack of skills as a propagandist. One instance, while minor, indicates an appalling disregard for the subtleties of press propaganda and gives an insight into how the military failed to deal adequately with the press.

In early November 1920 resignations from the RIC regular force were causing much comment in the press, as was the increasing numbers of recruits joining the RIC Auxiliary force. At this time the *Freeman's Journal* printed a report on 'Recruits who Resigned – Two Englishmen tell why they want to go home'.[125] The report concerned the entry into the Auxiliary Force of two new officers. Mr T.C. Sanson, who had once served as part of the London Metropolitan police, wrote the *Freeman's Journal* correspondent and Mr G.A. Smith who had fourteen years' service in the army. These men had apparently joined in the belief that they were to be members of an unarmed police constabulary and were shocked to see the military reality of the new Auxiliary Force. When they tried to resign and get passage back to England they claimed that they were told by General Tudor, the RIC Chief of Police, that they were needed as 'there is a war on' in Ireland. The *Freeman's Journal's* damning report was all the more effective for containing the testimony of actual members of the controversial new force. Marians wrote to Clarke suggesting that it would be 'useful to discredit the Freeman's source of information'. To this end, he produced a brief history of Sanson which showed that Sanson had been discharged from the navy 'on account of a fit', had been refused re-entry to the Metropolitan Police as he had been charged with assault on one occasion and had been fined for being 'drunk and incapable' on another. This, Marians argued, would show the character flaws of the *Freeman's Journal's* witnesses. Clarke scrawled tersely underneath Marian's letter that the *Freeman's Journal* would promptly add: 'But he was good enough for the RIC.'[126]

'Crying in the wilderness' – misinformation and propaganda

Clarke's efforts at creating favourable publicity for the Crown forces were also spoiled by the actions of the head of the British Government in Ireland, Greenwood. Clarke, Anderson, Sturgis, Cope and even Macready objected to Greenwood's approach to the press reports on reprisals and criticism of the activities of the Crown forces. Despite the mounting evidence and persistent claims of brutality and indiscriminate violence made against the Crown forces Greenwood consistently rejected all evidence of any such events. His performances as Chief Secretary in the House of Commons 'often carried him beyond the boundaries of fact so that he became as one crying in the wilderness', lamented Macready.[127] Therefore, when Greenwood accused newspapers of being mistaken or lying about reprisals he was in effect accusing the newspapers of being at best, dupes of devious republican propaganda and at worst, willing accomplices against the Crown forces.

The press reacted strongly to Greenwood who had, within months of taking the post of Chief Secretary, become something of a joke among journalists, denying the military reality of the Black and Tans, claiming that reprisals carried out by Crown forces were actually undertaken by 'Sinn Feiners' in captured British uniforms and even that the burning of Cork city centre was the work of the IRA.[128] By 1921 the Irish papers and the English press critical of the Government refused to believe almost any statement by Greenwood. The *Irish Independent* wrote that his statements in the House of Commons were 'outrages nearly as bad as the reprisals policy'.[129] The same paper described him in unflattering terms:

> He is cynical and callous, brutally brusque and overbearing, and even where some occurrence is so horrible to be incapable of defence by him – and this is saying a good deal – he conveys the impression that Irish people, even women, deserve no consideration.[130]

Such views were not only held by Irish newspapers. In December 1920 the Labour Commission (British Labour Party fact-finding mission) reporting on Ireland stated that the Chief Secretary's replies in regard to questions on Ireland 'have been characterized by a disregard for the truth'.[131] No paper jumped to Greenwood's defence while *The Times* backed the report claiming that it 'casts a doubt on the accuracy of Government information, which we have long shared'.[132] Macready was moved to write to Lloyd George's private secretary to say that Greenwood's over-optimistic reports on Ireland were damaging to the Irish Administration.[133] Even Greenwood's press secretary, Norman Loughnane, complained to Anderson in February 1921 'that the police reports from the country are on the face of them false in the main' and that he was being used in 'creating a smokescreen for the CS's parliamentary answers under cover of which these things [reprisals] can continue'.[134]

These comments from Loughnane lead us into the more shadowy realm of news production and propaganda. The creation of news was the remit of two men: Press Officer of the Information Section of the Police Authority, Hugh Pollard and Secretary of the section, Captain William Darling, both of whom also had leading roles in the production of the *Weekly Summary*. In effect their work would now be called 'black propaganda'. However, while the aim was undoubtedly black propaganda, the methods and results could often, be more accurately described as 'slapstick propaganda'. The most famous of their escapades was the production of a fake version of the Dáil Éireann published *Irish Bulletin*, an escapade which rebounded against the Irish Administration (see Chapter 2). As we have seen, their paper the *Weekly Summary*, while it may have offered some solace to the police, had resulted in much negative publicity for the Crown forces and the Irish Administration. Outside of that scheme there were a number of others.

A consistent campaign of insinuation against the hunger-striking Lord Mayor of Cork, Terence MacSwiney, had also been launched. MacSwiney had been arrested in August 1920 and was found to be in possession of RIC documents that implicated him as a member of the IRA. He refused to recognise the court or the right of the British Government to try him and on his transfer to Brixton Prison in London began a hunger strike which was to shock public opinion in Ireland and internationally, especially due its prolonged nature. The campaign against him generally consisted of reports that he was secretly taking food or that he had been involved in various murders. *The Times*, to take just one example, was insistent in its refusal to believe these reports, condemning 'as grossly unjust official suggestions that he was in reality guilty of other crimes'.[135] These official suggestions, called 'a campaign of innuendo' by the *Irish Independent,* met with limited success only in such papers as the *Morning Post*. Generally, the claims that he was being fed secretly were widely dismissed across the English press, although the MacSwiney family felt it necessary to issue a statement decrying the 'campaign of misrepresentation and falsehood that has been engineered by the English government'.[136] Many of the malicious rumours may have originated with Pollard and Darling as the *Weekly Summary* seems to have been where many of the false reports first appeared in print. Calls for MacSwiney's release and the praise given to his self-sacrifice among many English papers as well as the worldwide publicity given to MacSwiney's prolonged death were proof that any campaign against MacSwiney had failed.[137]

Initial exposures of propaganda attempts reflected badly on the Irish Administration. In November 1920, photographs appeared in English newspapers showing the 'Grim Reality' of the war in Ireland. The photos supposedly taken in Tralee showed the aftermath of the 'Battle of Tralee' where a group of Auxiliaries had bravely fought off an IRA ambush.[138] There was also an accompanying Pathé newsreel (Pathé film studio, which produced newsreels as well as movies) which had supposedly captured some of the fighting. The *Irish Independent*, on the following day, published the 'Battle of Tralee' photograph and underneath it another photograph taken from exactly the same location – in actuality Vico Road in Dalkey, County Dublin.[139] That there had been no 'Battle of Tralee' and that the photographs and newsreel had been staged was quickly exposed throughout the press. Despite this, Greenwood did not admit that no such 'battle' had occurred until the following February.[140] The photos had been created a few weeks earlier by Pollard and Garro-Jones (who worked in the London office with Street).[141] That Pollard did not consider how easily these photos could be exposed as fakes was remarkable. Pollard evidently had a low opinion of journalists. He definitely had a low opinion of Irish people and wrote with a prejudice not uncommon at that time that the 'typical' Irish person had two 'fundamental abnormalities, namely, moral insensibility and want of foresight'. These two factors, he assured his readers, were 'the basic characteristic of criminal psychology'. Therefore, on this logic, Irish people were inherently criminal.[142] Such opinions did not bode well for his propaganda techniques. Propaganda through prejudice would not fit well with Basil Clarke's hopes for a scheme of propaganda through news.

While there are many records in the Colonial Office files of propaganda attempts, the records are impartial and were poorly kept. This caused frustration at the time and one of Clarke's staff wrote to him, in December 1920, on the dangers of a 'lack of system':

> At present I do not think any record is kept of propaganda and only general measures are in use. As the position improves we may need vigorous counter-propaganda to remove illusions which have been accepted as fact, material for counter statements should be collected and a policy drawn up.[143]

This betrays the haphazard nature of much of the British propaganda effort. It also leaves us often unsure as to who wrote an item and whether it was successfully placed in a newspaper. Many of the articles are of a poor quality, some displaying evidence of Pollard's prejudice attitudes. One article from November 1920 was intended for use following the execution of Kevin Barry. It contains what was, apparently, the sworn testimony of a spirit medium, Mrs J.A. Holloway. Making tea in her kitchen one night, shortly after Barry's death, she heard 'a voice call out from the Heavens'. It was Kevin Barry. He told her that heaven had 'melted his wicked heart' and implored her to send 'a message to the people and friends of mine in Ireland'. His friends, he told her, needed 'to stop their wicked deeds'.[144] This was not an isolated article. That same month a report was created which told of a curse upon an IRA Volunteer named as Donovan (probably Thomas Donovan shot dead during an ambush in October 1920) in South Tipperary. This curse, allegedly placed upon the unfortunate man by the local parish priest, led directly to Donovan's death. His demise 'in such a manner' the report predicted would deeply affect the superstitious people of South Tipperary and 'they may view this as an ill-omen for the future of the IRA'.[145] An almost identical article appears in the files for early 1921. Again, a parish priest had placed a curse on IRA Volunteers. This time the targets were two unnamed brothers in Swanlinbar, County Cavan. The brothers survived but their family suffered grave consequences, falling ill and dying one by one, cursed by association. 'This has been a great blow to the IRA in the locality so far' the article concluded.[146]

Who was this propaganda directed at? Was it designed to play on the minds of the supposedly superstitious Irish? The Irish press would not print such drivel so it could not be disseminated throughout Ireland. Nor would the vast bulk of the British press print these types of articles. The only possible outlet for this type of propaganda would be those who already held such views of the Irish, namely a paper such as the *Morning Post*. It is more likely that the articles were never printed and were a waste of time and resources. One pile of articles written by Pollard, Captain Charles Tower and 'Military GHQ' (presumably Major Marians) shows that only 8 out of 35 were published. The published articles appeared in the *Belfast Telegraph*, *Daily Dispatch*, *Daily Mail*, *The Irish Times*, *National News* and *Yorkshire Post* – hardly a sign of great demand for their endeavours.[147] Undeterred, attempts to publish similar types of propaganda continued and a so-called 'Sinn Fein Oath' surfaced in 1921. The 'oath' declared undying vengeance against England and strangely Scotland ('for having given aid and succour to the Beasts'). The oath, a long sectarian rant, ended with the following incantation:

> Question: What do you think of the times; will they be good?
> Answer: I think they will.
> Question: At what time?
> Answer: When we have a general shower of Protestant and heretic blood.[148]

The statement accompanying the piece stressed that it was 'an exact copy of the Sinn Fein oath' and that the paper on which it was printed bore the seal of the Irish Republic. The whole thing including the oath and the seal was fake. It clearly fitted the pattern of the work of Pollard and Darling. Under the heading 'Feeble Propaganda' the *Freeman's Journal* carried a furious Dáil statement deriding the oath as 'a filthy and blasphemous libel'. 'The Irish Republic has decreed and insists upon absolute tolerance for all religious creeds' the Dáil reply assured.[149] While the Dáil was obligated to respond to such forgeries, again it is hard to see what success such propaganda could have or what benefit it would offer to the Crown forces. Seemingly, this practice of forged Dáil documents being created in Dublin Castle was becoming a regular occurrence. A few weeks later the *Irish Bulletin* devoted a whole issue to similar forgeries, including the use of captured Dáil Éireann notepaper to make forged Dáil proclamations as well as forged letters from Dáil Ministers.[150]

Similar lack of foresight had been displayed following the burning of Cork city centre (see Chapter 5). A map of Cork was printed which was doctored to show the City Hall as adjacent to the burned-out buildings on and near Patrick Street. The map was an attempt to minimise the reprisal by suggesting that a single fire could have spread to destroy all the buildings, rather than the reality which was the systematic burning of multiple buildings. While this map has since become infamous, at the time it was seen for what it was and was only given prominence in a few newspapers such as the *Daily Chronicle* (owned by Lloyd George).[151] Cork was not isolated, Martial Law had yet to come into full effect (see Chapter 5) and many foreign journalists were in the city. The British Labour Party's Labour Commission group was studying the situation in Ireland at this time. It visited Cork within two days of the attack and repudiated claims that the IRA had committed the arson attack. The false map was immediately seen as a not very clever attempt at deception. Clarke later warned against such overt propaganda: 'As soon as propaganda becomes evident or its existence is suspected, it is bad propaganda... The service must look true and it must look complete and candid or its credit is gone at once and it becomes suspect and very soon taboo.'[152] Yet on reading the newspapers throughout mid-1920 until July 1921 one will find the press repeatedly reporting on botched propaganda attempts from 'official sources'. Many of the articles which Pollard and Darling attempted to place were simply ignored and many others were used as a stick to beat the Irish Administration, especially by the nationalist papers in Ireland.

Macready had been troubled by one such episode in March 1921. A communiqué that was issued from Dublin Castle on 28 March stated that the Crown forces had uncovered consignments of IRA weapons being moved on a large scale through the unlikely medium of fish-barrels. The Crown forces had – the communiqué breathlessly informed the press – uncovered a huge cache of weapons. Not only was this a coup in itself but timely also, as the weapons were supposedly to be used that very day in an all-out IRA assault on Mountjoy Jail. The story appeared in *The Irish Times* and many English papers, as having come from military GHQ.[153] That same day Macready wrote to Anderson to complain about this 'long piece of propaganda' and the PIB's handling of it, noting that the report had not come from GHQ and that the PIB had most likely received the story from the police (again probably from Pollard or Darling). Macready told Anderson that the actual haul was 'five rifles and forty odd revolvers', continuing 'how Michael [Collins] and Co. would laugh' at this propaganda. More seriously, he warned that the propaganda attempts were reminiscent of the exaggerated and ineffectual propaganda attempts early in the First World War which had served 'to make the [propaganda] department a laughing stock'. The same fate was now happening to the PIB, 'it gets worse every day', Macready warned.[154] Anderson was undoubtedly worried by Macready's letter. Fearing that what he now knew to be a grossly exaggerated press statement would be quickly exposed Anderson wanted to distance the Irish Administration from the statement. On the following day, Dublin Castle issued another statement saying that although the fish-barrel story had come from an official in Dublin Castle, it 'was not official and was not authorised by General Military Headquarters'.[155]

As Macready and GHQ would not stand by the story, Anderson had no option but to disavow the statement, but it left the Irish Administration looking not only duplicitous, but incompetently duplicitous. The *Irish Independent* and *Freeman's Journal* both used the incident to once again deem all Government news to be mere propaganda, while to newspapers like the *Daily News* it was further confirmation of the underhanded methods being applied by Dublin Castle.[156] The Dáil Publicity Department made use of the fish-barrel story in its *Irish Bulletin* to detail what it considered to be a whole series of fraudulent and exaggerated stories that had been released by the PIB, as well as to personally criticise Basil Clarke for the 'embellishments which are so much more frequent than accuracy in the official reports'.[157] Other English papers made negative references to the strange nature of the story over the following weeks. With this story, however, Basil Clarke can be exonerated from any blame as he was on leave during this time but that fact did not stop him and his PIB being associated with the incompetence of another botched propaganda scheme from the RIC. As regards the PIB, the fact that Clarke's absence led to such an embarrassing few days for the Irish Administration shows that little operational improvement had been made by the PIB over the previous months.[158] It also suggests a general lack of ability among his staff.

The problems with 'official news' and its successes

Clarke's hopes of a viable propaganda branch were hampered not only by the 'hydra-headed monster' that sprang from the uneasy mixture of Dublin Castle, the military and the police but also the nature of the conflict in Ireland. The public in Britain, that is to say the public that cared, had been lost to British propaganda by the time the PIB was created. For example the *Irish Bulletin* was being issued since November 1919 and Eamon de Valera had begun a lengthy and well-publicised tour of America designed to spread news of the republican cause in June of that year. D.G. Boyce has argued correctly that 'the activities of the Republican forces provided ample material for counter propaganda by the British'.[159] However, practically all sections of Irish nationalist opinion were irreconcilable with British policy during these years and so were many sections of British opinion. A common attitude was expressed in Hugh Martin's book (and in the pages of the *Daily News*) on his time in Ireland:

Whenever there was an Irish ambush, any kind of attack or assassination, the English newspapers received full and elaborate accounts from official sources, so that nothing of that was hidden. What was hidden with every precaution of secrecy by Government officials with all their power over the transmission and interpretation of news, was the other side of the picture, the sinister use of evil passions which they inspired and excused, their policy of fighting down the Irish people through a reign of terror...[160]

Similar attitudes were displayed throughout the English press. When the Government defended reprisals it was accused by the *Manchester Guardian*, *Westminster Gazette* and many others of replicating the actions of the Germans in Belgium. Both Anderson and Macready complained that: 'the section of the public which opposes the Government is ready to seize hold of anything to the prejudice of the administration'.[161] While this statement is clearly self-serving and does a disservice to most of the Irish Administration's critics it does underline the fact that the bulk of press opinion in Ireland and England, at this time, was not amenable to British propaganda.

Furthermore, even with the restrictions placed on newspapers in Ireland, the country was not a closed society and a paper such as *The Times* could choose to ignore propaganda and send its own correspondents to Ireland. Clarke tried to combat this through his 'propaganda by news' and he was definitely an able propagandist but his department found it difficult to cope with an insurrection that was so closely interlinked with propaganda. Adding to the many hurdles he faced, Clarke was distrusted and ignored by the military sections of the Irish Administration. Moreover, the lawlessness of sections of the Crown forces manifesting itself in the form of indiscriminate reprisals against civilians and their property posed a problem that could not be overcome by Clarke's 'official news' when papers such as *The Times*, *Manchester Guardian*, *Daily News* and many others from Britain and further abroad were sending their own journalists to Ireland to scrutinise these incidents for themselves.

The system of official news did have some successes but these were few and far between and tended to occur when the newspapers were not in a position to verify the facts of an event independently. For instance, the official report of the Kilmichael ambush in County Cork was one such success for the PIB. Coming a week after Bloody Sunday, this ambush was of great importance to the IRA as it resulted in the first significant and successful attack on the new force. An IRA column led by Tom Barry succeeded in surprising and killing seventeen of an eighteen-man patrol. Kilmichael was an isolated location and journalists were forced to seek information as to what happened from the nearest Auxiliary base in Macroom. However, one Auxiliary, Bill Munro, stationed in Macroom, later recollected that in the days after the attack, journalists were 'barred from the town'. Although he stated that this was due to the indignation of the Auxiliaries 'at copy being made out of our disaster' it is reasonable to suggest that management of the news was the main reason for controlling the movements of reporters.[162] Trying to enter Macroom after the ambush, *The Irish Times* special correspondent telegraphed to Dublin: 'A visit to Macroom today was a strange experience. The Press representatives were "held-up" at various points and it was almost an impossibility to secure a narrative of the crime.'[163] There was no opportunity to talk with residents in the town or members of the Crown forces who may have held information.

Consequently, his newspaper report was identical with the official report. One of the paper's local correspondents also reported that '200 civilians' had taken part in the ambush. This was a claim of the official report. A graphic list of the wounds suffered by each of the dead Auxiliaries was also provided to the paper by official sources.[164] Whatever the reason for banning the journalists from the town, the remoteness of Kilmichael and the inability of journalists to obtain independent confirmation of the events of the ambush meant that the official report was given prominence across all the newspapers.[165] This report stated that the 'dead and wounded were hacked about the head with axes' and that 'they were savagely mutilated'. The local people were accused of 'terrible treachery' as they had known of the ambush party but had not informed the Auxiliaries.[166] This detail about the local inhabitants seems strange. Perhaps some locals may have known of the ambush and were either supportive of the IRA or too intimidated to tell the Auxiliaries. However, another possibility is that the PIB may have been engaged in damage-limitation, placing some blame on the locals so that they would be seen to be partly responsible for the reprisals that were believed certain to follow. The official report, in the absence of any other available information filled the pages of newspapers across Ireland and Britain. Even the *Freeman's Journal* and *Irish Independent* used it as the basis of their reports (although they clearly marked the reports as official) and for once, there was very little counter-argument from the newspapers.[167] The story of mutilation of the dead Auxiliaries went unchallenged, except in the *Irish Bulletin*. We can see here how the military control of a locality would greatly affect the content of newspaper reports and how the news could be reported (see Chapter 5 for a fuller discussion of how the press operated under Martial Law).

A similar success for the PIB was what was called the 'Exchange Court Tragedy' – the shooting dead, while in custody, of Richard McKee, Peadar Clancy and Conor Clune. This occurred in Dublin on the night of Bloody Sunday. What actually happened is unknown but as Mark Sturgis confided to his diary it was 'a strange and possibly unpleasant affair'.[168] Republican claims that the three men had been tortured and deliberately killed are not outside the realms of possibility, considering the febrile atmosphere among the Crown forces that day. More concretely, although a friend of Clune's who saw his body said he had not been tortured, a doctor who had the opportunity to examine Conor Clune's body reported that he had received thirteen wounds, which were unlikely to have been received in the manner indicated by the official statement (see below). McKee and Clancy were both key figures in the upper ranks of the IRA and well known to the Crown forces.[169] Their capture presented an excellent opportunity to those wishing revenge for the events of the morning. The PIB press release stated the men were shot while trying to escape. According to the press release the three men had discovered Mills bombs (hand grenades) under a bed in the guardroom where they were being held. Not realising that the grenades were not primed they then attempted to use these bombs in a frantic bid for freedom and were shot in the process.[170]

Detailed information was also provided on each of the three men, showing their respective histories within the IRA. Some of this information was false. Clune was not in the IRA. Clarke gave no indication where he had received the information on how the men died while the personal information on the men was based on a memo written by Captain Darling and sent to Clarke on 22 November. Darling vaguely described his information on the three men as having come from 'various sources'.[171] Clarke retained the basic structure of Darling's memo removing some of the more excitable of Darling's language such as 'Peter Clancy died as he lived a fanatic and a desperate and a daring criminal'. From here it was issued, on 23 November, to the press in Ireland and a copy was also sent to Major Street in London. The story in the statement does not hold up to scrutiny. James Gleeson, in his book *Bloody Sunday*, made the observation that McKee and Clancy were both experienced and knowledgeable with military equipment. They would have known if the grenades were not primed. They would also have known that to use the explosives in such a confined space would have meant their certain death. Gleeson also wrote that 23 other prisoners had passed through the room that night but not one of them had seen weapons of any sort in the guard-room.[172] Even with such contradictions, this PIB statement, again in the absence of any independent means of verification and despite the very suspicious nature of the men's deaths, became the core of the press coverage of this episode.[173]

These were relatively rare successes. Clarke had a definite theory of propaganda that may have met with more success if the British Government in Ireland and the Crown forces had spoken with one voice. Instead, there was a cacophony of competing voices, each trying to grab the attention of the press. Hamar Greenwood, as Chief Secretary, simply denied all evidence that he did not like or did not support his claims that conditions in Ireland were improving (conditions were always 'improving'). The military, in effect Macready, did not like or value Clarke's work. A secret memo sent in April 1921 from the British army's Judge Advocate General's office to Greenwood concluded that 'nothing could be done to reconcile public opinion' to the policy of reprisals.[174] The memo acknowledged that some IRA attacks were undertaken to goad Crown forces into wild reprisals but, unsurprisingly, the memo blamed the newspapers for reporting on them in a critical manner. It considered these critical reports to be the main reason for the poor reputation of the Crown forces. It did not even consider the option of maintaining discipline and not allowing troops and other members of the Crown forces to indulge in these reprisals.[175]

The propaganda of the RIC/Auxiliaries was just that – propaganda. The work of Pollard and Darling was sometimes too clever, more often not clever enough. Outside of Clarke, there was no vision of what could be achieved or of how propaganda could be improved. Anderson admitted privately to Macready in March 1921 that he could not see how the publicity problems facing the Administration could be overcome.[176] Anderson was not involved in publicity and propaganda but his comments do not express any great confidence in the PIB and Crown propaganda. Marians, Pollard and

Darling on the other hand were daily involved in publicity and propaganda work yet they all had a blinkered, politically inept attitude towards propaganda, producing work of poor quality and pointlessly placing it in sympathetic newspapers (of which there were few). Clarke made this very point to Greenwood's press secretary, Norman Loughnane, after he had noticed articles from the military appearing in the *Morning Post* (articles which had bypassed the PIB). In a short forceful letter he complained to Loughnane about the futility of this attitude:

> But it would be better that we should also have chances of a cut at the same stuff so it might be put to better and more fuller use. I deny that the Morning Post is the best outlet for this kind of matter; it is a poor job preaching to the converted. Such information should and could have a home in the more neutral and widely-read papers.[177]

Although Clarke stressed this point repeatedly and was supported by Anderson, he was ignored by Macready and Hugh Tudor, now RIC Chief of Police. When it came to the negative publicity surrounding these events Tudor was very much of the same mind as Greenwood: his response was to deny evidence of reprisals, no matter the level of proof.

That attitude was the most common theme of the Irish Administration and Crown forces' reaction to critical news reporting. The Crown forces had moved from a strict censorship of the newspapers to political intimidation through suppression, then violent intimidation, topped off with often obvious and unbelievable propaganda. We can clearly see how the British Government and its forces in Ireland had alienated newspapers and reporters across Ireland and England (as well as their readers). There will be more to be said on Clarke and the PIB in later chapters but having seen how the Irish Administration and the Crown forces tried to influence and control the press we must now turn to look at how republicans tried to do the same.

2

DÁIL ÉIREANN AND THE IRA

Throughout the War of Independence most Dáil Éireann and Sinn Féin propaganda was directed outside of Ireland. This was a result of the censorship imposed by the British Government which severely curtailed the extent and impact of republican propaganda within Ireland at this time. The Irish Administration in Dublin Castle had responded coercively to an increasingly confident Sinn Féin. All republican newspapers, including Arthur Griffith's popular *Nationality* were suppressed in 1919 and the Dáil itself was declared illegal in the same year. This policy had the result that 'from 1919 onwards the party's publicity was subjected to far more drastic restrictions than in the past and was correspondingly less effective'.[1] This is not to say that republicans did not attempt to influence and utilise the press in Ireland during these years and their actions will be examined below in the context of the wider republican propaganda strategy.[2]

Tearing down the paper wall

The Sinn Féin party had utterly dominated the 1918 general election in Ireland, one which had resulted in the concurrent demise of the Irish Parliamentary Party (IPP). In the words of historian Francis Costello:

> The 1918 elections can be seen as fundamental in providing the Republicans with the ability to claim in Britain, the Dominions, the United States and elsewhere, that they had the moral authority to govern Ireland and that the British Government did not.[3]

It was on this basis of these election results and the creation of the Dáil that republicans made Ireland's claim for independence. One of the greatest aims of leading Sinn Féin members was to internationalise events in Ireland and crack what Arthur Griffith had termed 'the paper wall' that, through censorship and propaganda, the British had erected around Ireland. Many members of Sinn Féin and the Dáil realised that international interest and sympathy had to be focused on events in Ireland. This was apparent in the opening of the first Dáil when much of the proceedings were also read in French and when the Dáil proclaimed a 'Message to the Free Nations of the World'. This sought to place the case of Ireland within the context of the emerging post-First World War world:

> Ireland to-day reasserts her historic nationhood more confidently before the new world emerging from the war, because she believes in freedom and justice as the fundamental principles of international law ... because the permanent peace of Europe can never be secured by perpetuating military dominion for the profit of empire but only by establishing the control of government in every land upon the basis of the free will of a free people, and the existing state of war, between Ireland and England, can never be ended until Ireland is definitely evacuated by the armed forces of England.[4]

This statement contained a number of ideas that would be replayed by republicans over the following years – specifically the ancient and inalienable right of the Irish nation for independence. It was to propagate these ideas that the Dáil founded a Department of Propaganda under the control of Laurence Ginnell (a former member of the IPP who joined Sinn Féin in 1917), although Desmond Fitzgerald (a member of Sinn Féin who had fought in the GPO in 1916) soon took over this position (see Appendix III). In addition, Sinn Féin ran its own Department of Propaganda under Robert Brennan while Piaras Béaslaí operated as the army Director of Publicity. Art O'Brien worked as the Department of Propaganda's press liaison in London. This new impetus was vital as the republicans faced a series of obstacles to successful propaganda, which they resolved to defeat in a number of ways. On the international stage British dominance of the news emanating from Ireland had to be combated. For conducting foreign propaganda, cooperation with Irish representatives sent as envoys to foreign countries was vital. In February 1919, Seán T. O' Kelly was sent to Paris as an envoy of the Dáil with the aim of convincing the Peace Conference to take up the case of Ireland. There he immediately set up an office from which he distributed articles relating to Ireland and through which he created contacts with European journalists. Although the Dáil Éireann delegation lobbied intensively for months and Seán T. O' Kelly and George Gavan Duffy presented a 'memorandum in support of Ireland's demand for recognition as a sovereign independent state', no Irish delegation was admitted to the conference.[5]

While the failure at the Paris Peace Conference was a blow for the Sinn Féin cause the lobbying and networking of the Irish delegates did establish a framework of contacts that could be used for propaganda distribution in Europe. One problem the republicans faced was that official France was obsessed with maintaining a continued strong relationship with Britain. There still existed a palpable fear of Germany along with an equally heartfelt desire to share in the war reparations. Gavan Duffy and O' Kelly remained in France to try and 'secure the support of the French press and indirectly to influence the French Government from Ireland's point of view'.[6] This seems to have had a bearing on some of the French papers as they were soon reported to be printing 'well informed and sympathetic articles on the claims of Ireland'.[7] In spite of these emerging signs of a more sympathetic French view of Ireland, George Plunkett, Minister for Foreign Affairs, reported back to the Dáil that the progress was extremely slow: 'The French press is very conservative and anxious to do nothing to offend Great Britain'.[8] This anxiety was aggravated by the French press' reliance for their news of Ireland on English press agencies. Gavan Duffy and O' Kelly continued their work and gradually began to impress themselves on French journalists so that by June 1920 the Dáil Éireann report on foreign affairs could claim 'their efforts have so far been attended with considerable success'.[9]

French Journalist Sylvain Briollay later backed up this claim. He praised Gavan Duffy for this change but Briollay was not the only person to recognise Duffy's success. The greatest measure of his achievement came in early September 1920 when the French Government gave Gavan Duffy notice to leave France. This order was made by the French Government under pressure from their British counterparts. Sylvain Briollay detailed the background to this decision:

> ... Messrs. O' Kelly and Gavan Duffy, Irish envoys at Paris, who had been at first repulsed because of the fervour of the Anglo–French Alliance, finally by taking advantage of a certain bitterness begotten by English selfishness, succeeded in

interesting French public opinion in the fate of Ireland... The Paris Press which had always refused to accept the communiqués of the Irish Bulletin ceased to pin its faith to the accuracy of Reuter's versions of events in Ireland.[10]

The *Irish Independent* similarly praised the work of the two envoys, claiming that because of their work 'the entire French press has displayed intense sympathy with Ireland'.[11] Examples of this new and rapidly increasing sympathy with Ireland were carried in the nationalist dailies throughout the second half of 1920. Articles from *Le Matin* and *La Lanterne* were published which expressed their disgust at British policy in Ireland. In October, *Le Petit Journal* printed a full-page drawing of Terence MacSwiney on its front page. The headline was '*Le Martyr Irlandais*' – The Irish Martyr.[12] Seán T. O' Kelly remained in France to continue the work of spreading news about Ireland and countering British propaganda. By the time of the truce he was able to write to Robert Brennan that: 'There is no doubt whatsoever that the sympathy of all elements of the population here is with us'. Despite this, he warned Brennan that the political situation allying the Governments of France and Britain remained the same and there was no real chance that the French Government would recognise an Irish republic.[13] Kelly's pessimistic but accurate assessment demonstrates that influencing press and public opinion was no guarantee of political success. The experience of trying to influence press and politicians in Europe as well as the varied contacts that the republicans had made convinced them that they needed their own platform for pressing their viewpoint. It was to fill this need that the *Irish Bulletin* was created.

The *Irish Bulletin*

Charles Hathaway, an American diplomat in Ireland during the early months of 1919, commented that the editorial hostility shown by many papers to Sinn Féin was not strange because: 'in Ireland Sinn Féin has no adequate press and practically all the newspapers whether Unionist or Nationalist are controlled by elements with small sympathy for the Independence program.'[14]

Many newspapers at this time were unsympathetic to republicanism but this was changing as the newspapers in Ireland became more receptive to a population that had deserted the Irish Parliamentary Party for Sinn Féin in the recent general election. Terence MacSwiney had proposed a Dáil motion to capitalise on this new mood in April 1919 when he suggested that a daily paper be established for the purposes of publicity.[15] At the time his idea was shelved but by November it was clear that republican propaganda was suffering from the continuance of DORA and the clampdown which had seen all republican newspapers suppressed. Exacerbating this problem was the fact that the old reliance on pamphlets and posters was proving ineffective in Ireland and on the international stage. Desmond Fitzgerald decided that some form of printed counter-propaganda was vital to republican aims and to take advantage of the popular success of Sinn Féin and the increasing international interest in Ireland. He was confirmed in this opinion after travelling to London to make personal contacts with the London representatives of the foreign press. While he considered the journalists he met to be 'interested and sympathetic', he found, unsurprisingly, that they were 'entirely dependent for their Irish news upon what they read in the English Press'.[16] During 1919, as could be witnessed by the derisory commentary on the opening of the first Dáil (see Chapters 3–7), Irish news sent to foreign newspapers was rarely published and events in Ireland were often covered in a manner detrimental to the republican cause. Furthermore in the aftermath of the First World War there was solidarity among the victorious powers, allied to the fact that many of these same powers still held vast colonial empires. At governmental level, Ireland was Britain's problem. The fact the Dáil delegation to the Paris Peace Conference had been so badly snubbed did not bode well for republican attempts at international propaganda.

To lay the groundwork for the change in republican propaganda, Fitzgerald made a series of five more visits to London in 1919 to personally put the republican case to foreign journalists. This was part of the wider policy undertaken by republican envoys on the Continent at the time based on the belief that 'the press will publish from a recognized correspondent a great deal that we could never get in otherwise'.[17] Fitzgerald had through his literary contacts and through tireless work made friendships with many French journalists operating in London, including the London editor of the *Echo de Paris* and the London representatives of *Le Journal*, *Le Matin*, *Le Journal des débats*, and *Le Temps*. According to Kathleen McKenna who worked directly for Fitzgerald he succeeded to such an extent that M. Valbert, the London editor of *Agence Havas* convinced his editors to make a special feature of Irish news.[18] Furthermore, this entry into the journalistic world paved the way for meeting many leading journalists from the United States, France, Italy, Holland, Spain, Greece, Denmark, Norway, Sweden, South America and Australia.[19] These contacts would be vital if Fitzgerald's proposed news bulletin was to have a viable audience. One essential breakthrough that Fitzgerald made was to make contact with the editors of the press agencies, such as the Press Association and Reuters, which supplied news to so many newspapers throughout the world. These informed him 'that they were bound to print the stories that were reported but they would also print any other bona-fide reports they could get'.[20]

Fitzgerald was supported by a meeting of the Dáil Éireann Cabinet. On the 7 November they agreed 'A scheme for daily news bulletin to foreign correspondents, weekly lists of atrocities, entertainment of friendly journalists approved and £500 voted for expenses under Mr Griffith's personal supervision.'[21] Four days later on 11 November 1919 the first edition of the *Irish Bulletin* was printed. Its initial print run was a mere 30 copies.[22] The paper was at this stage largely edited by Robert Brennan and Frank Gallagher and throughout the next two years Gallagher provided 'a large part of the copy' of each edition.[23] Griffith was involved in setting up the paper but his role as acting President meant that he had no time to devote to the new venture. In its early days the *Irish Bulletin*'s contents were almost always confined to lists of raids and arrests or any other examples of violence from the Crown forces. It was gradually expanded so that from early 1920 Fitzgerald had began to investigate and compile more detailed and dramatic accounts of incidents believing that these more vivid accounts would arouse more interest than a mere list of arrests and raids. The *Irish Bulletin* was always anxious to legitimise the activities of the IRA and their continuous attacks on the RIC and DMP: 'In Ireland the police force is a military organisation for the repression of every phase of the National Movement, such repression frequently resulting in the destruction of life and property and the destruction of the public peace.'[24]

The *Irish Bulletin* claimed that these police were involved in a campaign of terror against the Irish population. However, it asserted that 'the terror which was created to break the spirit of the Irish people has left that spirit stronger'. Sentiments like these were clearly designed to demonstrate to foreign readers the unity of the Irish people.[25]

This national unity in the face of British terror was a major theme in the *Irish Bulletin* throughout its publication. The sessions of the Dáil courts were covered in detail and newspaper cuttings from foreign newspapers (especially English papers) citing favourable comments were utilised to substantiate the claims of the *Irish Bulletin*. The comparison was all too easily made between Irish self-sacrifice and British repression. C.J.C. Street (attached to the London Office of the PIB) admitted this when he wrote: 'Reprisals are an impossible policy. It has none of the forms of law and lays itself open to attacks by even the dullest propagandist'.[26] The *Irish Bulletin* had to do little work to create an unfavourable impression of the Crown forces and the policy of reprisals. British actions were often sufficient. The *Irish Bulletin* placed reprisals in the context of a war of aggression by England against Ireland similar to that which the Germans had recently inflicted against Belgium. The *Irish Bulletin*'s concise matter-of-fact reports and blunt lists of English aggression were covered by headlines such as 'War on Irish Women and Children', 'War on Irish Trade', 'Murder in Ireland' and 'Policemen who Murder and Burn'. The Restoration of Order in Ireland Bill was, in the words of the *Irish Bulletin*, the 'Instigation to Murder in Ireland Bill'. These themes were repeated in the paper throughout the War of Independence. The whole policy of the British Government was portrayed as one of destruction aimed at the Irish people. It was for this reason, the paper claimed, that the Government sanctioned a special police force of Auxiliaries and the so-called Black and Tans 'to carry out the policy of terror by which it was hoped the Irish people would be compelled to surrender their demand for National Independence'.[27]

When describing the activities of the Crown forces, the *Irish Bulletin* could also be shockingly explicit, providing details that would only be hinted at in the mainstream newspapers, such as when it covered the deaths of two brothers in County Clare. Henry and Patrick Loughnane had been prominent local Sinn Féin leaders while the elder, Patrick, was also in the IRA. While working on the family farm they had been arrested by the RIC before being handed to the local Auxiliaries. At their hands they suffered an appalling fate:

> On Dec 6th, the bodies were found in a pond. The skulls were battered in and the flesh was hanging loose on both bodies. The two men were evidently tied by the neck to a motor lorry and dragged after it until they were dead. Before the bodies were hidden in a pond an effort was made to burn them.[28]

The paper also regularly reported on Crown forces' violence and intimidation of Irish women. In April 1921 a whole issue was devoted to 'Outrages on Irish Women' which included sworn affidavits by women accusing the RIC and British army of rape and assault. The Labour Commission on Ireland, who attempted to investigate similar claims, believed such attacks to have occurred but reported that 'the women of Ireland are reticent on such matters'.[29] The *Irish Bulletin* also claimed to have sworn testimony from dozens more women who did not want their cases to be publicised.[30] Again, this level of detail was only hinted at in the newspaper press, but by providing the information and making it known to journalists they would undoubtedly have influenced how these journalists viewed the Crown forces. The *Irish Bulletin* only provided such stories where it had some documentary evidence. This was a result of the manner in which Fitzgerald and later, following Fitzgerald's arrest in February 1921, Erskine Childers edited the paper. Ernest Blythe, who knew Fitzgerald well, wrote of his bravery and how he:

> ... resisted the pressure to which he was constantly subjected to from most quarters in favour of painting outrages by British forces in a blacker hue than was justified by the facts and also the pressure of accepting without investigation every report of an outrage which came in from the country. The result of this attitude and the personal impression which he made was that independent foreign pressmen who admired and trusted him did ten times as much to make Ireland's case known throughout the world as would have been done if the advocates of heavy expenditure had their way or if a less transparently honest man had been in charge of propaganda.[31]

Blythe was certain that this is how the *Irish Bulletin* developed such a high reputation for accuracy for what was, after all, a propaganda sheet. The Department of Propaganda was greatly aided in obtaining the vital documentary evidence against the Crown forces by Cumann na mBan (established in 1914 as an all-female auxiliary group to the Irish Volunteers). Fitzgerald's own wife, Mabel, was the propaganda director for this organisation and she oversaw a nationwide, often unseen, network of members, who reported back any evidence they had of reprisals and associated violence by the Crown forces.[32]

Imitation being the sincerest form of flattery – the fake *Irish Bulletin*

By mid-1920 and throughout 1921, the *Irish Bulletin* was being quoted by many foreign newspapers as well as making it onto the news pages of the *Freeman's Journal* and *Irish Independent*. Even papers such as *The Times,* which had its own reporters in Ireland, used it on occasion. Its reputation for accuracy was taken up by critics of the British Government who used the *Irish Bulletin* regularly as a stick with which to attack Lloyd George and Greenwood in the House of Commons. The spiralling fame of the *Irish Bulletin* resulted in constant raids by the police and military, desperate to locate the site of its publication. This necessitated regular changes of address and by March 1921 the paper's staff and equipment resided in its ninth hideout.[33] Inevitably, one of these raids succeeded. The discovery was potentially devastating for the Propaganda Department of Dáil Éireann and the *Irish Bulletin*. Kathleen McKenna later wrote of the extent of the damage done: 'All of our equipment had been captured; all our documents; all our newspaper files; all the spare copies of the Bulletin, our primitive addressing machine with relative name-plates, and Ernie O'Malley's account of his torturing (by Crown forces).'[34]

The information gathered by the raiding party included the addresses of all recipients of the paper, information that was quickly utilised by the police. Dublin Castle issued its usual report of the day's raid but did not mention that the office of the *Irish Bulletin* had been discovered. This apparent anomaly was soon explained by the emergence of a second fake *Irish Bulletin*. William Darling, a member of Tudor's (RIC Chief of Police) staff composed the counterfeit bulletins in Dublin Castle and forwarded them to the usual subscribers of the paper.[35] It was a brilliant idea but as so often with the propaganda attempts of Dublin Castle the application of the idea was poor. The forgers put the wrong number on the fake edition. Fortunately, for the Dáil Department of Propaganda, the raid occurred on a Saturday and Monday's edition had already been posted. This also meant an extra day in which to restart production. Publication of the real *Irish Bulletin* continued and it was successfully issued on the following Tuesday.[36] The first edition of its unwanted twin appeared on the following day. This was listed as Vol. 4, No. 56 (30 March). In the real *Irish Bulletin*, that was the number of the previous day (29 March). The forgers remained unaware of this anomaly and continued to issue false editions with incorrect volume numbers.

Slight aesthetic differences between the two bulletins also existed. Anybody who had been used to reading the *Irish Bulletin* would have quickly deduced which of the competing editions was the fake. The first edition of the fake *Irish Bulletin* was very badly written. It consisted entirely of long quotes from the RIC's *Weekly Summary*, each followed by a short and unsatisfactory reply.[37] The second issue more closely resembled the style of the actual *Bulletin*, detailing lists of aggression by the Crown forces but grossly inflating the figures, speaking of 'thousands of murdered men, women and children' and the 'millions of ruined homes'.[38] The following editions were similar, even containing false Dáil proclamations and reports. Childers and his Department moved quickly to counteract the forgeries, issuing a detailed response on 7 April. A whole edition of the *Irish Bulletin* was devoted to helping readers differentiate the real from the fake.[39] By this stage, keen observers such as the *Daily News* were already deriding the 'Crude forgeries of the famous Sinn Féin sheet'. It printed extracts from the impostors to highlight this: 'The destruction of no less than 35 ricks, stacks and outlying farm buildings by Sinn Féin in one day is indeed no mean achievement. All this seems to have been accomplished without loss of human life, but there is no occasion for despondency'.[40] As the quote demonstrates, the forged *Irish Bulletins* were often extremely crude, almost satirical in nature, but they did have some initial success. Art O'Brien was forced into releasing a circular to all newspapers and press agencies in London warning them of the forgeries.[41] Childers reported in May that 'The forgeries do however cause some confusion for foreign readers'.[42]

Many newspapers were initially fooled. The *Daily News* had published a report from one of the forged *Irish Bulletins* to the effect that the Dáil had 'convened a committee for negotiations with enemy countries'.[43] The implication was that the Dáil was tiring of conflict, maybe even losing its resolve and was preparing to make peace. The forgers would have been delighted to know that this report even tricked de Valera. He had not seen that day's real or fake *Irish Bulletin* but on reading the *Daily News* report he fired an angry letter to Erskine Childers demanding that the statement 'should be corrected in the next issue of the Bulletin'.[44] Childers' reply does not survive but de Valera was doubtlessly informed of the truth very quickly. Other papers picked up on the story including the *Irish Independent* but that paper reported it 'was officially informed' that no such statement had appeared in the *Irish Bulletin*.[45] The paper does not expound on what it means by 'officially informed' but it probably means that a representative of the Dáil Department of Propaganda, perhaps Childers, visited the paper and presumably others in an effort to quell the potential damage of the forgeries.

After this early success for the fake version, the English and Irish press realised that forged *Irish Bulletins* were being circulated and, once exposed, the forgeries were widely denounced as yet another example of the nefarious techniques being applied by the Crown forces in Ireland. The *Irish Independent* wrote that 'the clumsy forger is a fool as well as a knave'.[46] In the longer term the forgeries badly damaged both the credibility of the Crown forces as well as the work of Basil Clarke and the PIB he controlled. (There is no evidence, however, that he had any part in the counterfeit productions – the forgeries seem to have been entirely the work of the police.) The newspapers had been publicly tricked and many editors and journalists were made to look foolish by their original acceptance of the forgeries. The *Irish Bulletin* exploited this situation and used the affair to place all the blame for the forgeries with 'the Publicity Department at Dublin Castle'.[47] Most journalists agreed with this analysis. Although the forgeries were a police operation outside observers just viewed them as another example of British Government propaganda. The sentiments of the *Daily News* were widely shared across the press: 'It is scarcely necessary to comment on the character of a Government organisation which permits itself to use this contemptible and dishonest means of confounding a nation. It fits in exactly with all of our official dealings in Ireland.'[48]

While damaging to the PIB, this episode ultimately enhanced the *Irish Bulletin*'s reputation. By January 1921 the Dáil Report on Propaganda was able to state that: 'The Foreign Press makes considerable use of the *Irish Bulletin*'.[49] By March it was reported that the *Irish Bulletin* was being circulated daily 'to two hundred English newspapers and public men', and 'weekly to three hundred other persons including many Continental and Colonial newspapers and journalists'.[50] By May, after the forgeries, this figure had increased to 650.[51] By August the surge upwards had reached 900 'newspapers and specially selected individuals'.[52] The *Irish Bulletin* was clearly successful and largely accepted as a legitimate source of news on events in Ireland but it is noticeable that most of these reports concern foreign circulation. There is little in the Dáil reports on the press in Ireland.

Dealing with the Irish newspapers

The effort put into Irish newspaper propaganda lagged far behind that directed abroad. There were a number of valid reasons for this. The Irish Administration and the Crown forces were actively suppressing newspapers and intimidating journalists. Owing to the suppression of republican newspapers since 1919 there was no natural home for republican newspaper propaganda. Further, the Dáil was confident that it had the support of the vast majority of the people and that it was vital to direct its limited resources onto the international stage, especially Britain, Europe and the United States. These limited resources needed to be used as efficiently as possible. Fitzgerald was determined to keep costs down and he was suspicious of schemes that would require large portions of the budget devoted to publicity. This caused a number of resentments within the Dáil. Seán MacEntee, TD for South Monaghan, was consistently critical of the work of Fitzgerald and the Department of Propaganda. On a number of occasions he accused them of leaving the press in Ireland 'in the hands of the enemy'.[53] Fitzgerald repudiated this and explained how he saw the situation regarding newspaper propaganda in Ireland:

> The remnant of the Irish Press was terrorised, so that internal Propaganda could only be done by posters or through organisations, and any such Propaganda must have the active support of the people to be successful. He failed to see how they could carry out Propaganda in Ireland unless they had machinery for it. His idea was to run the Department on as little money as possible. Most people engaged in National Propaganda spent huge sums. His Department's methods had been to use other people and other people's money as far as possible.[54]

The Dáil agreed to vote the Department an extra £5,000, some of which was to be used for work in Ireland.[55] In March 1921, Childers (Fitzgerald had been arrested in February) informed the Dáil that: 'Steps have been taken to maintain closer touch with the Irish Press and to supply it, so far as can be safely done, with information of an authoritative character.'[56]

One step was to try and improve relations with the national newspapers. There was the ongoing strong relationship with the *Freeman's Journal*. In early 1920 Martin Fitzgerald, the owner of that paper, agreed to let his Dáil namesake, Desmond, use the paper's telegraph wire to send out around 300 words a day to newspapers and press associations on England and the Continent. The two men had agreed on this after Desmond Fitzgerald had met with representatives of the press agencies from France. These had informed him that they would use reports from republican sources if it could be forwarded daily by telegraph.[57] The two men had also agreed a secret deal whereby more wire services would be supplied if the *Irish Bulletin* was ever put out of commission by the Crown forces.[58] In return, the paper had also received a few major news stories, such as the speech of D.C. Smyth to the RIC in Kerry, from Michael Collins and the Department of Propaganda (see Chapter 3). De Valera now ordered that when such news stories were available, the *Irish Independent* should be given equal prominence as its 'wider circulation should be availed of to the full'.[59]

Another development was that correspondents from foreign newspapers who wanted interviews with leading figures such as de Valera, Collins and Griffith would now have to agree to provide full copy of their interviews to any Irish newspaper who wanted to print the interview.[60] The correspondents seemed happy to agree and throughout 1921 the Irish press carried a stream of such interviews from major American and other newspapers and press agencies. This was important as it allowed the republican leaders to speak directly to the Irish public. By May, Piaras Béaslaí could report that:

> ... he would be able to answer any questions that would arise regarding the [Publicity] Department as he was in touch with it every day from the Home Propaganda aspect. The scope of their work had been greatly extended. The Military and Civil sides were brought more into touch than before, and the 'Bulletin' was now issuing a review every week of the military operations. 'An t-Oglach,' the official organ of the Army, would be used as a Propagandist organ, and steps were being taken to have it circulated to outside publicity institutions. Extracts from it were being published in American papers, and he was trying to get them into the Irish, English and other daily papers also. A number of leaflets were being prepared and printed at the present time to counter the Enemy Propaganda at home.[61]

Although Béaslaí and Gallagher began to work more closely together to keep in contact with the Irish press, *An t-Óglach* was never used by the Irish press to any great extent. Problems with Irish-directed newspaper propaganda persisted. De Valera had written to Childers a few weeks earlier giving a more pessimistic assessment than Béaslaí: 'I had a talk yesterday with the M.D. [Cathal Brugha, Minister of Defence] relative to propaganda. He thinks, and I agree with him, that there has been so far very little evidence in the Irish press that it has been influenced by our new organisation.'[62]

Certainly, the *Irish Bulletin* was not a major factor for Irish newspapers, although it was used occasionally by the *Freeman's Journal* and *Irish Independent*. The surviving lists of the recipients of the *Irish Bulletin* from mid-1921 show that it was widely distributed across Britain, Europe, America and Britain's Dominions. It even reached Japan and China. In Ireland, however, it did not venture outside the Pale. Not one regional and only three Irish newspapers are listed as recipients, the *Freeman's Journal*, *Irish Independent* and *The Irish Times*.[63] It is doubtful whether the paper would have been used by the regional press even if it had been sent to them. The Irish Administration's nationwide suppression of newspapers in September 1919 for carrying the Dáil loan prospectus had a profound effect on the press. Regional papers that had previously printed news sent to them from Sinn Féin, suddenly ceased to do so.[64] As the intimidation of newspapers by the Crown forces increased throughout 1920 the papers became understandably wary of placing Dáil material within their columns. This wariness turned to outright fear as Martial Law was extended throughout the eight most southern counties of Ireland in 1921.

This was confirmed by P.S. O'Hegarty in a letter to Richard Mulcahy (IRA Chief of Staff). O'Hegarty had been working for Mulcahy in trying to improve relations between the IRA and the regional press. He had met with many reporters but he warned Mulcahy that his dealings with press men had convinced him: 'that little can be done with local correspondents, save in a few outstanding cases. A good number of them are unsympathetic or hostile, the majority are too intimidated to be of any use.'[65] Mulcahy did try to rectify this problem and establish more formal relations with the regional press. This can be seen from his General Order Number 23 (these General Orders came from IRA GHQ and were applicable to all IRA members) in May, which ordered local Brigade Commandants to use a suitable Volunteer as a 'special reports officer' whose job would be to supply 'the local press and local press correspondents with information which it is desired to make public'.[66] There is little evidence that this had much of an effect over the months leading to the Truce. O'Hegarty had also noted how the intimidation administered by the Crown forces to journalists and newspapers was having an effect. This he believed was a major factor for local correspondents of Dublin-based and foreign newspapers.

Accounts of fights and shootings are usually telegraphed to Dublin. The local man has to hand in his message at the local P.O. [Post Office] and present a pass signed with his name. This makes him an easy target for Black and Tans if he reports anything they object to.[67]

There was nothing that Mulcahy and the IRA could do to combat this kind of fear and intimidation.

Even the members of the Dáil Department of Propaganda were unable to meet with Irish journalists, as they had hoped to do. Piaras Béaslaí and Frank Gallagher bemoaned the fact the sheer volume of work prevented them from dealing with Dublin journalists other than through written correspondence.[68] Both men were aware of the value of good personal relations with journalists as was the case between the Department and foreign correspondents. In July 1921 calls were still being made for a stronger focus on Irish-directed propaganda: A memo was sent to Piaras Béaslaí from the office of Richard Mulcahy: 'It is desirable to increase the Irish Circulation of the 'Bulletin' because its articles are just the sort of material required to improve the morale of large sections of the people'.[69]

The fact that such a statement could be made in July 1921 shows that much of the republican propaganda efforts were directed abroad over the previous two years and shows also how the combined effects of British censorship, intimidation of newspapers and press control throughout Ireland had very much inhibited republican newspaper propaganda in Ireland. It was not until November 1921 during a re-organisation of the Department of Propaganda that a section was devoted specifically to the Irish newspapers.[70]

Republican attitudes to propaganda and press influence

There is no doubting the importance with which the republican leaders regarded propaganda and the skill with which they applied it. In this sense the Dáil had an advantage over the PIB. While there were debates and disagreements within republican circles about the extent and success of propaganda, figures such as Collins, de Valera, Griffith, Mulcahy and the various staff of the Department of Propaganda had remarkably similar notions of what was the best way to publicise the case for Independence and the war against the Crown forces. There was a lot less of the petty bickering and distrust that marred the efforts of the Irish Administration in Dublin Castle. The counter state symbolised by the Dáil was itself an enormous propaganda exercise designed to show the Irish people and the world that the party could provide a viable alternative to British rule. The activities of the Dáil courts were reported widely in many, though not all, of the newspapers. These courts were vital in keeping the reality of a counter state alive in the minds of the population. This was especially important to the Dáil, which met rarely in the period between October 1919 and July 1921 as many of its members were either imprisoned or trying to avoid prison. Arbitration courts were set up to deal with the potentially explosive and intractable issue of land disputes and rule from Dublin Castle became less and less a factor in the lives of people in many areas. Horace Plunkett (the driving force behind the co-operative movement in Ireland) told the American journalist, Carl Ackermann, that 'You now have in Ireland two governments, a de jure government repressing a de facto government, which has the greater force of the people's will at its back.'[71]

The Republic was now being experienced by people as tenuous but tangible reality. A Limerick unionist chronicled in June 1920:

> Sinn Fein rules the County and rules it admirably...The fact is that everybody is going over to Sinn Fein, not because they believe in it, but because it is the only authority in the County; and they realise that if their lives and property are to be secured they must act with Sinn Fein.[72]

Praise for the counter state was common in 1920 from Irish papers like the *Irish Independent* and the *Freeman's Journal* as well as English papers such as the *Daily News, Manchester Guardian, Observer* and *The Times*.[73] Mary Kotsonouris has described the reaction of the Provincial press: 'The provincial papers in July and August [1920] carried a steady stream of reports of parish courts being set up all over and gave the names of the justices appointed as well as full accounts of proceedings.'[74]

These Dáil Courts and the Volunteer police filled the space left by the retreating RIC. Darrell Figgis, a prominent Sinn Féin member described what it was like to travel through Ireland in 1920:

> ... one saw roofless walls, stark and black, of burnt-out police barracks, loose casements rattling unheeded in the wind, sandbags piled in the windows, through which the sky was seen, and steel, loop-holed sheeting, often twisted by fire, over the friendless deserted doors. They were with all their paraphernalia of defence, a sign and mark of the change that had come.[75]

The RIC barracks that remained occupied were no longer a part of the local community. They had become isolated and militarised fortresses. This was a coherent part of Dáil and IRA policy, although its effects seem to have bypassed the British Government despite repeated warnings by *The Irish Times* on the vital need to not only support the police militarily but also to reoccupy the abandoned barracks. As *The Irish Times* saw it, 'if the police go, everything will go'.[76] The cumulative effect of these changes must have had a more powerful effect on the Irish population, both nationalist and unionist, than any rhetoric about Irish independence, no matter how stirring, any press propaganda, no matter how expertly judged or any assurances from the British Government about restoring 'law and order', no matter how strongly worded. By May of that year even *The Irish Times*, although still utterly opposed to the Dáil, spoke of the 'bold and not unchivalrous law-givers of the Republican movement'.[77]

The 'Dáil Loan' initiated in June 1919 was another example of practical propaganda. This was a direct appeal to the Irish people to finance the republican counter state and by the September 1920 Michael Collins was able to report that £370,000 had been raised in Ireland.[78] For the purpose, the Dáil had even created a short cinema film. It showed Collins sitting at a table in his role as Minister for Finance as the other Dáil members beginning with Griffith subscribed to the loan. For added symbolism, the table behind which Collins was seated was the block on which Robert Emmet had been beheaded.[79] The time to write Emmet's epitaph was close at hand. Other schemes designed to promote the counter state such as the Dáil's Commission of Inquiry into the Resources and Industries of Ireland continued to work and report throughout the whole of the War of Independence, although Irish newspapers were banned by the Irish Administration from reporting on its proceedings.

This skill was not only evident in the political arena. Ned Broy, who worked closely with Collins and was one of his spies in the DMP, later wrote of Collins' awareness of the consequences of the IRA's actions:

> In 1919, assassinations could have damaging political consequences. Broy remembered that he would always work out how the public would react to the shooting of a G-man first. Then he would hang back for another while before he'd have another shot.[80]

This not only shows that republican leaders like Collins had a natural aptitude for propaganda but also helps explain the relatively low level of attacks on police in 1919. As we shall see nationalist newspapers were not supportive of these attacks, especially at that time (see Chapters 3, 4 and 5). Neither was the Irish public, Figgis wrote, ready for open warfare on the RIC. This fact was widely appreciated among republicans in 1919. He describes the Sinn Féin-inspired social boycott of the RIC, which had been in place since 1917, as a means of 'propaganda' to prepare the Irish people for the war that was to follow. It was part of 'a much larger and more ambitious campaign' that would culminate in attacks upon all the Crown forces.[81]

Collins was not the only member of the upper echelons of the IRA to possess this awareness of the political aspects of the IRA campaign. Richard Mulcahy held similar beliefs. According to historian Maryann Valiulis: 'Mulcahy had an abiding concern that the IRA act in a way which would visibly disprove the British view that those who were waging the war of liberation were nothing more than murderers, thugs and common criminals.'[82]

This concern was evident regarding the burning of large estate houses. As the regularity of Crown force's reprisals increased IRA units began the policy of destroying local estate houses. The Cork number 2 Brigade proposed an intensification of this policy so that where a reprisal by British forces has occurred 'a similar number of houses belonging to the active enemies of Ireland be destroyed'.[83] As most of these houses were owned by Protestants, any such increase in attacks would have provided ample opportunity for British propagandists to claim a sectarian aspect to the IRA campaign. This could have been extremely damaging from a propaganda perspective. Richard Mulcahy's response in General Order No. 26 was that arson attacks on estate houses should occur only if the owners were 'the most active enemies of Ireland'. It was further stressed that: 'For the purposes of such reprisals no one shall be regarded as an enemy of Ireland, whether they may be described locally as, Unionist, Orangemen, etc, except they are actively anti-Irish in their outlook and actions.'[84]

To further prevent the policy from getting out of hand, sanction for such attacks had to be obtained from the Brigade Commandant, who had to seek permission from Divisional Headquarters, which would inform General Headquarters of the action.[85] A similar scheme proposed by Liam Lynch (Commandant 1st Southern Division) to shoot a local loyalist for each IRA prisoner executed or shot by Crown forces was also dismissed by Mulcahy.[86] In the Dáil a scheme proposed by Seán McEntee that for 'every citizen of the Irish republic executed by the enemy, a subject of the enemy Government shall be executed by us' could not find any other member present to second it.[87]

Although the shooting of spies did not command anywhere near the amount of press coverage afforded to reprisals, Collins, Mulcahy, Childers and others were worried about the effects of these shootings, especially of women spies. The IRA execution of Mary Lindsay had resulted in much negative publicity. Lindsay was suspected of informing on a battalion of the Cork IRA leading to the death of one volunteer and the subsequent execution of three others from that battalion. Her death in March 1921 was well publicised in the English papers as she was an elderly woman and had been executed in reprisal for the execution of six IRA men in Victoria Barracks, Cork.[88] Following detailed reports in English and Irish newspapers of another execution of a supposed female 'spy', Kitty Carroll, Childers wrote to Collins in April 1921 asking which of the following he should place in the *Irish Bulletin*: 'Shall we say, (a) the execution of women spies is forbidden, and that Kitty Carroll was not killed by the IRA? Or (b) Kitty Carroll was killed in contravention of the IRA'.[89]

Kitty Carroll had been shot dead by the IRA in Monaghan. *The Times* reported the 'poor Irishwoman' was 'put through a farce of a trial after which she was found "guilty" and then shot dead through the head'.[90] IRA GHQ had provisions in place to try and prevent such occurrences. General Order No. 13 from November 1920 had ordered deportation for women spies, rather than execution, although there was some debate about this in the IRA. A Commandant in the Roscommon IRA wrote to Mulcahy in early 1921 ask whether GHQ had 'yet decided whether Capital punishment should be inflicted on women spies'.[91] It does seem that the policy towards women spies was modified over the following months and there are reports of the shooting of a few women 'spies'. These included Kitty Carroll and Mary Lindsay. Mulcahy was especially insistent that the correct procedure should always be followed when dealing with those considered spies and informers. The procedure involved a court of inquiry, after which sentences had to be ratified by the Brigade Commandant and then passed to the Adjutant General in GHQ. Mulcahy retained the final decision.[92] General Order No. 17 from April 1921 allowed the death penalty only on 'written covering authority from General Headquarters'.[93] Once again, it must be stressed that this policy proved hard to implement in more violent areas where the pace of events meant that local commanders often ignored procedure and acted of their own accord. The execution of Mary Lindsay had not been sanctioned by IRA GHQ, for example. What the General Orders signify is the political and publicity concerns of the GHQ leadership.

By May 1921, Mulcahy had given General Order No. 23. This dealt exclusively with 'War Publicity' and contained a number of important initiatives. Brigade Commandants were to promptly forward to GHQ reports of 'conflicts, ambushes, attacks, execution of spies and enemy outrages in their district'.[94] It seems that the transmission of such reports was not common beforehand. The Department of Propaganda was closely involved in the creation of the Order. It would bear all costs of sending a member of a Brigade to GHQ to provide such information.[95] While a large part of this initiative was to gain further evidence against the Crown forces, another aspect was the control of potentially damaging news stories such as the execution of spies. This was highlighted again by a letter Childers wrote to the Minster of Defence, Cathal Brugha, weeks later. He stressed the need for regular reports from the IRA. This information was vital as it was required 'to combat enemy propaganda arising from such cases as Kitty Carroll'.[96] He also asked that he be kept informed of any IRA change in policy with regard to burning houses as counter-reprisal, execution of prisoners and other events that could be used against the IRA.[97]

While some figures such as Brugha were wary of the work of the Department of Propaganda and did not have an understanding of how publicity and propaganda worked, both Collins and Mulcahy instinctively realised the political aspect of the violence in Ireland. Being in the crucible of Dublin rather than an area of more sustained IRA success such as Cork, they realised that the IRA were not capable of an outright military victory. As such it was vital to attack the enemy on the political and propaganda fronts in the hope that their will to wage war would be sapped. This point had been noted in 1920 by the writer and politician Stephen Gwynn while working as a special correspondent for *The Times*: 'The shrewder brains understand the military realities of the position and manoeuvre to maintain a state of affairs in which the Government cannot count upon public support in Britain for a real use of military force.'[98]

Charles Townshend has written correspondingly about IRA violence:

> Collins and Mulcahy were the principal representatives of the new realism, which had emerged after the Rising. Though not pure terrorists, they may be said to have conceived the Volunteers' military campaign primarily as armed propaganda. Collins in particular pursued a campaign in which violence was at bottom symbolic.[99]

Consequently, Collins and Mulcahy were always aware of the needs of the Department of Propaganda. Others within the Dáil were not so aware.

The Department faced a number of criticisms regarding its propaganda. Some of these criticisms came from within the Department itself. After Fitzgerald's arrest, Art O'Brien wrote to his replacement, Childers, asking for more funds and making it clear he had 'some little misunderstandings' with Fitzgerald on this issue.[100] Art O'Brien argued that more efficient and concerted efforts were needed to maintain relations with foreign journalists working from London. As far as O'Brien was concerned, his section was grossly understaffed.[101] Fitzgerald, however, remained sure of the need to keep costs down and he dismissed many schemes as too costly and liable to backfire. Seán MacEntee, J.J. Walsh, TD for Cork city and Cathal Brugha, Minister of Defence, made a number of representations for large-scale propaganda campaigns to be conducted in England. Other TDs requested that the Department of Propaganda buy advertising space in English papers or distribute 50,000 posters per week throughout England. This, Joseph MacDonagh TD for North Tipperary, claimed would have 'a demoralising effect on the British Government' although he never explained what these posters would contain that would so frighten Lloyd George and his Cabinet.[102] J.J. Walsh wanted the Dáil to instigate 'a propaganda campaign on a scale likely to affect the internal harmony of England'.[103] Any such scheme as that proposed by Walsh to affect the internal harmony of England was not only grossly impractical and ruinously expensive but would also have left the Dáil and Sinn Féin open to accusations of 'Bolshevism'.

The Bolshevik seizure of power in Russia had occurred only a few years earlier and newspapers like *The Times* were publishing pamphlets such as 'The Horrors of Bolshevism'. Henry Wilson, the Commander-in-Chief of British Land Forces, and the British Cabinet were gravely worried by the possibility of large-scale labour strikes in England. Nevertheless, Sinn Féin and the Dáil were never seriously tarred with the socialist brush. *The Irish Times* occasionally made half-hearted references to supposed links between the Dáil and socialist groups, while British propagandists made some efforts in 1921 to turn diplomatic correspondence between Dáil Éireann representatives and the Bolshevik Government of Russia into proof that the Dáil was part of a vast socialist conspiracy.[104] These claims were ignored by the mainstream Irish and British press. Perhaps one reason such claims failed to damage Sinn Féin and the Dáil was because it was obvious that the leaders as well as the vast majority of both organisations were not socialists. Even Lloyd George rejected this when he told Unionist politicians that it would be a 'mistake' to conclude 'that Sinn Fein is purely a Bolshevist conspiracy against Great Britain'.[105] Another reason was that foreign journalists could come to Ireland, see events for themselves and bypass propaganda, if they so wished. They would have seen no such links. Whatever the reasons, the Department of Propaganda backed by Cabinet members such as Collins, Mulcahy and de Valera, as President, were not willing to sponsor propaganda campaigns like that suggested by Walsh. A recurring theme of republican propaganda was that Ireland had no quarrel with the English people and that a free Ireland would be independent but friendly with England and any such schemes would have run counter to this notion.

Death was another symbol that could be utilised in the promotion of one's cause. In the aftermath of Bloody Sunday the Crown forces gave a sombre and imposing accompaniment to the coffins of the dead officers as they made their slow journey to a boat in Dun Laoghaire. When the dead men arrived in Britain, Lloyd George was in attendance to witness the passing of the funeral cortège. Despite such a display, republicans were the masters of the propaganda of martyrdom. Following the death, in 1917, of Easter Rising leader Thomas Ashe, Collins took the opportunity to organise a massive funeral[106] with 3,000 uniformed Volunteers accompanied by a crowd of tens of thousands in attendance.[107] Scenes like these were repeated during the War of Independence on many occasions (if not on such a large scale) even though the Irish Administration was determined to prevent funerals becoming mass participation propaganda events. This determination was manifested in the aftermath of the death of Terence MacSwiney when the army tightly controlled Cork on the day of the funeral. Despite these controls MacSwiney's tricolour-draped coffin had already travelled slowly through the streets of London as thousands of Londoners watched in silence.[108] The *Manchester Guardian* described the extraordinary scenes: 'Here was all the assistance of the police and the city authorities to carry through a great demonstration, with rebel flags and rebel uniforms and the whole greeted with respect by the English people.'[109]

As MacSwiney lay in Cork City Hall, another journalist from that paper observed:

> The austere figure within it is clothed in the uniform of the Brigadier of the Republican Army. It is the only uniform there, but Volunteers in mufti stand rigidly on either side of the coffin and form a cordon along the street outside.[110]

Notwithstanding the Bishop of Cork's repeated condemnations of the IRA (see Chapter 5), 'eight bishops and hundreds of priests' accompanied the thousands of other mourners on the journey to the cemetery.[111] Other funerals also became huge, sombre public events. For example, the *Freeman's Journal* and *Irish Independent* gave large reports on the 'impressive funeral scenes in Dublin' as hunger striker Francis Gleeson was taken to his 'martyr's grave' in May 1920.[112]

In Ireland, even though many were uneasy about the violence of the IRA the deaths of young Irish men at the hands of the Crown forces stirred such deep emotions that much of the press began to see the conflict as a war between two nations. The execution of Kevin Barry shows this process of change as the Irish papers called for the execution to be rescinded due to the fact that Barry was a 'prisoner of war' and not a common criminal. Barry's age (he was eighteen) also allowed the Crown forces to be portrayed as the bloodthirsty killers of Irish youth. Barry, a medical student at University College Dublin and a member of the IRA, had been arrested in September 1920 at the scene of a fatal IRA ambush of British soldiers. The British Government and the PIB tried to publicise the fact that one of the soldiers killed in the ambush (two more died soon after) was of similar age. However, while the *Irish Bulletin* portrayed the unfortunate British soldier as a paid mercenary, Barry was seen as the embodiment of a nation struggling to free itself from foreign oppression. Irish nationalist newspapers, independently of the *Irish Bulletin* and the Dáil Department of Propaganda, took the same line. When Barry's sentence became known, both Griffith and Childers had long letters published in English newspapers. Both letters covered similar themes. Childers wrote:

> This lad Barry was doing precisely what an Englishman would be doing under the same circumstances and with the same bitter and intolerable provocation – the suppression by military force of their country's liberty. To hang him for murder is an abuse of power and, an unworthy act of vengeance, contrasting with the forbearance and humanity invariably shown by the Irish Volunteers towards prisoners captured by them.[113]

But even without such letters, there was little anger at death of the three young soldiers in the English newspapers. As historian M.A. Doherty has written, 'Privates Whitehead, Washington and Humphries remained faceless names and numbers'.[114] There was sorrow that the men had been killed but the situation had changed violently in the weeks since Barry was captured. His capture happened on the same day as the Balbriggan reprisal which had focused so much attention on Ireland. Even in the weeks since that reprisal, the Crown forces were increasingly seen as vengefully violent and servants to a Government policy which was ultimately embittering Ireland and destroying Britain's international reputation.

Reporters: how to win friends and influence people?

What of republican intimidation of the press? This was undoubtedly an aspect of the IRA campaign in many areas; however, in the absence of more evidence it is hard to judge the level of this intimidation. From the evidence that does exist, it seems very probable that republican assaults on press freedom did not reach anywhere near the level of those practised by the Irish Administration and Crown forces, which had the ability to mount legislative attacks on the press through the Criminal Law and Procedures Act 1887, DORA, the ROIA and Martial Law. Furthermore, in regard to attacks on newspapers the Crown forces and especially the Auxiliaries were extremely active in the final year of the conflict. This was because, on balance, the press in Ireland was far more critical of the Irish Administration and the actions of the Crown forces than their Dáil and IRA counterparts. However there are examples of serious republican intimidation of the press. When the *Irish Independent* published a report of the IRA ambush on the Lord Lieutenant, French, which criticised the IRA, its offices were attacked within days. Dan Breen recalled in his memoir that the IRA Volunteers involved in the ambush were particularly upset at the criticisms of an Irish-owned paper 'that depended on the support of the people who had voted for the establishment of the Irish Republic' (see Chapter 4).[115] The same fate befell the *Cork Examiner* one year later in December 1920 following that paper's consistent condemnations of IRA violence. In both instances, severe damage was caused to the printing machinery. Also in Cork, the IRA attacked the premises of the *Skibbereen Eagle* and the *Cork Constitution*.[116] *Cork Constitution* editor, H.L. Tivey, was ordered to leave the country but he refused, bravely maintaining his role as editor and continuing to criticise the IRA.[117] There were certainly other such incidents elsewhere.[118] This is clearly implied by a discussion in the Dáil between TD from Cork West, Seán Hayes and Piaris Béaslaí (TD for Kerry East and editor of *An t-Óglach*). Hayes asked:

> ... if any action could be taken against provincial papers, such as the *Cork Examiner*, whose propaganda was hampering the work of the Republic and weakening their position throughout the country by advocating a policy of moderation.[119]

Béaslaí commended Hayes for raising the matter and continued: 'The *Independent* and *Freeman* were pursuing a policy of the same nature and the Department would try to devise some scheme for getting at such papers. They recognised that it was largely a military question.'[120]

Yet there is no indication that any action was taken against these papers. At this time the Department of Propaganda supported by de Valera was involved in making attempts at providing Irish papers with news and reports. Intimidation of newspapers would not have been compatible with this policy. The only violent action taken against these papers during 1921 was taken by the Crown forces. There was undoubted frustration among some members of the IRA and Dáil with attitudes of the Irish press. Especially upsetting to some was newspaper commentary that advocated a level of settlement closer to Dominion Home Rule rather than an outright Republic. Both the main dailies, the *Irish Independent* and the *Freeman's Journal* followed such an editorial line. Piaras Béaslaí wrote a number of disapproving letters to these papers criticising their coverage and language. The letters were critical but made no threats against either paper.[121] Again, it must be said, the level of intimidation was certainly far less than that practised by the Crown forces. The national dailies report very few instances of republican intimidation. For example, *The Irish Times* makes no reference to IRA attacks on provincial papers despite its willingness to use Dublin Castle's 'Official Reports'. The Colonial Office files display a similar lack of such reports. Of all the PIB press statements issued to the press from August 1920 to July 1921 there are no statements relating to intimidation of newspapers bar one attack on *Cork Examiner* employees and as we shall see below this attack was almost certainly undertaken by Crown forces.[122] An IRA GHQ report on all IRA activities from March 1921 until the Truce, mentions no attacks on newspaper offices or journalists.[123] Nor is there any report of republican intimidation of foreign journalists comparable to that of Hugh Martin's reports of his experiences in Ireland. When Greenwood was asked to substantiate claims he made in the House of Commons that the IRA had forced foreign correspondents to leave the country, he was unable to provide any names.[124] Nor did any journalists come forward to say they had been expelled from Ireland by the IRA. What can be said is that violent attacks on the *Irish Independent* in 1919 and the *Cork Examiner* in 1920 show that there existed sections of the IRA who were willing and able to try and intimidate newspapers whose reportage they sufficiently disliked.

There was one attack on *Cork Examiner* employees in May 1921 which seems at first glance to be a likely example of IRA intimidation. The attack was made on a group of four *Cork Examiner* staff returning home after work. The group comprised two composers and two proofreaders. The paper reported that a bomb was thrown into the group and this was followed by revolver fire. One of the men, Stephen Dorman, lost a leg and died the next day.[125] In an earlier article the author had written on this topic it had suggested that the suspicion of responsibility for the attack lay with the IRA as the facts seemed to strongly suggest an IRA ambush. After all, the paper had been attacked by the IRA previously and there were many instances of civilians being shot as spies and informers. The IRA in Cork had few qualms about attacking those it considered enemies and many of them were angered by the paper's criticisms of the IRA.[126] Historian, Peter Hart, writing about this incident argued that 'the *Cork Examiner* staff were gunned down after the paper refused various IRA demands'.[127] However, the belief that the staff members were attacked by the IRA has been 'fatally undermined' by the work of John Borgonovo. He clearly shows that the dead man, Stephen Dorman, was a member of the IRA's Second Battalion in the city. He then, convincingly, places the attack within the context of an ongoing British reprisal campaign against IRA members.

Dorman was targeted because he was a member of the IRA, not because he worked for the *Cork Examiner*. The attackers were unknown members of the Crown forces.[128]

Indeed, for the most part, the Dáil Éireann Department of Propaganda worked tirelessly to create and maintain contacts with journalists reporting about and from Ireland. Fitzgerald developed contacts with many foreign journalists and Briollay speaks of American, Australian, English, French and Spanish journalists coming to Ireland in 1920. Many of these made contact with Sinn Féin and the Dáil with a view to ascertaining the situation in Ireland.[129] Bennett has written of how the Dáil Department of Propaganda facilitated this by taking journalists on what Dublin Castle called the 'republican scenic railway':

> Desmond Fitzgerald called on you at the Shelbourne Hotel, and with an elaborate show of secrecy arranged an interview with Arthur Griffith ... You had invitations for tea from Mrs Erskine Childers, Maud Gonne McBride and Mrs Stopford Green, who described atrocities they claim to have seen. Then you went to Thurles to see the Archbishop of Cashel ...[130]

What Griffith and Collins also played upon was the romance of secret meetings between journalists and the most wanted men in the Irish counter state. There was an elaborate series of arrangements to be followed before a reporter could meet with a leading republican figure. Ernie O'Malley, one of the IRA's outstanding organisers, who regularly delivered reports of Crown reprisals to the Department of Propaganda, met many foreign journalists in the company of Fitzgerald: 'It was a mild adventure for some, an exciting thrill for others, to talk to men of the hidden government, for whom Castle officials, seen earlier in the day, were hunting.'[131]

One brilliantly designed example of this type of republican propaganda involved the unmasking of British spy, Frank Hardy. Hardy had arrived in Ireland with the aim of capturing Collins but the goal of his mission became known to IRA intelligence. Collins lured him into a meeting chaired by Arthur Griffith and Desmond Fitzgerald in which Hardy was to offer his services to Collins' intelligence network. Arriving at the meeting Hardy was met by Griffith and what he was informed were the assembled leaders of the IRA's Dublin Brigade (in actuality journalists). While Hardy expounded on his plans as a potential counter-spy, the 'IRA leaders' read a dossier compiled by

Collins. This dossier detailed how Hardy had been convicted of a succession of fraud and forgeries and had been convicted to five years' imprisonment in 1918. When he had finished speaking, Griffith informed Hardy of the trap and told him that he had better leave the country that day. Hardy departed from Dun Laoghaire that very afternoon. The *Freeman's Journal* and *Irish Independent* presented a full account of the 'English Spy Unmasked', commenting on it in both their editorials and their news sections.[132] The incident was also good propaganda for republican claims that the British were using criminal elements in their war in Ireland as both papers detailed the multitude of forgery offences of which Hardy had been convicted. The drama of the staged exposé made such a good article it would have been irresistible to the newspapers and Briollay detailed that among the supposed IRA leaders there were American, Spanish, English and French journalists.[133] Indeed, *Irish Independent* journalist Michael Knightly recalled that he and Seán Lester, news editor of the *Freeman's Journal*, were the only Irish journalists there. He wrote that the American journalists in attendance were amazed while 'the English journalists were disgusted' by the tactics of the Crown forces.[134] This all points to Collins' tactic of keeping close contacts with journalists and his heavy involvement in the exposure of other stories damaging to the Crown forces, such as an inflammatory speech by an RIC Divisional Commissioner in Kerry during 1920 (see Chapter 3).[135]

The growing number of foreign journalists in Ireland throughout 1920 and into 1921 can be gauged from the Irish press which carried the interviews of leading Dáil figures such as Collins, de Valera and Griffith with foreign newspapers. From December 1920 and de Valera's arrival back into Ireland from America the Department of Propaganda seems to have organised these interviews. In the following months until the truce de Valera was interviewed by papers as diverse as *L'Oeuvre*, the *Manchester Guardian*, the *New York Herald* and the Swiss paper *Neue Zeitung* as well as meeting with representatives of the press agencies such as United Cable Service (Australasian). Collins also held interviews with American papers such as the *New York American* and with Carl Ackerman of the *Philadelphia Public Ledger*. In these interviews the republicans usually adopted a hardline position with de Valera ruling out Dominion Home Rule, claiming a republic as the only acceptable outcome, and Collins playing up to his image of the military hawk telling Ackerman that: 'Ireland had been fighting for 750 years and there was no reason why she could not go on a long time still'.[136]

Statements such as these have to be taken in the context of ongoing secret negotiations aimed at creating a truce. Republicans had obsessively worked over the past year to prevent any negotiations or rumours of negotiations from being portrayed as a weakening on the part of the Dáil or the IRA to continue the war. They were not always successful. In November 1920, Wexford TD Roger Sweetman, proposed an end to IRA violence as well as peace negotiations between the Dáil and the British Government.[137] This was followed within days by acting President of Sinn Féin, Father Michael O'Flanagan's telegram to Lloyd George also proposing a peace conference.[138] The telegram had no backing within Sinn Féin or the Dáil and came as a huge surprise, not only to the press and public but to Sinn Féin and the Dáil. Although acting President of the party, O'Flanagan's influence was minimal. Understandably, the press picked up on the telegram and the *Irish Independent* as well as some regional papers reported that 'the call for a truce in Ireland meets with more and more encouraging support'.[139] The incident did force Collins as acting President of the Dáil (de Valera was still in the United States and Griffith had recently been arrested) into responding via the Irish newspapers. He wrote that: 'At the present moment there is a very grave danger that the country may be stampeded on false promises and foolish ill-timed actions. We must stand up against that danger.'[140]

Other leading members of Sinn Féin also moved to dismiss O'Flanagan as acting without authority and it became quickly apparent to the press that there were no immediate prospects of a truce. But the story did have some of the consequences that republicans feared.[141] Although Lloyd George was intrigued by O'Flanagan's telegram and Sweetman's letter, the reaction within the British Cabinet and the upper echelons of the British military was that the Dáil was indeed desperate for peace. In a typical misreading of the situation Greenwood told the Prime Minister that 'The SF cause and organisation is breaking up … there is no need to hurry in settlement'.[142] On his return from his publicity tour of the United States in December 1920, de Valera was determined there would be no repeat of that fiasco. In a letter to Childers, he stressed how reports of peace and negotiations should be handled by the Department. He suggested that reports of negotiations be dismissed and that the following line be maintained at all times:

England has no right whatsoever in Ireland. The presence of her forces here is an invasion of the rights of the Irish people. They must be removed. The Irish people must be recognised as an independent nation with a right to determine freely its own government. Interference or dictation from outside must be ended. That done, England and Ireland might well be the most friendly of nations.[143]

When he got back to Ireland de Valera took an immediate hands-on interest in Dáil Éireann propaganda. Within months he had taken the decision to rename the Department of Propaganda the 'Department of Publicity'. 'Propaganda has acquired an evil odor these days' he explained to Childers.[144] After Fitzgerald had been apprehended by the Crown forces de Valera moved quickly to install Erskine Childers as his replacement. De Valera seems to have had a closer relationship with Childers than he had with Fitzgerald and both men were very much of one mind when it came to influencing the news. On replacing Fitzgerald, Childers had stressed the importance of a change in the republican propaganda campaign. He wrote:

> Nothing struck me more, when I first got insight into the publicity department, than the failure of the political side to take responsibility for the Army and its work ... it was only by insisting that it [IRA] was waging a legitimate war of defence and by basing propaganda on that principle could one meet the torrent of defamation.[145]

Childers displayed a characteristic that seems common to all good propagandists: paranoia. There was no 'torrent of defamation' as he described it but he was determined to counter all opinion that was not fully sympathetic to the aims and methods of Dáil Éireann and the IRA. De Valera agreed. He was especially worried about British propaganda which attempted to portray the IRA as 'the murder gang'. This phrase had been Lloyd George's and the British Government's mantra throughout the previous year. In March 1921, de Valera gave one of the most important interviews of this period to the press agencies, the International News and the Universal Service. For the first time Dáil Éireann, through de Valera as President, took responsibility for the actions of the IRA. Of the IRA, de Valera said: 'One of our first governmental acts was to take over the control of the voluntary armed forces of the nation ... This army is, therefore, a regular State force under the civil control of the elected representatives ... It is the national army of defence.'[146]

As Childers had advised, this action allowed de Valera to defend IRA ambushes of Crown forces as a war of national defence. De Valera told the journalists:

> If they [Crown forces] may use their tanks and steel armoured cars, why should we hesitate to use the cover of the stone walls and ditches ... If German forces had landed in England during the recent war, would it have been wrong for Englishmen to surprise them?[147]

These arguments were replayed in all de Valera's extensive series of interviews at this time. Another recurring theme was the Dáil's refusal to consider anything less than an outright republic and its determination to continue fighting until this was achieved. Questions on the six counties of the northeast and the unionists within were always answered in a similar manner:

> We have shown that we stand for civil and religious equality, for equal security and equal opportunity for all citizens, for giving to minorities full proportional representation. Provided the unity and independence of Ireland is preserved, we are ready to give such local autonomy to Ulster, or to any other part of Ireland, as would be practicable, if it would make for the contentment and satisfaction of the citizens resident there.[148]

They were noble sentiments but they did not consider how to deal with unionists who refused to countenance incorporation into any 32-county state. More problematically for the Dáil, the northern state was up and running, although de Valera tended to treat the new state as a temporary measure in interviews, as an attempt by the British Government to cause rancour and division. The typical republican argument was that a negotiated settlement for the whole island would solve this problem.

These interviews were facilitated by the close contacts that Fitzgerald, Gallagher, Childers and others had created with journalists. Arthur Griffith was especially well respected by reporters. A lifelong journalist, he understood what the newspapers required. Desmond Ryan, on the staff of the *Freeman's Journal* at the time wrote that 'journalists always spoke very highly of Griffith. He was most approachable and kindly'.[149] Erskine Childers was perhaps the most active of all. His diaries detail meeting after meeting with journalists from all over the world. Before becoming Director of Propaganda,

Childers had travelled all over Ireland to meet with journalists, bringing copious notes. He also regularly travelled to Britain, where he was well known as a writer and journalist, not only to meet with the Department's representative, Art O'Brien, but also to press the Irish case with British politicians.[150] It may well have helped their work that both Childers and Fitzgerald were English and with English-made reputations. Fitzgerald was also well known and respected by journalists in England. This was very apparent after Fitzgerald's arrest in February 1921. Many English newspapers carried complimentary reports on Fitzgerald's character and work.[151] Kathleen McKenna gives an insightful account of the closeness of some of these contacts in the aftermath of Fitzgerald's arrest:

> Mrs Fitzgerald immediately contacted Guy Moyston, representative of the United Press in America, and Mr Boyd of the Manchester Guardian, both excellent friends of ours, highly sympathetic with Ireland's cause and fond of Desmond in a personal way due to meeting him frequently in MacGilligans. They at once got in touch with Basil Clarke, the Castle publicity and press man.[152]

The efforts of the two journalists, who warned Clarke that they would publicise any violence done to Fitzgerald while in custody, ensured his safety. They also point to the kind of relationships that influenced the press in Ireland. Moyston, who could often be seen in a pub with the Dáil's Director of Propaganda, was the representative in Ireland of an American press agency that supplied 1,200 newspapers in the United States.[153]

It was with good reason that Fitzgerald had told the Dáil in January 1921 that 'the point of view of the pressmen usually improves the longer they stay here'.[154] Hugh Martin, for example, was initially very sceptical about reports of reprisals in Ireland, considering them to be exaggerated republican propaganda. Within a few months of returning to Ireland he reported in the *Daily News* that the word 'reprisals' now only meant one thing 'to the whole of the English-speaking world' and that was the violence that the Crown forces were inflicting upon Ireland.[155] Another reporter, Donald Boyd, of the *Manchester Guardian* who was also sceptical of the stories of reprisals, 'reformed greatly' according to Frank Gallagher during his stay in Ireland. Gallagher may well have played a significant role in Boyd's reformation. The two men had become firm friends over the previous months.[156]

Over in the PIB, Basil Clarke must have been aware of the disadvantage his department suffered in this regard. He developed the idea of housing correspondents with sections of the Crown forces in the hope that these close contacts would enable the reporters to see the Crown forces at first hand, develop a rapport with the men they were covering and ultimately report on the Crown forces 'more intimately, accurately and probably, therefore, more sympathetically'.[157] The idea went nowhere. That was in August 1921 and the journalists would not have given up the freedom they had enjoyed to become what would later be called 'embedded reporters'. Perhaps the clandestine manner in which republicans like Fitzgerald and Childers were forced to operate gave them the opportunity to establish these more informal and friendly ties with the journalists they sought to influence. These incidents do show the crucial importance personal contacts played in the Department of Propaganda's success. These contacts were vital in the propagation of republican views at home and abroad.

Having seen how the competing protagonists attempted to deal with newspapers and reporters, it is to the press that we must now turn.

3

THE *FREEMAN'S JOURNAL*

The *Freeman's Journal* was one of the two most widely read and influential nationalist papers in Ireland (the other being the *Irish Independent*). It had a long history of support for the Irish Parliamentary Party (IPP) and Home Rule for Ireland. Indeed, since 1912 the paper had actually been subsidised and run by the IPP but by 1919 that party was discredited and almost totally without influence in Ireland. The IPP which for so long had dominated Irish politics had been comprehensively defeated at the polls. In its place stood a triumphant Sinn Féin, refusing to take its seats in Westminster and advocating complete separation from Britain. Following these elections there was much residual bitterness directed at Sinn Féin from IPP supporters. The *Freeman's Journal* had even commented in their aftermath that there was nothing to choose between Sinn Féin and the unionists since neither were going to represent the nationalist population at Westminster.[1] Of more pressing concern for the paper were the financial difficulties that were becoming more apparent. Exacerbating these problems and in tandem with the decline of the IPP, the circulation of the newspaper was falling. The paper's printing works had been very badly damaged during the 1916 Rebellion and since then the paper had been in poor financial health.[2] It was in such a condition that the *Freeman's Journal* began 1919.

1919 – New owners
The first major events of the War of Independence have come to be seen as the opening of the first Dáil in Dublin and the Soloheadbeg ambush in Tipperary. Both events occurred on 21 January 1919. The ambush took place in Tipperary where Dan Breen and Seán Treacy led a group of Volunteers in an attack on an RIC party transporting gelignite. Two RIC men, Constables James McDonnell and Patrick O'Connell, were shot dead in the attack following their courageous

refusal to surrender the explosives. Of these two events, the paper gave the opening of Dáil Éireann far more coverage and the two events were not seen as linked by the paper. In this regard, the paper was correct. Breen had organised and carried out the attack without orders from the Volunteers (as the IRA were called at this time). Unsurprisingly, given that it was a Sinn Féin body, the paper expressed clear anxiety regarding the first Dáil, envisioning a no-win situation for Ireland. The editorial argued that if the instigators of the Dáil did not seriously consider giving effect to the measures they proposed – such as abstention from Westminster and the creation of an Irish republic– they would humiliate the Irish nation whereas if they were serious then, 'we are on the eve of one of the most tragic chapters in the history of Ireland'.[3] The criticism of the Dáil was mirrored by an attack on the 'stupidity of British officialdom in Ireland' and their continued policy of newspaper censorship.[4] The censorship which prevented both the Declaration of Independence and the Democratic Programme outlined in the Dáil from being printed in Irish newspapers irritated the *Freeman's Journal* greatly. The paper 'resented' the way in which regulations designed for wartime use such as DORA were now 'being used for the Government's political purposes in Ireland'.[5]

This criticism, not only of the continued censorship, but also of almost every decision by the Irish Administration, continued throughout 1919. By June of that year the paper had become bold enough to carry a full statement of the 'Memorandum in support of Ireland's claim for recognition as a sovereign independent state'.[6] This was a Sinn Féin memorandum handed to Georges Clemenceau, the President of France, accompanied by a letter signed by Eamon de Valera, Arthur Griffith and Count Plunkett. The memorandum and letter were designed to gain support for Ireland at the Versailles Peace Conference. In criticising the Administration the paper was echoing other influential sections of Irish society. The following day the Irish Hierarchy's condemnation of the Irish Administration was carried. This statement by the Bishops admonished the 'rule of the sword' emanating from Dublin Castle that was 'supremely provocative of disorder and chronic rebellion' in a country that was 'a distinct and ancient nation'.[7]

As the second half of 1919 approached it was apparent that Ireland was increasingly restive. The Irish Administration responded with more coercive measures. This increase in tension encouraged some elements to suggest possible settlements for Ireland. One of the first inklings of the possible nature of a new settlement seems to have been *The Times'* proposals in July for the dissection of Ireland into two legislatures, one of which would contain the nine Ulster counties (see Chapter 7).[8] The *Freeman's Journal* was dismissive of the plan, especially the proposed partition. Another plan that was proposed by the *Spectator* in mid-October proposed a six-county 'Ulster' state. The *Freeman's Journal* took the opportunity to warn that 'the six-counties fiction is once more emerging'.[9]

However, the ongoing financial problems soon re-emerged as the main worry for the paper. As support for the IPP fell away, the circulation of that party's main press supporter had declined with it and in a further blow the paper's production costs were greatly increased by the worldwide shortage of paper in the years after the First World War.[10] The paper's financial situation was now beyond repair and the remnants of the IPP were unable to keep financing the paper. A liquidator was appointed to the paper in September and a report in the *Irish Independent* stated that during the previous May the *Freeman's Journal* had been unable to pay its debtors and that the paper's solicitors were forced to admit that the company was 'unable to meet its current liabilities'.[11] The financial problems were so pressing that in October the *Freeman's Journal* was sold and came under the proprietorship of Martin Fitzgerald, (a prominent Dublin businessman) and R. Hamilton Edwards (a British journalist). Neither man had links with the IPP.

Under the new ownership, the paper's editorial tone began to change measurably, showing increasing sympathy in many important respects towards Sinn Féin. In addition, the Irish Administration in Dublin Castle endured the paper's increasingly vicious criticisms over the following months. The staff of the paper had already comprised many republican-minded journalists such as Seán Lester and Hugh Allen to whom the new owners now gave more freedom. Lester, who had by this time become news editor, had been a member of the Irish Republican Brotherhood (IRB) and of the Gaelic League.[12] Allen, a reporter, had been fired from his first reporting job, as the lone Catholic reporter of the *Belfast Telegraph*, for making a fiery speech at an election meeting of the IPP.[13] Another reporter, Desmond Ryan, was to join the paper's staff in early 1920. Ryan had fought at the GPO in 1916 and had been later interned with other republican prisoners at Frongoch in Wales.[14] These men were to play an important part in guiding the paper in a new direction. While this new editorial strategy may be seen as an attempt to revive a flagging circulation, the level of antagonism the paper was to arouse from the Irish Administration and the Crown forces in the following eighteen months suggests the owners, specifically Fitzgerald, were motivated by a strong desire for change in Ireland.[15] Desmond Ryan later recalled that Fitzgerald hated the Dublin Castle Administration and 'told his staff to go ahead and let the Castle know what he thought'.[16] The staff lost no time in following Fitzgerald's orders. The increasing militancy of the Irish Administration was seen in such rulings as the new motor permit whereby licensed owners of automobiles had to obtain a military permit to possess and operate their vehicles, something which greatly inconvenienced business. This and other new laws were portrayed by the paper as an attempt to foster rebellion in Ireland (a claim also tentatively advanced by *The Times*).[17] Both papers wondered aloud if there existed a 'hidden hand', some 'design in the sustained series of so-called blunders and stupidities that have reduced Ireland to chaos'.[18] The suggestion was that there was a coterie of so-called 'hawks' within the military keen for the 're-conquest' of Ireland.[19] This torrent of criticism so incensed the Irish Administration that, in December 1919, they made the draconian decision to suppress the paper (see Chapter 1).

The changing nature of the *Freeman's Journal* reporting can be seen in its coverage of the ambush on the Lord Lieutenant in December 1919. This was the IRA's most daring action so far, involving a large-scale ambush on Lord French near Ashtown in County Dublin. The ambush narrowly failed and came as a great shock to the Crown forces. By this stage the *Freeman's Journal* had been suppressed for almost one week. However its sister paper, the *Evening Telegraph*, had begun to produce 'Early Morning Editions' using the *Freeman's Journal*'s staff to replace the suppressed paper. This paper was to act as the de-facto *Freeman's Journal* over the period of the suppression. Despite the extraordinary pressure that this paper was under, it still managed to put a different perspective from other newspapers on the events surrounding the ambush. Firstly, Martin Savage, a Volunteer and the only fatality of the attack, was termed the 'young man shot dead' as opposed to the *Irish Independent* and *The Irish Times* who described him as an 'assassin' and a 'murderer'.[20] More noticeable was the coverage of the attack itself. This different use of language continued in the *Evening Telegraph*'s description of the attackers as 'delinquents' rather than 'assassins'. Whereas the two other national dailies had simply portrayed French's escape as a brave fight against inept attackers, the *Evening Telegraph* wanted to know how the ambush party had made their escape. Posed also was the question as to how the attackers had 'obtained the knowledge they possess as to movements of their victims'.[21] According to the paper only French's staff in the Vice-Regal Lodge was to know that he was even in Dublin. These were courageous comments by a paper that had seen its sister paper suppressed for asking similar questions of the military and the Irish Administration.

1920 – A year of confrontation

Although officially suppressed, the paper, through the *Evening Telegraph*, continued to openly oppose the increasing militancy of the Crown forces and the Dublin Castle Administration. Each day, 'Double column leaders howled defiance at the Castle' recalled Desmond Ryan in his memoirs.[22] Equally fervent loathing was directed towards what was to become one of the dominant themes in Irish affairs, the proposed 'Bill for the better Government of Ireland'. This Bill was created by a committee headed by Walter Long (a former Chief Secretary of Ireland). It proposed the partition of Ireland, although there was some scope for a future unification of the 32 counties under a Council of Ireland, involving representatives from both parliaments. Initially, the committee had hoped for all of the nine counties of Ulster to comprise the Northern parliament but this was vehemently opposed by James Craig and northern Unionists. They wanted a secure Unionist majority and persuaded Long and the committee to propose a six-county northern state. Such a state would have a far larger Unionist majority than a nine-county state, therefore making certain of a Unionist majority at all times. This would also destroy one of the stated aims of the Bill, the hope for the eventual reunification of Ireland.

From early 1920 as more and more details into the workings of the proposed Bill became known, the hostility shown by the *Freeman's Journal* increased substantially. Unsurprisingly, the most unpalatable clause was the proposed partition of the six north-eastern counties from the rest of the country and the paper now used every opportunity to attack the 'partition bill'. An excellent opportunity to do just this came with the results of the municipal elections of January 1920 when Sinn Féin, the Nationalist Party and Labour took 273 of the nine-county Ulster's 560 seats, with a combination of nationalists taking control of Derry City Corporation. The editorial of 19 January 1920 was exultant in its claims that despite Edward Carson's warnings to unionists to vote the straight party line, proportional representation had 'justified its existence by exposing once and for all the fallacy of a homogenous Ulster upon which Lloyd George bases his latest Home Rule proposals.'[23]

The *Freeman's Journal* reappeared on 28 January after over six weeks of suppression. It thanked the British press for the help and support which they had offered to the paper. The editorial then warned the Administration that although the suppression was an attempt at 'extinction not punishment' the paper would not be intimidated.[24] Certainly, the paper showed no let-up in its criticisms of the Crown forces and the despised Government of Ireland Bill, writing that though Carson's name would not be on the Bill his 'handwriting will be found all over it'.[25] The same editorial warned that the Bill, while on the surface a scheme to give self-government to Ireland, was in reality designed to 'give legislative effect to the principles of the Ulster Covenant'. This crusade to expose what it considered the fallacy of Ulster's homogeneity also encompassed fears for the future of any nationalist minority within a partitioned state. According to the *Freeman's Journal* the population of Ulster excluding Belfast city contained 397 more Catholics than all other denominations together. Furthermore, in the zone of supposed unionist homogeneity, Tyrone, Armagh, Fermanagh and Derry, Catholics were in a minority of only 53 people.[26] There was only one way to defeat this proposed partition, argued the *Freeman's Journal,* and this was through trade, or more precisely, a lack of trade with the partitioned counties. The paper's editorial advised: 'Ireland holds a power of blockade as effective as the fleet that the impulsive but shifty Mr Churchill threatened to mobilise on the morrow of the Curragh revolt.'[27]

This power of blockade involved a suspension of trade with the 'charmed circle of the Covenanter's territory'. The paper held that Ulster banking and trade would be destroyed by such a boycott, which would then force the 'hard-headed businessman' within unionist circles to realise that partition meant 'embarrassment and decay'.[28] By this stage the paper's previous IPP sympathies were but a memory and its new attitude corresponded very closely with that of Sinn Féin, who later that year sanctioned a boycott of goods emanating from Belfast.

The text of the 'Bill for the Better Government of Ireland' was released on the evening of 27 February and in common with the other dailies in Ireland the *Freeman's Journal* expressed anger at what it called 'an audacious fraud' designed for the 'plunder and partition of Ireland'.[29] The text of the Bill was published under the heading 'Partition in its worst form – Two parliaments: both in chains and powerless for good'.[30] Commenting on claims that the Bill provided for eventual Irish unity, the paper countered that this was entirely 'when Ulster pleases'. Other sticking points were the fact that Irish Acts were to 'be subject to Acts of the UK Parliament' and that the Viceroy could choose (or veto) the heads of all Irish departments. The hostility the *Freeman's Journal* displayed towards the Bill mirrored that of practically all nationalist Ireland as well as southern unionists (see Chapter 6). This groundswell of negative opinion greatly comforted the paper who confidently predicted that the Bill was 'doomed to early dissolution', simply because it tried to govern 'with the dissent of the governed'.[31]

Alongside criticising the Government of Ireland Bill the *Freeman's Journal* continued its attacks on the Irish Administration throughout 1920. Lord French and the Administration under John Taylor were berated with editorials and reports calling them the 'most abject failure in the history of Irish Government'. In February the *Freeman's Journal* linked an extensive but largely failed raid on Sinn Féin members to the 'German Plot' of 1918, which had been an attempt by the Irish Administration to break Sinn Féin through mass arrests. The 'plot' was a creation of Dublin Castle and became notorious throughout nationalist Ireland. The paper replied to the Government actions by warning that 'nationality is too sane to be deceived by these stale tricks of defeated coercion'.[32] The paper claimed a few days later amid speculation that Lord French was to leave Ireland that his legacy was a country 'dragooned even more thoroughly than General von Bissing dragooned Belgium'.[33] It made many similar comparisons with Germany's treatment of Belgium during the First World War. The incarceration of the Sinn Féin Lord Mayor of Dublin, Thomas Kelly, who was arrested as part of a mass arrest of republicans, was treated as matching the German deportation of the Mayor of Brussels.[34] In mid-February an editorial attacked the Government inaction over the examples of military and police action. The shooting dead, in Limerick, of a young woman, Lena Johnson who 'was murdered by a policeman who fired without orders' was held as a particular example (see also Chapter 4).[35] The use of the term murder is insightful for at this time the *Freeman's Journal* had come to call shootings of policemen 'appalling tragedies' and the like rather than 'outrages' and certainly not 'murder'.

From this time onwards violence throughout the country began to intensify and the death toll climbed quickly. This rise was signalled by two deaths: Tomás MacCurtain, Lord Mayor of Cork and Resident Magistrate, Alan Bell, in Dublin. The first of these deaths came on 20 March when MacCurtain was shot dead in his home by unknown members of the RIC. The *Freeman's Journal* unequivocally blamed 'a conspiracy of vengeance, formed by enemies of the Sinn Fein movement and supporters of British rule in Ireland'.[36] Unlike other nationalist commentators such as Bishop Cohalan in Cork and the *Cork Examiner* who utterly condemned the murder of the Lord Mayor but also blamed republicans for the current state of affairs, the *Freeman's Journal* saw the British Government and Irish Administration as the real instigators of the current violence and dissatisfaction in Ireland. The paper accused the Government of antagonising the whole Irish nation with a repressive and draconian system of military rule commentating that 'when law is administered in a system of lawlessness, then, as Burke says, the end is anarchy'.[37] This is not to say that the paper condoned violence, as it called on the citizens of Cork 'not to allow themselves to be tempted into a campaign of retaliation'.[38]

Despite such pronouncements the paper was accused of encouraging violence only a few days later (26 March 1920) with the death of the Resident Magistrate, Alan Bell. Two IRA Volunteers took the elderly Bell, who was travelling with no guard, from a tram and shot him dead. Bell was killed on the orders of Michael Collins because of the potentially disastrous effects of his investigations into republican funding. The *Freeman's Journal* had reacted fiercely to Bell's appointment just weeks earlier. He had been given wide-ranging powers to examine otherwise private bank accounts and the paper had accused him of being part of a plot to destroy the commercial fabric of the country. While none of the other papers had published anything like this level of detail, the *Freeman's Journal* scrutinised every aspect of his work.[39] Michael Collins and IRA intelligence knew of Bell and would have killed him with or without the publicity afforded to his current work. Bell had a long history of intelligence work in Ireland and outside of his current investigations of republican funding he had also supplied intelligence on republican suspects to Lord French and Basil Thompson, the head of British Intelligence.[40]

Nevertheless, the conviction arose that the publicity surrounding Bell had made his death more likely and *The Times* and other English newspapers gave substantial exposure to the *Freeman's Journal* coverage of Bell. The future GOC of the British Army in Ireland, Nevil Macready, also held the belief that the paper was partly responsible for Bell's death.[41] Macready's antipathy towards the *Freeman's Journal* was to have severe consequences for the paper, as we shall see below.

Undeterred, the *Freeman's Journal* continued its criticisms of the Administration and rejoiced when the Chief Secretary and long-time target, Ian Macpherson, was removed from Ireland in April 1920. While the new Chief Secretary, Hamar Greenwood, was to quickly become an implacable foe of the paper, he was initially warmly greeted in an editorial which claimed him to be 'a believer in civilian control and self determination'. The report also stated, without any corroborating evidence, that if the new Chief Secretary had a free hand he would 'be an advocate of Dominion Home Rule'.[42] Disillusionment set in very quickly among the journalists of the *Freeman's Journal*. Within two weeks the paper ran a scathing editorial titled 'Wanted - Sanity and a Policy'. The paper said it realised now that new personnel meant no change in Castle policy and that Greenwood was: 'so ignorant of Irish facts and so indifferent to Irish opinion that he is telling the electors of Sunderland that there is a sufficient body of moderate opinion in the south and west of Ireland to work the partition and plunder Bill.'[43]

The disillusionment was exacerbated by the beginning of a mass hunger strike in Mountjoy Jail by untried members of the public arrested on suspicion of involvement in IRA activities. The *Freeman's Journal* devoted most of its news sections to the hunger strikers and their imprisonment by what the paper termed 'the army of occupation'. It also supported the Irish Labour Congress' calls for a general strike in support of the 'imprisoned Irishmen fighting for freedom'.[44] This strike was carried out peacefully and successfully and the prisoners were released on 14 April 1920. This was greeted by the banner headline: 'Mountjoy Battle Won: Castle's Unconditional Surrender'.[45] The paper now calling itself 'Ireland's national newspaper' was now seen as pro-Sinn Féin both within the Castle and elsewhere. At this time *The Times* was quoting from *The Irish Times* to demonstrate 'southern Unionist opinion' and using the *Freeman's Journal* as the gauge of 'Irish Nationalist opinion'.

The Irish Administration was becoming more irate with the

Freeman's Journal's reporting. A foretaste of future pressures on the paper may have been that on the day of the prisoners' release, the *Freeman's Journal's* telegraph wire to London was cut (the wire was taken, apparently, because Dublin Castle required all available wires to London). The *Freeman's Journal* took the event as a direct assault on the paper and as 'the Castle's answer to the flagellation which the *Freeman's Journal* had administered to it'.[46] This was not hubris. One of the first acts of the new GOC of the British army in Ireland had been to meet with Irish and English journalists in General Headquarters, where he specifically criticised the *Freeman's Journal's* reportage. Macready generally disliked the press but had taken special exception to an article in the paper that argued that soldiers who indulged in revenge and reprisals were 'no longer soldiers but a mob'. The article was reprinted the following day under the banner headline: 'Macready appoints himself critic of the Freeman'.[47]

The paper continued to invoke the ire of the Irish Administration. While ignoring or treating with suspicion the Castle-inspired 'daily lists of outrages' the paper carried occasional news from the *Irish Bulletin* and also carried many reports on 'the activities of Irish Volunteer patrols and sessions of Sinn Féin courts'.[48] The editorials and reports that filled the paper during these months clearly illustrated that the paper's owners believed it to be the only newspaper in Ireland 'fighting single handed, at great cost, the cause of Ireland'.[49] This was done in a series of open-letter editorials to various figures in the British Parliament. These letters accused them of lying about the situation in Ireland while English newspapers were attacked by the *Freeman's Journal* for producing 'lie after lie regarding conditions' in Ireland. Almost daily, the paper corrected erroneous reports that had appeared in English newspapers.[50] These reports were seen as proof that there was a 'campaign of calumny' being organised against Ireland: 'This campaign is so consistent and so malevolent that is obviously an organised effort… Which of the Government propaganda bureaux is responsible? Is it the one that was lately set up within the Castle Walls?'[51] The paper believed also that ongoing and secret attempts were being made to suppress it. Events in the following weeks were to make such a move more likely.

The *Freeman's Journal* takes centre stage

On 10 July 1920 the paper published an article concerning disaffection in the ranks of the RIC in Listowel, Co. Kerry. The detailed report was from an account in the *Irish Bulletin* and carried a speech supposedly made by the Divisional Commissioner for Munster, Gerard Smyth, and the ensuing resignation of fourteen local constables. The *Freeman's Journal* claimed that Smyth urged the Listowel RIC men and presumably other members of the force to retaliate for barrack burnings by destroying the best nationalist houses in the locality and throwing the occupants into the gutter. 'Let them die there – the more the merrier,' he allegedly said and continued to urge that his men should shoot suspicious characters on sight. While he said all this he was in the company of RIC chief of police, Hugh Tudor. Smyth continued:

> You may make mistakes occasionally, and innocent persons may be shot, but that cannot be helped, and you are bound to get the right parties sometime. The more you shoot the better I will like you and I assure you that no policeman will get into trouble for shooting any man.[52]

While it is impossible to know if the printed text of Smyth's speech was a word-for-word account, what he said was inflammatory enough to provoke 25 constables to refuse to carry out his orders. The military had to be called to take control of the barracks, whereupon fourteen of the constables resigned their positions.

As well as the original report in the *Irish Bulletin*, the *Freeman's Journal* had the opportunity of meeting with an eyewitness to the affair. Michael Collins, eager to gain maximum publicity for the incident, had introduced one of the resigned constables to editor Patrick Hooper and Martin Fitzgerald. Constable Jeremiah Mee was questioned by Hooper and Fitzgerald for three hours.[53] Both the editor and owner were satisfied with Mee's account and his input provided the basis of the paper's reporting of the affair over the following days. They had also tried to obtain a response from the RIC. Before printing the article, the *Freeman's Journal* made inquiries with RIC headquarters, military headquarters and Listowel RIC barracks for an official reply but due to the many faults within the British propaganda structure there was none.[54] The article was published without contradiction. The resigned officers later drew up and signed as accurate a report that confirmed the account of the incident in the *Freeman's Journal*. It seems therefore that, at the very least, the spirit of what Smyth said was conveyed accurately in the report. Although Smyth vehemently denied the allegations, his claims of innocence were treated with understandable suspicion by the press. It was, after all, the word of Smyth, one member of the RIC against fourteen other members of the same force.[55]

Smyth's denials appeared in the pages of *The Times* that same week, as the story of the 'mutiny' had by this time reached the English press.[56] The *Freeman's Journal*'s claims were also denied by Greenwood in the House of Commons. Greenwood read aloud an account by Smyth in which he had written that his speech 'has been twisted by the *Freeman's Journal* into incitement to murder'.[57] Smyth visited Dublin Castle to discuss the matter with John Anderson, but a prosecution of the paper was ruled out. According to Sturgis, Anderson strongly believed that the paper should be prosecuted for false information. Fortunately for the *Freeman's Journal*, the Irish lawyers were 'dead against it' as they believed that a successful prosecution could not be guaranteed.[58] The fourteen officers who resigned would have been called to testify and they had already supported the *Freeman's Journal* version of the speech. Just two days after this meeting and one week after the publication of the *Freeman's Journal* article, Smyth was shot dead by the IRA in Cork city. The *Freeman's Journal* was quickly blamed for Smyth's death – criticism followed from other newspapers and the House of Commons while the news was treated with dismay in Dublin Castle.[59] Mark Sturgis' diary for this time contains the blunt entry: 'The Freeman killed Smyth' adding: 'It seems to make a prosecution of the Freeman easier'.[60] But again, no prosecution was undertaken – most likely for the same reasons as detailed above. Legally as well as from a publicity viewpoint it would not have reflected well on the Irish Administration. After all, the Chief of Police was with Smyth when he had made his speech. If, as seems likely, the fourteen officers were correct in what they said then it would seem that Smyth's speech was official RIC policy. We do know that Tudor was a strong supporter of police reprisals (see Chapter 1). Despite this reprieve, the *Freeman's Journal* was now under intense scrutiny and literally one misplaced story away from prosecution.

In late July 1920 the paper again aroused official attention when it advocated a settlement for Ireland involving 'Dominion Home Rule based on the constitution which Canada won'.[61] The editorial also appealed to Lloyd George to call a truce and set a meeting between 'representatives of British control and an equal number of republicans as equals'. This was a bold move by an Irish paper. While the *Freeman's Journal* was generally supportive of Dáil Éireann and Sinn Féin, the call for Dominion Home Rule fell short of the republic that those organisations were pledged to achieve. These proposed negotiations would then succeed if they led to 'a full and complete measure of Dominion Home rule'. This would mean that:

> The Irish must control their own fiscal, judicial, and domestic arrangements; their own taxations; their own police, and their own military - should they need them. The question of Ulster – or rather the four counties which are dominated by the Orangemen – may be left to county option. It would be quite safe that way.[62]

There is no evidence that the newspaper had any knowledge of peace initiatives by Sinn Féin or the Dáil (although it is almost certain that leading journalists would have some knowledge, however scanty, of such developments) and it seems quite possible that the paper was acting of its own accord. Perhaps the owners and editor were aware of the efforts of some within Dublin Castle to investigate the possibilities of a settlement. Mark Sturgis wrote that these articles were largely written and influenced by Jeremiah 'Jerry' McVeagh, a journalist and Cork businessman but, more significantly, a Nationalist Party MP for South Down from 1902 until 1922.[63] Apparently, William E. Wylie, legal adviser to the Irish Administration, a member of the Irish Supreme Court and a friend of McVeagh, had urged him to use his influence to try and bring an end to the violence.[64] This was not an official request from the Irish Administration. Wylie seems to have been acting on his own and in despair at how the situation in Ireland was developing rather than following orders from his superiors or taking part in any master plan by the Administration.

The effect of the articles seems to have begun some secret peace moves. The proposals were widely publicised and treated sympathetically by large sections of the English press.[65] A few days after the article, *The Irish Times* published an editorial also strongly supporting Dominion Home Rule and remarkably changing its previous position (see Chapter 6).[66] Thomas Jones (Lloyd George's Private Secretary) details how Lloyd George was aware of what the Prime Minister called 'these remarkable articles'. Jones' diary also contains the following entry dated 04 August 1920: 'The man who writes the articles was employed by the Daily Express, which was a conservative paper in Dublin. He made up his mind that Ireland was going to destruction and joined the Freeman to try and prevent it.'[67]

It was also remarked that this man 'was outside the door' waiting to meet Lloyd George. It is hard to judge how significant this meeting was but it is interesting that an editorial writer from the *Freeman's Journal* was able to meet Lloyd George. It is not known whether McVeagh was travelling under his own auspices or those of the *Freeman's Journal* as individual journalists in such situations often become conduits and intermediaries between opposing forces. In saying that, his editor and the owners would surely have known of his journey. That same week, Patrick Hooper of the *Freeman's Journal* and the editor of *The Irish Times*, John Healy, along with Captain Henry Harrison, secretary of the Dominion Home Rule Group, met with Under Secretary Anderson to state their various proposals in person.[68] But peace moves at this stage were destined to come to nothing, despite a receptive atmosphere in the higher levels of the Irish Administration, including from Anderson and Macready.[69] D.G. Boyce has detailed how Conservative Cabinet members were still completely opposed to any form of Dominion Home Rule for Ireland.[70] Furthermore, military chiefs had convinced Lloyd George that the IRA could be completely vanquished if the military were given a freer hand.[71] The Restoration of Order in Ireland Act (ROIA) was to be passed barely a week later.

Regardless of the new legislation, which clearly signalled an escalation of the violence, in the week that followed these meetings the *Freeman's Journal* gave its readers hints that a major development was about to happen. It reported on Saturday 14 August that the British Cabinet had 'capitulated' and that the 'Government seems converted to Dominion Home Rule'. There was no indication of this in any of the other papers but the *Freeman's Journal* assured its readers that it had 'intimate knowledge' of events. Andrew Bonar Law (leader of the Conservatives and a historic opponent of Irish Home Rule), the paper reported, was due speak in the House of Commons on the following Monday and give a statement that 'would leave partition and coercion far behind'. Monday came and went with no such developments. The paper responded on the following day that it had been 'betrayed' by the British Government. It is hard to judge if the paper was deliberately misled by Dublin Castle. The owners, editor and McVeagh may simply have misjudged the situation. McVeagh would not have been the first or the last person to have met with Lloyd George and taken away a viewpoint of the meeting at variance from that of the Prime Minister. Perhaps the paper had overestimated its influence with the Government or the Irish Administration. Was it a deliberate piece of misinformation from somebody in Dublin Castle or the British Government? We do not know but we can say that it was an embarrassing and bitter blow to the *Freeman's Journal* whose editor, Patrick Hooper, feared that their calls for a truce and Dominion Home Rule 'meant running the risk of their office being raided and wrecked by extremists'.[72] While Hooper may have believed this, especially in the aftermath of IRA attacks on such prominent newspapers as the *Irish Independent* and the *Cork Examiner*, it is highly unlikely that the IRA in Dublin would have been given sanction to attack a newspaper that was, for the most part, so vigorously supportive of Sinn Féin policies and critical of the British Government. In the event, any such perceived risks were undertaken for nothing.[73]

The introduction of the ROIA signalled an intensification of the conflict in Ireland and was a tacit declaration of war upon the IRA and Sinn Féin. The key provisions of the Act for newspapers have been outlined in Chapter 1, but it also empowered the authorities to impose severe restrictions on the movement of people and traffic, imprisonment on suspicion, and – most controversially – allowed the replacement of coroner's inquests with secret military courts of inquiry.[74] The *Freeman's Journal* bristled against this display of 'naked militarism' probably realising also that its newspaper was under more danger of suppression and legal prosecution under the new legislation.[75] The paper's response was to emphasise its support for Sinn Féin and Dáil policies. In late August it published an editorial concerning 'the scheming of Belfast' which was 'the cause of all the trouble'. 'But for Belfast' the paper stated, 'Ireland would be a peaceable, happy country, controlling itself'. The paper had a prescription for curing this trouble: 'The financial and commercial boycott of that part of Ireland which is causing all the trouble ... The rest of Ireland does not need Ulster or her products... The rest of Ireland should withdraw her money from the Northern Banks.'[76]

This call was repeated to its readers only eleven days after the Dáil had sanctioned an official boycott of goods emanating from Belfast. The continuing support for Sinn Féin and concurrent criticisms of the Administration from the *Freeman's Journal* and other papers did not go unnoticed and the Under Secretary John Anderson felt it necessary to write to the editors of the Irish newspapers warning them against publishing 'misleading statements'. The letter was given prominence in the paper under the heading 'A Threat and a Challenge'.[77] Hooper issued the challenge to 'the Castle' to point out any article, which had been published in the *Freeman's Journal* designed 'to provoke discontent and disaffection'. The challenge went unanswered.[78] Two days later, the paper again challenged the Irish Administration saying that it would publish anything in accordance with its 'political faith' and that this faith 'embraced the point that Castle Government is not necessary to the welfare of this country'.[79] Again there was no reply.

The following months were tumultuous for both the country and the increasingly pressurised *Freeman's Journal*. Reprisals and Terence MacSwiney's prolonged hunger strike were the dominant themes of the next few months' reportage. Taking its lead from the *Irish Bulletin*, the *Freeman's Journal* began publishing sections from the newly instituted *Weekly Summary* (see Chapter 1), which the paper condemned as designed to condone and incite reprisals. The more vicious sections of the police forces needed little incitement to attack the *Freeman's Journal*. By late September, Black and Tans were travelling around Dublin defacing *Freeman's Journal* posters that proclaimed there had been 'one hundred and one acts of reprisal in Ireland carried out by the forces of the Crown since September 1919'.[80] The paper was also regularly receiving threatening letters from the RIC camp at Gormanstown. However, the paper did establish a working relationship with an ex-Black and Tan who had resigned following the large-scale reprisal in Balbriggan, County Dublin (20 September 1920). This reprisal resulted in the deaths of two civilians. Former Constable, Alfred Flint, told the *Freeman's Journal* that he was present as the RIC wrecked the town and murdered a man called James Lawless: 'Lawless was called out. But he first received a smash on the head with butt of a rifle and then was turned outside and shot.'[81]

As Flint would have had to be prosecuted as well as the newspaper in this instance, it is doubtful whether the officials in Dublin Castle considered a prosecution of the paper viable, not only as the allegations were seemingly true but probably more importantly, the reprisal had been so widely covered in the English press. However, in late October, the paper received three summonses in the space of a week for various reports on Crown forces' activities (see Chapter 1). In response, the *Freeman's Journal* published an editorial deriding the 'Official sabotage that has succeeded official censorship'.[82]

Even in the face of this 'official sabotage' the *Freeman's Journal* had continued to print stories attacking the British Government or blaming the Crown forces for violence, when it had sufficient proof. Desmond Ryan later wrote how the news editor Seán Lester advised him how to handle a story in which the paper had evidence against the Crown forces. In this case, it was the shooting dead of Sinn Féin Councillor John Lynch. Lynch, visiting Dublin from Kilmallock in County Limerick, had being staying in a Dublin hotel when a group of armed men entered the room and shot him. Lester told him to 'let rip in the story and say out that it was murder'.[83] The paper also showed its sympathy and respect for republicans. The paper praised the recently deceased Terence MacSwiney as well as the Cork hunger strikers, Michael Fitzgerald and Joseph Murphy, as typifying 'the divine essence of nationality'.[84] Protest was made also against the 'extreme sentence' imposed on Kevin Barry. The paper claimed that the sentence was illegal as the ambush 'was conducted according to the rules of open war', a claim that signalled the paper's acceptance of the IRA as a legitimate army.[85] The sentence was carried out in Mountjoy Jail on 1 November 1920 in spite of mounting calls for its reversal. The *Freeman's Journal* praised, in a series of unusually emotional reports, what it called 'Barry's Heroic Sacrifice – Kevin Barry Yields His Life for Ireland Without Flinching'.[86]

The paper also accused the Government, echoing John Dillon after the executions of the 1916 leaders, of letting loose 'the River of Blood'.[87] Overwrought, perhaps, but not inaccurate. Bloody Sunday, which came soon after, was a profound shock to the paper (see Chapter 1). The paper's agonised editorial compared the events at Croke Park to the 1919 Amritsar massacre in India. In that instance the British army had massacred hundreds of unarmed Indians at a public meeting. However, the paper reminded its readers that the excuse used by the British army at Amritsar (the crowd at Amritsar, while unarmed, was technically breaking a law banning large assemblies) could not work at Croke Park as the crowd had been doing nothing illegal.[88] There were 'no proclamations, no warnings, no legalities defied by the assembly in Croke Park'. The Auxiliaries went in search of trouble and found it: 'The slaughter was a classic sample of a Government reprisal – the innocent were shot down in a blind vengeance.'[89] The paper rebuffed the official explanation of the Croke Park reprisal that the Auxiliaries had been fired on by unknown members of the crowd as 'a patent and infamous falsehood'.

Carrying reports from those at the scene the paper continued: 'Every scrap of evidence goes to show that the crowd, instead of fighting, stampeded wildly when the uniformed men burst into the field.'[90]

Republicans were not excused from blame. The paper acknowledged that the Croke Park attack was a reprisal for the shootings that morning of fourteen officers supposedly involved in intelligence work against the IRA. It asked that they consider their tactics as 'reprisal begets still worse reprisal'. Speaking of the Dáil insistence that it was pledged to the creation of an independent Irish republic, the *Freeman's Journal* wrote that: 'The people do not expect miracles – they would expect peace with honour, peace with full freedom in those affairs that are their aim.'[91]

November 1920 – Court Martial

The *Freeman's Journal* had been a consistent foe of the Irish Administration despite the Administration's determination to silence the paper. The intensity of the Administration's desire to strike back at the *Freeman's Journal* can be gauged by the fact that it was the first paper in Britain or Ireland ever to be tried by court martial.[92] This meant that not only would the paper be tried by the army, whose GOC, General Macready, was a known and vehement critic of the *Freeman's Journal* but the court martial had the added benefit, from the Administration's viewpoint, of removing the paper, its owner and editor from the normal protections of civilian law. The trial began in a Dublin still reeling from the appalling violence of Bloody Sunday. The *Freeman's Journal* had two charges to answer (six counts of spreading false reports and causing disaffection under each charge): one charge on the reported shooting of two RIC constables by Black and Tans and the other charge related to the paper's reporting of the mistreatment of a man named Arthur Quirke in Portobello Barracks (the third charge had been dropped by this time). Former IPP MP T.M. Healy defended the paper, but the progress of the court martial showed that the military court was always going to believe the sworn testimony of fellow soldiers and police than that of the *Freeman's Journal* editor, owners and witnesses.[93] After a morning session to lay the charges against the defendants, the court took a break in proceedings to pay respects to the funeral cortège of the officers shot dead on Bloody Sunday. The court martial resumed in the afternoon. The matter in hand was the *Freeman's Journal* report of the Tullow reprisal and death of two regular RIC constables at the hands of Black and Tans. The paper had reported a rumour from the locality that the men had been killed by Black and Tans. The defendants, Hamilton Edward and Martin Fitzgerald, were quickly acquitted on four of the six counts on this charges (all counts on this charge against the editor, Patrick Hooper, had already been dropped as he was in Canada at the time of publication).[94] The process was repeated with all three men on the second charge relating to the reporting of the ill-treatment of the man named Arthur Quirke in Portobello Barracks. They were again acquitted of four of the six counts on this charge (Hooper was back in Ireland when this report was published).

The two charges that remained concerned whether the paper printed a 'false report' and if this report 'was designed to cause disaffection against His Majesty'. These charges became the crux of the trial. On the first charge Edwards and Fitzgerald were found guilty. The Crown counsel conceded that the story which the *Freeman's Journal* had printed was widely known and a 'persistent rumour' in the locality. However, the court martial judged the rumour to be false and although the paper had printed the rumour, as a rumour, and without claiming it to be true, the paper was found guilty on both counts.[95] On the second charge Healy put in a strong defence disputing the make-up of the court martial and attempting to show that it would not produce a fair judgment. During the court martial it was proven that the photograph of the injured man published in the paper was not a fake while Quirke, in the words of the *Manchester Guardian*, 'bore out his statement [that he had originally made to the *Freeman's Journal*] in detail'. The only 'error' in his evidence was that he was unable to identify which of the soldiers assaulted him.[96] As he had reportedly been beaten while tied face-down to a bed, this was understandable. However, the real intent of the Crown case could be seen in the speeches throughout the trial of counsel for the Crown, James Rearden KC. In one statement he told the court martial: 'It was only necessary to prove the gravity of the offence to call attention to the large circulation of the *Freeman's Journal* and then the thousands of ignorant, gullible, impressionable people who read papers.'[97]

Before publishing Quirke's allegations, the *Freeman's Journal* had had Quirke examined by a Dr McDonnell, the Coroner for Dublin, Dr Louis Byrne and a 'renowned surgeon', Dr McArdle.[98] Despite this and the fact that one of the prosecuting counsel, Cecil Fforde, conceded that Quirke's injuries were real, the court martial of seven military men found the defendants guilty of the two charges of 'spreading a false report' and of 'causing disaffection'. The *Freeman's Journal* had little chance of avoiding a conviction on the count of 'causing disaffection'. Under the RIOA regulations the press provisions were very clear. The members of the court martial were undoubtedly influenced by Rearden's arguments when he reminded them in his closing statement:

> Did the court believe the military witnesses, or did they think that Quirke was not the type of young man who was only too glad of an opportunity to blacken the reputation of the British Army … Even if every word that appeared in the *Freeman's Journal* was true, the defendants would be guilty of an offence against the regulations if the Court came to the conclusion that the true report was likely to cause disaffection.[99]

This assertion had been the mantra of the prosecuting counsel throughout the course of the court martial. Having been found guilty of the two remaining charges the three defendants were ordered to be detained in Mountjoy Jail to await sentencing. Pressed on this by the defence counsel, the president of the court martial stated that the competent military authority would detain the men as it was this body that was responsible for convening the trial.[100] As the papers were, in the words of Fforde, 'being prosecuted as soldiers' the men were now effectively outside of civil law. On 6 December 1920 Edwards and Fitzgerald were sentenced to six months' imprisonment on the first charge. On Christmas Eve all three men were sentenced to one year in prison from the second charge. The *Freeman's Journal* was also fined a total of £3,500.[101]

Searching for peace

While this legislative attack was under way the *Freeman's Journal* premises suffered a series of violent attacks in the same month, including one attack in which explosives were thrown into the paper's office.[102] The financial costs of these must have been crippling especially when added to the large fine imposed by the court martial. These problems affected the paper's reportage negatively. Under attack, its owners and editor jailed, facing huge financial penalties and damaged machinery, the paper was struggling to cover the news. Following the burning of Cork city centre (see Chapter 1) by Auxiliaries the paper ran a report on the 'Irish City in Ruins' but the report, which was limited and perfunctory, lacked the detail of a typical *Freeman's Journal* report (and that of reports in other newspapers).[103] These problems are apparent throughout the rest of that month, although the paper did rouse itself to write a detailed condemnation on the passage of the Government of Ireland Bill into law at the end of December 1920 (see also Chapters 4 and 5).[104] With the recent introduction of Martial Law (see Chapter 5) in the south, a large increase in reprisals and an increasing spiral of violence, the paper and the country had every reason to fear that the following year could be just as dark.

This year began with some better news for the beleaguered *Freeman's Journal*. Such was the reaction of the British press allied to the recent publication of the Labour Commission report on events in Ireland (which was very critical of the Irish Administration and Crown forces) that the Irish Administration was forced by Downing Street to grant an 'unconditional release' to the jailed journalists. The paper thanked its supporters and criticised its main competitors: 'The English Press and, in fact the Press of all the world, with the exception of the daily newspapers in Dublin, condemned the sentences as unwarranted, vindictive, savage and vicious.'[105]

Bolstered by this support and the return to some sort of working normality, the *Freeman's Journal* quickly resumed its combative reporting. The paper did not let the attacks of the previous months deter it from its willingness to publish reports of violence or to criticise what it saw as the real reason for the state of Ireland: the Irish Administration, the campaign of reprisals and the Government of Ireland Act. It deplored the failure of the British Government to publish the Strickland Report into the burning of Cork (see Chapter 1).[106]

Such headlines as 'Cork Man Shot during Military Search' commonly appeared in the *Freeman's Journal* at this time.[107] The paper reported deaths in differing ways. All deaths were considered 'tragic' but the deaths of British soldiers, RIC constables and IRA members while 'on duty' were considered a risk and consequence of war in Ireland. Reprisals and the wild actions of Auxiliaries and Black and Tans aroused the anger of the paper most of all as these were directed mainly against peaceful and often completely innocent civilians in what the paper sometimes termed an 'Amritsar Policy'. The *Freeman's Journal* also considered the executions of captured IRA Volunteers as illegal and contrary to the conventions of war. The execution of six IRA men in Cork during February was reported as 'a noble and brave sacrifice'.[108] A large banner headline on 'How Six Young Irish Boys

Died' accompanied the report, in March, of the hanging of six more IRA Volunteers in Mountjoy Jail.[109] The paper's editorial accused the British Government of terrorism but warned that the country would not be intimidated. It quoted the words of Terence MacSwiney that 'Not to those who can inflict most but to those who can endure most will victory be given'.[110] Its position at this time could be seen from an editorial it had printed in December:

> The Freeman's Journal stood and stands for constitutional methods. It believes with the Bishop of Cork that it is possible for Ireland 'to advance by peaceful evolution to a full ideal of freedom'. But it never ceases to proclaim that if Ireland no longer believes in a constitutional movement, the responsibility rests on the Carsons, the Bonar Laws and the 'Galloper' Smiths.[111]

During the following months until the truce the paper's coverage of events in Ireland did not differ in nature from what it had printed throughout 1920. The activities of the PIB and other British propaganda attempts were a constant bugbear while the paper continued to openly report on events such as the 'murder of the Lord Mayor of Limerick'. In March 1921, the Sinn Féin Mayor George Clancy and former Mayor Michael O'Callaghan were attacked in their homes and killed. Another man, Joseph O'Donoghue – a prominent member of the Gaelic League – was also shot dead by Crown forces on the same night.[112] The military were clearly implicated by the paper who reported that men, presumably soldiers, were seen leaving the army barracks under cover of curfew, 'a little before the murders began'. Relatives of the dead men, who saw what had happened, said that the men were shot by the soldiers and police.[113] Again, the criticism of the Crown forces caused consternation among the Irish Administration. General Macready wanted to initiate more legal proceedings in March (and also against the *Irish Independent*) but was persuaded by Anderson that this was not viable or desirable at this time. The paper did not continue unscathed. At the end of April the Auxiliaries raided the premises and forced all the staff onto the street. During questioning a number of the staff claimed they were treated roughly. Their claims were backed up by several foreign correspondents who were using the paper's offices for a meeting at the time of the raid. These reporters were also manhandled. Indeed, a number of the male staff were beaten with revolvers. Guy Moyston, representative of the Associated Press, was recognised by the Auxiliaries. One of them warned him that he should take the next boat back to America.[114] On this occasion, Greenwood was forced to deny the claims in the House of Commons. During curfew hours, the Auxiliaries raided the offices for a second time that day breaking windows and damaging equipment.[115]

Directly touched by the violence, a means of ending the conflict was to be the *Freeman's Journal* main concern until the July truce. In a tone very similar to the public comments of Eamon de Valera the paper repeatedly stated its belief that the Irish and English people (the paper rarely referred to Britain) were not enemies but allies with more 'interests in common than divides them'. This friendship could only blossom through a just peace and the freedom for Ireland. Generally, the paper suggested that Dominion Home Rule was the least that could be accepted by the Irish people. Unfortunately, the paper believed, too many people in England were either not aware of or did not understand this claim. It repeatedly criticised Lloyd George and Greenwood for their defence of the reprisals carried out by the Crown forces and their claims that the IRA were a 'murder gang'. Appreciative prominence was given in the paper to a House of Commons' speech by MP Sir Robert Woods:

> Englishmen have failed in dealing with Ireland because they have not tried to imagine the Irish man as something other than a kind of Englishman gone wrong. That Irish patriotism should have Ireland and not England as the object of its affection seems to them outrageous…[116]

Over the Christmas period there had been secret attempts to broker a peace deal but these came to nothing. The attempts at creating a truce had centred on Archbishop Clune from Perth who had acted as an intermediary. Following Clune's interview with the French journal, *La Liberté*, the *Freeman's Journal* placed the blame entirely on Lloyd George's insistence that the IRA lay down their weapons before any negotiations could take place.[117] The paper had recently given much support to de Valera's statement that 'The British Dominions have had conceded to them all the rights that Irish Republicans demand'. This, the paper claimed, was a 'real peace offer'.[118] Nothing came of it and there was no progress until after the elections of May 1921.

The May elections were the first elections held in Ireland since the introduction of the Government of Ireland Act and while the elections in the south were a formality for Sinn Féin as every constituency was uncontested (barring the four seats granted to Trinity College), the six counties of the northeast were another proposition. Sinn Féin and Nationalist Party candidates agreed a common anti-partition platform. This agreement was enthusiastically supported by the *Freeman's Journal*, which urged the voters to utilise the proportional representation and give their second preferences to anti-partitionists. If this was done, the paper prophesied, then: 'The Partition Parliament will be a torn and ragged and unrepresentative institution from its birth. It will carry the seeds of dissolution in its cradle.'[119]

Even though almost one-third of first preferences were cast for either Sinn Féin or the Nationalists the parties shared equally only twelve of the fifty-two contested. The *Freeman's Journal* was particularly disappointed with what it called 'the Gerrymander's victory' blaming the intimidation of Catholics at the polls and falsely constructed electoral boundaries.[120] However, these very elections that so disappointed the *Freeman's Journal* had indirectly improved the chances of peace. As historian Michael Laffan notes, now that northern Unionists and their Conservative backers were satisfied and public opinion in Britain was alienated at the way in which the war was being fought, Lloyd George was finally ready for serious negotiations with the Dáil.[121]

The *Freeman's Journal* was involved in the negotiations leading to the truce although the exact details may never be known. In early May, Sturgis noted in his diary that Andy Cope had met with Patrick Hooper as part of Cope's attempts to arrange a truce (he also had arranged meetings with the *Irish Independent, The Irish Times* and *Cork Examiner*). Clearly, Cope was trying to utilise the influence of the leading newspapers in creating a truce. According to Sturgis, Cope had 'a most interesting talk with Hooper' and reported that Hooper was very open to the idea of a settlement as he was especially fearful of how the violence would increase if no settlement was forthcoming.[122] With this aim, Martin Fitzgerald somehow became an intermediary between the British Government and the Dáil, meeting on numerous occasions with Andy Cope and Michael Collins over the following weeks.[123] In early July Sturgis also met with Fitzgerald who told him that 'the thing [negotiations] is going splendidly'. He also told Sturgis that members of the Dáil were due to have an important meeting 'at his place' (presumably the offices of the *Freeman's Journal*).[124] While none of this appeared in the columns of the paper, its reports at this time were full of hopeful commentary and hints to readers that the long-awaited truce was in the offing.[125] This truce eventually came into effect on 11 July 1921 and the *Freeman's Journal* shared the widespread joy at the new-found peace. It took its lead from 'President de Valera' and urged the Irish people to be disciplined and keep calm in the face of any provocations that might arise. The paper further showed itself at this stage to be very much aligned with Sinn Féin:

> Ireland's four delegates are well chosen. Mr de Valera, Mr Griffith, Mr Austin Stack and Mr Burton represent at once the intelligence, the fighting spirit, and the self-sacrifice of Sinn Fein. What they put their hands to, the country will countersign.[126]

What we can see is a paper that was effectively an arm of the IPP in 1919 was by now a firm backer of the Dáil and Sinn Féin. The paper had also challenged the Irish Administration consistently and made clear its belief that Ireland should have, at a minimum, complete Dominion Home Rule. The new owners had played a large part in this change but so had the violence of the Crown forces and the coercive response of the British Government.[127] We will now look at the *Freeman's Journal*'s main competitor, another nationalist daily, the *Irish Independent*, to see how that paper's journey compared to the *Freeman's Journal*.

4

THE *IRISH INDEPENDENT*

The *Irish Independent* had condemned the leaders of the 1916 Rebellion, indirectly calling for the execution of James Connolly. On that evidence, it would seem an unlikely supporter of Sinn Féin but in the two years prior to 1919, the paper had moved closer to that party. One of the major catalysts of this change had been the 'conscription crisis' of 1918. Following the mass of public opinion in Ireland during that year, the paper and Sinn Féin had both utterly opposed the British Government's plans to introduce conscription throughout Ireland. Yet it remained to be seen how the *Irish Independent* would address the powerful Sinn Féin party that had grown from the 'conscription crisis' and the general election of the same year. The paper was also an opponent of the Irish Parliamentary Party (IPP), which made it a political, as well as a business, rival to the *Freeman's Journal*. The paper's owner, William Martin Murphy, had initially been a very prominent member of the IPP and a supporter of Charles Stewart Parnell. However, when the knowledge that Parnell had been co-respondent in a divorce case became a public scandal, Murphy followed the great majority of the party during the IPP split, joining the anti-Parnellite faction.

Murphy was to prove unsuccessful at the polls and suffered a humiliating series of election defeats which saw him turn to newspaper ownership as his means of gaining political influence. Political machinations within the IPP, especially the refusal of some senior party leaders to back Murphy as an election candidate in Mayo, later resulted in Murphy becoming an implacable adversary of John Dillon and then John Redmond. Following its master, the *Irish Independent* became a constant critic of both men as well as the IPP. In a later obituary of Murphy *The Times* commented that while he 'was certainly not a Sinn Feiner' he 'used every weapon to defeat the old party and all Sinn Fein's attacks on it received full publicity in his newspapers'. In 1919 the paper was still edited by Tim Harrington who had written the famous editorials denouncing the leaders of the Rising. Owned by a true press baron and describing itself as broadly nationalist, the paper had the largest circulation of the Irish dailies and the reputation of being the most receptive to the desires of the mass-market.[1]

1919 – 'Broadly nationalist'

In common with the other national dailies the *Irish Independent* doubted if the new Dáil would be able to carry through its resolutions, for example, the creation of an independent Irish republic. If not, then the drafting of measures it could not enforce 'would be to risk ridicule more fatal than opposition'.[2] The paper feared that if this came to pass it would have potentially disastrous consequences for Ireland's claims to self-government. The 'shocking outrage' at Soloheadbeg was not linked to the gathering of the first Dáil at Dublin's Mansion House.

The *Irish Independent* was highly critical of the violence carried out by the Volunteers throughout 1919. Following the deaths of two RIC men at Knocklong, County Tipperary, the paper gave extensive coverage to Archbishop Dr Harty's condemnation of the shooting as a 'Crime against God and Ireland'.[3] Other Volunteer activities – such as derailing trains and raiding post office vans – were termed 'outrages', 'dastardly crimes' and so on. The incidences of violence during 1919, while sporadic compared to the following eighteen months, were totally condemned by the paper. Fatal attacks on soldiers, police and officials such as Resident Magistrates were always termed 'murders'. In parallel with these reports the paper continued to give extensive coverage to Dáil and Sinn Féin meetings, publishing reports of speeches and photographs of Dáil members. In April, it covered in detail the Sinn Féin Árd-Fheis and gave prominence to a photograph of the Dáil Assembly with Collins, Brugha, Griffith, de Valera and Cosgrave seated in the front row.[4] Such contradictory coverage was probably a result of the paper's belief that there existed a battle within Sinn Féin between 'moderates' and 'extremists'. In September the paper quoted approvingly from the *Drogheda Independent* concerning the recent 'murders and outrages':

> Oppression always produces reprisal, but no cause can be advanced by immoral methods, and there are no Irishmen responsible for their actions who can hope to advance their

political beliefs by methods of cowardly and cold-blooded assassination.[5]

During the previous June William Martin Murphy, the owner and driving force of Independent Newspapers, had died. His son, William Lombard Murphy replaced him as Chair of the group and immediately assured readers that 'there will be no departure from the policies hitherto pursued in these journals. In the future as in the past the Independent Newspapers will be nationalist journals in the broadest sense, detached from parties, independent, outspoken and fair'.[6]

No change in editorial policy was apparent in the months after the changeover in power. However, in tandem with the rest of nationalist Ireland the *Irish Independent* began to be much more critical of the Irish Administration. The paper had no delusions about the discontinuance of press censorship in Ireland. As long as DORA operated, the newspapers would suffer under the 'dictates of the competent military authority'.[7] The paper later used the 'drastic' suppression of the *Cork Examiner* as an example of the military intimidation to which the Irish newspapers were forced to acquiesce, what it called 'dragooning of the press'. The *Irish Independent* had avoided suppression at that time by not printing the Dáil Loan Prospectus and this cautious, at times self-censoring approach, was to remain a factor in the paper's news reporting. Events in Fermoy during September, where perhaps the first military reprisal of the conflict occurred, were reported by the paper as a 'night of terror'. In response to an earlier attack by the IRA the local British army contingent burned and looted houses in the town. The paper's 'representative' reported directly from the scene that 'a large body of soldiers took part in the wrecking of the town centre without any attempts to prohibit them'.[8] This type of criticism continued throughout the year. The declaration of the Dáil as an illegal organisation was also condemned and the paper quoted Arthur Griffith as saying that the move 'proclaimed the whole Irish nation an illegal assembly'.[9] De Valera's tour of the United States was regularly and comprehensively covered.

The coverage of Sinn Féin was becoming increasingly positive and while this had much to do with the failure of British rule in Ireland there were also a number of other reasons. The more sympathetic coverage was also a response to the change in editorial policy undergone by the *Freeman's Journal* under its new ownership. Both papers were competing for the same readership, a readership that had abandoned the IPP for Sinn Féin in the 1918 general elections and one increasingly repulsed by the actions of the Irish Administration.[10] In addition, the Murphy family was bitterly resentful of the IPP and support for Sinn Féin was another nail in the coffin of that ailing organisation.[11] Moreover, the paper's staff and journalists were not detached from the events they covered – such a large paper undoubtedly had many staff supportive of Sinn Féin and the IRA. Indeed, chief proofreader, Martin Pender and drama critic David Sears were both long-time republicans[12] while a sub-editor, George Gormby, was a member of the IRA.[13] Reporters Ned Lawler and Michael Knightly had both provided information to the IRA.[14] Knightly, who had fought in the 1916 Rebellion, was heavily implicated in the shooting dead of RM Alan Bell, having provided Michael Collins with an up-to-date photo of the Magistrate (see also Chapter 3 for information on Bell).[15] Knightly later stated how he viewed his role as a reporter in testimony to the Bureau of Military History. His job allowed him to combine:

> ... newspaper work with intelligence work for the IRA ... Newspaper work also afforded opportunities of helping the cause in the political field and I was always glad to assist in this way.[16]

Knightly was so heavily involved with the IRA that on a tip-off from an *Irish Times'* journalist he was arrested by the Crown forces in early 1920 and charged with being a member of the IRA. It is unknown if he was convicted (many prisoners at this time were neither charged nor convicted) but he spent seven months in Mountjoy. On his release he was immediately re-employed by the *Irish Independent*. Clearly, being a known member of the IRA was no barrier to a job with the paper. Perhaps it even was of use to the paper. For example, the *Irish Independent* was the first paper to cover the capture of Kevin Barry. Michael Knightly was aware that the ambush was going to take place and he had arranged with one of the ambush party, Tom Kissane, to provide an account of the attack as soon as it was over.[17]

As the end of the year approached the paper began to turn its attention towards the proposed Home Rule Bill, arguing that 'any settlement based on partition would fail'.[18] This had been the position of the *Irish Independent* throughout 1919. Earlier in the year it had dismissed the plans of *The Times* for two legislatures in Ireland, professing that Home Rule for the whole of Ireland was the only viable solution.[19] While very critical of the Irish Administration and the British Government the *Irish Independent* avoided personal attacks on figures such as Lord French and Ian Macpherson and as such the paper's criticisms seem muted in comparison to the *Freeman's Journal*. This may have helped the *Irish Independent* avoid the unwanted attentions of the Irish Administration. Yet its criticisms of the Volunteers led to unwanted attentions from that quarter. The paper had continued its policy of condemning the shootings of policemen, calling the shooting of DMP Constable Downing in November, 'brutal and purposeless'.[20] This vein of reporting was to provoke retaliation from the IRA.

Following a report on the ambush of the Lord Lieutenant (see Chapter 3) the IRA attacked the offices of the paper on 21 December 1919. The *Irish Independent* had given huge coverage to the 'miraculous escape' of French. The editorial called the attack 'a deplorable outrage' while the correspondent covering the event compared the 'thrilling nature of the sensational occurrence' to the Phoenix Park murders of 37 years before.[21] The comparison is revealing: the Phoenix Park murders had almost derailed Parnell in his quest for Home Rule. Offence was taken by the IRA at the editorial of the previous day that had called the ambush 'a dreadful plan of assassination' and the dead Volunteer, Martin Savage, 'an assassin'.[22] The paper reported that the leader of the 'masked men' (Peadar Clancy) informed the editor that his paper was being suppressed for having 'endeavoured to misrepresent the sympathies and opinions of the Irish people' through its coverage of the ambush. The men then proceeded to cause 'enormous destruction' to the printing machinery.[23] Dan Breen wrote in his memoir that the intention was to cause so much damage that 'no edition could appear for some time'.[24] Despite the damage and intimidation the *Irish Independent* was able to publish and reprinted the offending editorial on the following day.[25]

1920 – 'Heartless Government'

The *Irish Independent* continued to deride the Irish Administration and the Government of Ireland Bill into 1920. The paper was particularly vociferous in its condemnation of the increasing raids that the 'iron-rule of oppression' was forcing on Ireland. The introduction of the Dublin curfew was used to charge England with 'martyrising Ireland through a policy of self interest'.[26] Accusing the 'present castle rulers' of strangling liberty and justice the paper warned that 'Martial Law will fail and will leave behind it bitterness and hatred. The first step towards any amelioration or settlement should be the resignations of Lord French and Mr Macpherson'.[27] The continuance of the DORA war regulations aroused much criticism because supposedly transitory measures were being 'used against Ireland as if they were part of the common law'.[28] Regarding the Home Rule Bill, the paper claimed that Ireland was by 'every test a nation, one and indivisible'. Lloyd George was accused of committing himself:

> ... once more to the unconstitutional doctrine that the minority must rule the question at large in Ireland, though when the railway strikes took place in England he declared that the government could not permit a minority to defy and upset the nation.[29]

Furthermore, the paper was highly supportive of the proportional representation local government elections that had recently taken place and in which Sinn Féin saw a significant degree of success. In these elections, the paper argued the vast majority of the country had voted against partition.[30] In addition to this, the *Irish Independent* publicly supported Horace Plunkett's framework of an Irish settlement (Plunkett was also a founding member of the Irish Dominion League) which proposed that any Irish settlement would have to be based on three basic principles: the unity of Ireland, recognition of Irish nationality and the right of the Irish people to the government they desired.[31] Clearly this proposal differed greatly from the Government of Ireland Bill. When the terms of the Bill became known the *Irish Independent* called it the 'Irish partition and plunder scheme', a scheme so ludicrous that 'the only papers to treat it seriously are the unionist journals' and adding that even these rejected the terms of the Bill.[32] The Bill, argued the *Irish Independent*, was designed to ensure that 'Ulster is safe' and because of this was, at its core, an embarrassing sop to Carson, a man who had once resisted the Union through the threat of force. The editorial deplored the 'reward' handed to men 'who were prepared to arm and drill against Britain'.[33]

The *Irish Independent* by now supported many of the positions articulated by the *Freeman's Journal* and ultimately Sinn Féin. The motor permit regulations, the Dublin curfew and the 'denationalising' Education Bill were the subject of strong condemnation.[34] As the paper had previously carried reports of the Hierarchy's condemnation of the Volunteers it now carried reports of the Bishops' denunciation of the 'cruel and unjust rule' that spawned the 'coercion regime' of the military.[35] Editorials now asked the British Government why they refused to grant Ireland her 'just rights' when they had supposedly fought a war for the defence of free nations. Why was it necessary to coerce Ireland? The paper argued that it was a result of the inherent wrong of the British position best encapsulated by the 'desperate' raids in Dublin and across the country:

> Thus the stupidity of British welt-politik is fittingly reflected in the bungling of its administration. We protest against the cruelty and injustice of the secret raids. Men are torn at midnight from their families. No charge is made against them. They are kept in prison without trial.[36]

The *Irish Independent* practically accused the police of murder in the case of Lena Johnson and R. O' Dwyer in Limerick, both civilians caught in gunfire from an RIC patrol that was moving through the area with army support. While the police claimed to have been attacked, witnesses who spoke to the paper disputed claims that the patrol had been fired on. The paper reported that the police 'got out of hand and fired indiscriminately'.[37]

The level of violence increased steadily throughout 1920. In March following the shooting dead of Tomás MacCurtain, the Lord Mayor of Cork, the *Freeman's Journal* was ready to blame the forces of the Crown within days of his death but the *Irish Independent* was more cautious. Not cautious about who had committed the murder but about publishing it explicitly. While the paper dismissed claims that he was shot by members of Sinn Féin it was content to let the story evolve through the inquest deliberations that took place over the following month. This inquest resulted in a verdict of murder against 'unknown members of the RIC'.[38] Whereas the *Freeman's Journal* had run the story of MacCurtain's death as 'The Murder of the Lord Mayor of Cork', the *Irish Independent* was content to make a call for Home Rule, stating that in no self-governing country would 'tragedies like this, and the others that have occurred recently, take place'.[39] This was characteristic of the paper's reportage over the next year. The paper, while highly critical of the Irish Administration and the Crown forces, was very careful in how it published its stories, often avoiding the bluntness that characterised the reports of its main competitor. This policy helped the paper avoid the direct confrontations with the military and the Administration that characterised the history of the *Freeman's Journal* and many of the regional newspapers at this time.

The *Irish Independent* was also careful to link events to one another. Following the death of Alan Bell at the hands of the IRA the paper considered the recent violence:

> Just a week ago today Lord Mayor MacCurtain was done to death; a few hours previously a policeman was shot dead in Cork ... and yesterday morning Mr Alan Bell R. M. was taken off a tram car and shot dead in Ballsbridge... These terrible deeds by whomsoever committed are extremely deplorable...[40]

However, a shift in the paper's reportage at this time can be detected. It continued to deplore all violence but judged now that the Irish Administration and the British Cabinet who had subjected Ireland to 'an iron rule of oppression' must 'bear full responsibility for the consequences throughout the world'.[41] The *Irish Independent* could be seen as following the general contraction of the 'extremists' and 'moderates' of Irish nationalism into a single entity: an entity created by the failure of the Irish Administration and the British Cabinet to foster any other policy than coercion of Ireland in the years since the 1916 Rebellion. Editorial attacks on the Irish Administration continued throughout the year and were to become more aggressive and sustained. For example, the arrival of Nevil Macready as GOC was greeted with the headline 'Soldier Dictator for Ireland'.[42] This new vigour in the *Irish Independent's* reportage was typified by the paper's coverage of the hunger strikers in Mountjoy Jail during April. Following large-scale arrests of suspected republicans earlier in 1920, hundreds of people were held in jail for months. Many of them had not been tried; some had not even been charged. A mass hunger strike was begun by the prisoners in Mountjoy as a protest against their incarceration.

The *Irish Independent* urged the release of the men. Those that had been tried, the paper argued, had been convicted of political offences and should not be subjected to 'the rigours of ordinary prison life'.[43] The paper was making a clear distinction that it had not made during 1919 between political and non-political crimes. A mass feeling of anger had been created amongst the populace at the treatment of the prisoners (large demonstrations continued every day outside the prison) and the *Irish Independent* captured this mood with a bitter attack on the British Government:

> It is an impertinence on the part of the mere Irish to claim that they should be accorded any of the rights of human beings. God made the Irish to be victimised; trampled upon and maltreated

by British Governments which have actually passed laws making the ill-treatment of beasts a penal offence. The champions of liberty for small nations have become the champions of subjugation and inhumanity in this ancient nation ... Trying though the ordeal is our people will, we have no doubt, preserve patience and restraint.[44]

The paper supported the national strike called by trades unions to support the prisoners. Following the success of this strike and the release of the prisoners the paper congratulated the people for 'smashing government tyranny'.[45] It warned the Irish Administration that only one concession would satisfy Irish people: 'give the Irish people real self-determination' and 'the power to manage all their own affairs uninterfered with, unhampered, unafraid'.[46] Over the following months the *Irish Independent* printed a series of powerful editorials and reports which accused the British Government of preparing for the 're-conquest' of Ireland.[47] Part of this preparation, the paper claimed, was the new 'official reports of outrages' instigated by General Macready, designed as the paper put it 'to poison minds against Ireland'. These editorials accused the Irish Administration of being 'a cruel and inhuman regime'.[48] A regime which bore the sole weight for the violence in Ireland: 'The one glaring evil; the one outstanding crime in Ireland is British misgovernment. It is the root cause of all the trouble and discontent. Remove that cause and Ireland at once becomes a contented country.'[49]

Were it not for even more aggressive attacks by the *Freeman's Journal* on the Administration and the Crown forces, which had diverted so much of the Irish Administration's attention, it is likely that the *Irish Independent* would have been in direct conflict with the Crown forces and Dublin Castle. In August 1920 the West Galway RIC County Inspector reported:

> ... the mainstay of the Sinn Fein movement in this county is the *Irish Independent*. It is this paper which creates, fosters and foments hatred of the English Government from day to day, from week to week, from year to year. It never lets it alone.[50]

The *Irish Independent*'s large (and growing) circulation of over 130,000 copies per day and its clear disgust with British rule in Ireland made the paper a potent critic of the Administration and the Crown forces whom it was now terming 'the army of occupation'.[51] Consequent to the paper's belief that the British Government was to blame for the

violence in Ireland, what had also changed throughout the previous
year were the descriptions of IRA attacks on the Crown forces. Terms
such as 'crime' and 'murder' no longer appeared above or in these
reports. Such events were now reported as 'Four Policemen Killed' or
'Police Inspector Shot Dead'.[52] 'Appalling Tragedy' was the soubriquet
that now replaced 'Dastardly Crime'. The *Irish Independent* was also
regularly reporting on the 'activities of Sinn Féin Courts' as well as
quoting from the *Irish Bulletin*. Of the Dáil courts the paper claimed
that they 'command confidence and their decisions are respected and
obeyed'.[53] Dan Breen claimed that this change was a direct result of
the 'salutary lesson taught to the Independent' by the IRA's attack on
the paper's office at the end of 1919.[54] This is debatable. The *Irish
Independent* had reprinted the offending editorial on the day after the
attack and continued to condemn violence throughout the war. The
change in language began to become apparent from the spring of
1920 and could be seen as a response to both the changing climate
caused by the rapidly increasing coercion of the Administration and
the increasing confidence of the IRA.

The *Irish Independent* continued throughout the following months
to attack the 'Prussianism' of the British Government. This manifested
itself, according to the paper, in the increasing militancy and
lawlessness of the Crown forces, the insistence of the British
Government on pushing through the 'Bill for the Better Government
of Ireland' and through the Government's clear partiality towards
northern Unionists. The paper was especially concerned for the fate
of nationalists in the northeast of the country following severe
fighting in Derry. Reports in the paper detailed Catholic districts
under siege by 'Orangemen, fully armed with rifles and revolvers':

> Had the forces of the British Government intervened on
> Saturday or even on Sunday they could have put a check or a
> stop to the operations of the Orangemen ... In the
> circumstances the passivity of the Government must be ascribed
> to sympathy with and approval of the Orangeman's war plans
> against Catholic and Nationalist citizens.[55]

The paper deplored the 'Orange partisanship' of the British
Government, which allowed constant sectarian intimidation of
Catholics throughout Derry and Belfast.[56] Over the following weeks,
many reports appeared in the *Irish Independent* detailing massive
evictions of Catholics from their homes and their jobs.[57] In a piece

entitled 'Pogrom Plans' it quoted, in apparent agreement, from an *Irish Bulletin* report by Eoin MacNeill which stated that the object of the attacks on Catholics was to displace the Catholic population 'so as to create the homogenous Ulster of British spokesmen'.[58] In most instances, it was reported, that the Crown forces offered no help or protection to the victims.[59] Assessing the situation, the *Irish Independent* wrote that the events in Derry and Belfast were proof of the dangers of partition: 'Other methods [than partition] could be found for safe-guarding minority interests. Partition in any shape or form is hateful to all Irishmen and should be strenuously rejected.'[60]

That partition was not in fact 'hateful to all Irishmen' was proven by the actions of Carson and northern Unionists who had by now given their support to the proposed Government of Ireland Bill (see Chapter 3). However, the *Irish Independent* welcomed the decision of southern unionists and *The Irish Times* to call for Dominion Home Rule for a united Ireland.[61] The *Irish Independent* had no doubts that minority interests could be safe-guarded in a united Ireland. In fact, a united Ireland was vital to the protection of these interests. It compared the situation in the northeast to that in the rest of Ireland: 'If in the South and west such a furious and unChristian vendetta had been pursued against Protestants, the followers of Sir Edward Carson would have placarded before the world as proof of the bigotry and intolerance of Irish Catholics.'[62]

The reality, the paper claimed, was that sectarianism was almost non-existent outside of the northeast. It reminded its readers that no 'Nationalist Leaders' had emulated the 'degrading standard set by Sir Edward Carson when he urged his followers to emphasise the religious issue'.[63] In 'the south and west ... all creeds have lived there in amity and neighbourliness' and reported that, despite claims by Greenwood and Bonar Law, 'Protestants in almost every Catholic county have borne tribute to the tolerance of their Catholic fellow-countrymen'.[64]

Such tolerance was not forthcoming from the British Government, the paper claimed. What Ireland was getting instead was Crown colony government, signified by the introduction of the Restoration of Order in Ireland Act (ROIA).[65] This 'new coercion act' was portrayed as part of a series of campaigns, which had 'consistently flouted the majority of the Irish people and are today repressing them with a ruthlessness never before paralleled in any civilised country'.[66] With the escalation of violence that followed the ROIA, reprisals by

Crown forces began to take up more and more space in the paper's reports as the year progressed. Headlines such as 'Scenes of Blood and ruin in Balbriggan', 'Terror in the West and South', 'Soldiers run amok in Limerick' and 'Terrible Wreckage in Mallow' were regular occurrences and the police and military were judged as responsible in these reports.[67] In September, the *Irish Independent* ran an editorial titled 'Government Terrorists' which accused the Government of inciting reprisals through the publication of the *Weekly Summary* and continued to say; 'There can be no doubt as to the responsibility for the killing of two civilians and the burning of Balbriggan'.[68]

The *Irish Independent* often reported on reprisals in such a manner, not actually blaming the Crown forces but leaving its readers in no doubt that they were responsible. It explained the reasons to its readers: 'Under present conditions, Irish nationalist newspapers cannot express their opinions freely'.[69] The *Irish Independent* considered reprisals not as spontaneous acts of revenge but, echoing comments of Arthur Griffith, 'a calculated campaign of indiscriminate vengeance against the Irish people'.[70] Even with the self-censorship necessitated by the intimidation of the Crown forces there was a new directness in the reports of reprisals as could be seen from the report carried on the death of Ellen Quinn in Gort, County Galway. The local parish priest, Fr Considine, reported to the paper that she had been shot by members of the Auxiliaries. Quinn had been shot in the stomach and left to die. Aged 23, she was seven months pregnant. When she was shot, she had been holding her first child in her arms. Considine's testimony to the paper was appalling. He described following a trail of blood to find 'the poor woman lying on her back with blood oozing through her clothes'. The circumstances of her death were truly horrific. In great pain she told the priest how a party of Auxiliaries had fired at her as they passed by on a military transport.[71] The paper spared little detail and openly accused the Auxiliaries of murder.

The *Irish Independent* also displayed deep sympathy towards republicans imprisoned by the Crown forces and repeatedly demanded leniency in the case of Terence MacSwiney calling him 'a martyr in the sacred cause of freedom'.[72] His death and the deaths of the Cork hunger strikers, Joseph Murphy and Michael Fitzgerald was mourned as the 'supreme sacrifice'.[73] The paper ran with black borders for four days. The death of Kevin Barry, 'the Boy Martyr', was also covered sympathetically and the paper had called for a repeal of the death sentence due to Barry's youth and the fact that the execution was contrary to the rules of war.[74] This was an acceptance by the paper that it now considered the IRA a legitimate army. These events were precursors of the violent end to 1920. Like every other newspaper the *Irish Independent* was shocked by the events of Bloody Sunday and it provided vivid accounts of the confusing events of that day reporting on the 'Eleven Officers of the Crown Killed' and the 'awful death roll' at Croke Park that left twelve dead. Detailed coverage was given to both attacks. The paper reported that shortly after the Auxiliaries arrived 'volleys of rifle fire were heard' which caused a mass stampede. Twelve people were reported dead, with eleven seriously wounded and 54 others suffering varying degrees of injury. Of the twelve dead the *Irish Independent* reported nine had died from bullet wounds and a fourteen-year old boy had been bayoneted to death.[75] The paper wrote an impassioned plea to the British Government:

> The real cause of all the terrible happenings to which we have alluded [violence of the past year] is incapacity or deliberate refusal on the part of the British Government to perceive that the disease is political and that the cause is a measure of autonomy conceding to the people unfettered control of their own affairs ... this is the only road to peace so needed by our distracted country.[76]

Republicans were again urged to show restraint as any action would only end in reprisal: 'In our view, force, by whomever so committed can produce no good results'.[77] Days after Bloody Sunday the paper countered Greenwood's claims that the Auxiliaries had been fired on when entering the ground by asking 'how can he explain that not one dead or wounded person was found with arms'.[78] After the Cork city reprisal the paper again dismissed Greenwood's claims. This time he had declared that Sinn Féin members had burned the city. Reporting from the scene the paper's 'special representative' reported that all the people he spoke with including 'staunch Unionists' ridiculed Greenwood's claims. That day's editorial claimed that by supporting the policy of reprisals in Ireland 'they [British Government] have created a Frankenstein monster which they may be unable to control'.[79]

1921 – 'The Partitionists'
Unsurprisingly, the proposed Government of Ireland Bill that had

sailed through parliament in 1920 was a continuing cause of concern. Every aspect of the Bill was a step towards the 'partition and plunder of Ireland' claimed the paper. *Irish Independent* editorials stated repeatedly that full Dominion Home Rule 'the smallest measure of freedom we are willing to accept' was the only means of ending the conflict in Ireland.[80] Aware that possible peace negotiations could soon begin, the paper made a demand to the British Government for 'an honourable peace'. But, the *Irish Independent* insisted, the Government of Ireland Bill was no basis for that peace.[81] When that Bill was passed, at the end of 1920, the *Irish Independent* demanded that Ireland remain 'one and undivided' and that any offer of a settlement based on partition was futile. In no sense did the paper believe the passing of the Act to be the final say on the future government of Ireland. Similar to many of the other nationalist papers, there is a sense that the paper missed the importance of the Act, believing it to be a temporary measure as it was so clearly unacceptable to all sections of society bar unionists in the northeast.[82]

Throughout 1920 and 1921 the newspaper still regarded the taking of human life as wrong and repeatedly counselled the 'extreme wing of Sinn Fein' or sometimes 'the extreme wing of the popular movement' to be steady and refuse to answer what it termed the 'provocations of the army of occupation'. It also questioned the benefit to Ireland of ambushes that brought the terror of reprisal and coercive legislation on the local community. In the aftermath of the Auxiliaries' huge reprisal in Cork in December 1920 the paper had asked: 'What is the mentality of the men who plan or carry out ambushes or take part in the kidnapping of individuals when it is clear to them that appalling consequences flow from these activities.'[83] However, the paper refused to blame the 'extreme wing' for events in Ireland as it stated that these men were provoked beyond self-restraint by the iniquities of British rule.

Consequently, it reserved nearly all its spite for the British Cabinet and the Irish Administration. Each day reports appeared listing wrongdoing by the Crown forces and the Administration.[84] The paper repeatedly called for the publication of the Strickland Report. In early March, when it reported on the murders of the Lord Mayor of Limerick and two of his colleagues, the paper stated that they were 'riddled with bullets as they lay prostrate and writhing on the ground' and dismissed Government claims that they were killed by republicans, writing that it was inconceivable 'that they were killed by Sinn Feiners or men belonging to any section of their fellow citizens'.[85] By this time the *Irish Independent* had become so critical that General Macready accused both it and the *Freeman's Journal* as 'nothing less than daily propaganda of rebellion'.[86] What had upset Macready so much was the paper's reporting of the army in Ireland. The paper had published many reports of civilians shot 'while trying to escape' and had a week before claimed that 48 civilians had died in such suspicious circumstances.[87] A further aspect of the paper's reportage was comparisons between the punishments meted out to captured IRA members (still called 'Volunteers') and that given to soldiers and police involved in reprisals. The paper asked 'Is it one of the ordinary rules of civilised warfare to shoot prisoners?' and continued:

> The British Administration in Ireland has made no real attempt to bring to justice many of the perpetrators of these outrages, although there can be very little doubt that they could easily be traced... When members of the Crown forces take life, as they did at Balbriggan, Gort, Abbeyfeale and a dozen other places, what steps have been taken to bring the culprits to justice?[88]

The forthcoming general elections (North and South) were depicted as a military exercise designed to force through the provisions of the 'Partition Act'.[89] The paper asked how fair elections could be held given that 'in the North of Ireland Sinn Fein organisers have been arrested' while 'in the South a gathering of six persons is illegal and the press is subject to a strict censorship'.[90] To an even greater degree than the *Freeman's Journal* the issue of partition dominated the editorials and reports of the *Irish Independent* during the election. In an editorial titled 'The Nation's Verdict' the paper welcomed the success of Sinn Féin in the 26 county elections:

> Mr De Valera in his proclamation said Sinn Fein would take part in the election in order to give an opportunity to the people of proving once more their loyalty to the principle of Irish Independence...Today the world will learn that Ireland rejects with scorn the great measure of partition.[91]

The paper commented that even while being an illegal organisation Sinn Féin had surpassed Parnell 'at the zenith of his success'.[92] Turning its attention to the elections for the six-county legislature the *Irish Independent*, like most nationalists, believed it possible that, despite the intimidation of their candidates, Sinn Féin and Nationalists would take up to twenty seats in the Northern elections. This, the editorial forecasted, would be a 'smashing blow for the partitionists'.[93] The paper was forced to reassess this forecast after the election when pro-partition Unionists took 40 of the 52 seats: 'Partition has been victorious in Northern Ireland … but it is not surprising considering the campaign of terrorism to prevent Catholic people recording their votes, which operated in many areas.'[94]

The northern election results were the 'Reward for Gerrymandering' lamented the newspaper in a series of reports and editorials over the following weeks.[95] It was especially fearful for the fate of 'isolated' Catholics under the control of the new northern parliament: 'Much as we deplore strife and feuds and desire peace between Irishmen, unfortunately the Catholics of the Six Counties seem to us to have no option but to band themselves together for self-defence.'[96]

A deep gloom pervaded the editorials of the paper following the Northern elections. In May the paper had reported that 'all Ireland is to be put under martial law' and that an 'immense army' of tens of thousands of extra troops was to be sent to Ireland.[97] The paper carried similar reports in the following weeks. The violence was now at fever-pitch and an endless stream of deaths and destruction filled each edition. Events that would formerly have merited great coverage as 'thrilling' or 'sensational' developments were now confined to a few short lines. Indeed, in February the paper had stated that it had not enough space to cover the daily rush of events. For example, the burning of the Custom House in an IRA attack was well covered but by the next day was no longer a main story. This attack which would have been deemed 'sensational' six months earlier and would have dominated the paper's reportage for days was very quickly superseded by the next major event. It also stated that it had evidence and files of far more cases of 'crown misdemeanours' than it had actually printed.[98] The *Irish Independent* was seemingly unaware of the peace moves which were slowly gathering pace. In June a despairing editorial it asked if the 'English Government' thought it could break 'the will of our people':

> It may kill, but it will not conquer; it may produce a wilderness by such methods but it cannot contrive a peace … The Irish people has determined that its country is not a province, by that determination it will stand…If English men and women want our friendship they can have it; at the moment it would almost

seem that they want – and they are certainly earning – our ceaseless and bitter hatred. Is that the legacy they want to leave to their children and to ours? The English people and ours have more interests in common than they have for rivalries, more reason for friendship than for antipathy. But friendship can be rooted not otherwise than in freedom.[99]

Even in such an impassioned editorial, the paper still believed that friendship between Ireland and England was not only necessary but natural. In this, it mirrored the *Freeman's Journal* and other nationalist newspapers, and also very closely resembled a recurring theme in the statements of de Valera and republican propaganda. Yet, the paper was deeply pessimistic about the immediate future. The gloom was such that King George's speech at the opening of the Northern Parliament (in which he called for 'forbearance and conciliation' in Ireland) was welcomed yet treated with suspicion. Recognising that the British Cabinet had written the speech the paper countered that the Cabinet's 'military policy' was 'not the way to bring about conciliation, goodwill and friendship between the two nations'.[100] Yet within a few days these negotiations became public knowledge when Lloyd George invited de Valera to a conference.[101] Two more weeks saw these negotiations end in a truce.

Its coverage of the truce differed little from the other papers. The *Irish Independent* praised de Valera and Griffith, for their work in securing a truce. Praise was also afforded the four 'minority' peers, led by Lord Midleton who had acted as intermediaries between the Dáil and the British Government.[102] The editorials expressed much gratitude towards de Valera for his 'statesmanship' and recognised him as the leader of the Irish nation: 'In the natural order, belligerent nations having declared a truce, settle down to discuss terms of peace. The real negotiations between Mr Lloyd George's Government and Irish Republican leaders have yet to take place.'[103]

De Valera was further acclaimed for challenging Lloyd George to end violence by stating that an end to bloodshed was the 'essential condition' of peace negotiations. This had created the conditions for a truce, stated the editorials.[104] The paper offered him its full support as he and the 'peacemakers' began their series of meetings with Lloyd George. In the days after the truce, the paper printed many reports of 'stirring stories' from the violence of past months including stories from the *Irish Bulletin* on 'How the IRA men fought'.[105] Amidst the relief and new peace the paper reported that the northeast was 'the one dark spot' but overall the paper was full of hope.[106]

The *Irish Independent* had become increasingly antagonistic towards British rule in Ireland between 1919 and 1921 and like the *Freeman's Journal* it had allied itself much more closely with the public aims and statements of Sinn Féin and the Dáil. The fact that the circulation of the paper continued to rise over this period suggests that it was in tune with public opinion in its criticisms of the Administration and Crown forces. However, also like the *Freeman's Journal*, it opposed violence and believed that full Dominion Home Rule, not a republic, was the most achievable goal of Irish demands for independence. Both papers were agreed on the necessity of removing British rule and British forces from Ireland as a necessary condition of any viable and lasting peace. Having looked at the main countrywide national dailies, we will now move to Cork to see how the country's foremost regional newspaper covered events. [107]

5

THE *CORK EXAMINER*

The *Cork Examiner* was owned and edited by the Crosbie family (as it had been since the 1870s). The Crosbie family were well known and respected within the newspaper industry across Ireland and Britain. They and their paper had a long commitment to Home Rule and constitutional nationalism and by 1919 the *Cork Examiner* was an independent nationalist paper, widely read across Munster. Its ability to continue publishing independent news was to be severely tested in the following years as it operated in what became the most violent county in Ireland during the War of Independence.

1919 – Repression in Ireland

Unlike many of the other nationalist papers the *Cork Examiner* was supportive of the events in Dáil Éireann. The paper praised the 'decorum and sense of responsibility' of the Dáil deputies and proceeded to accuse the British Government of 'pledge-breaking' in regard to Ireland. The opening of the Dáil was portrayed as a 'new departure' in that 'it connotes the breaking away from the methods that secured the full adherence of some of the greatest Irishmen of the past half-century'. This was an inevitable result 'of the methods several British Governments have employed in their dealings with this country'.[1] These methods had warranted the new Dáil in 'discarding the constitutional methods that have been associated with Butt, Parnell, McCarthy and Redmond'. The events at Soloheadbeg were reported as a 'tragedy' but as with the other papers they were not linked to the enrolment of the first Dáil.

The *Cork Examiner* continued to criticise the 'pledge breaking' Government over the following months and it warned that 'until Ireland is granted the self-government which is her right she will continue to maintain her struggle for freedom'.[2] However, it quickly became apparent that the paper did not support violent action in the name of this struggle for freedom. In early April a group of IRA Volunteers attempted to free fellow Volunteer Seán Byrne from Limerick Union Hospital. Byrne, who had been arrested by the RIC, had been placed there following a three-week hunger strike. The rescue attempt resulted in Byrne's death and the death of RIC Constable Martin O'Brien.[3] After deploring the attack from what it considered a moral and Christian viewpoint the editorial continued that the attack was not only wrong, but futile: 'Can any reasonably minded man of any party suggest that the premature deaths of an Irish Policeman and a Sinn Fein prisoner will compel the Government which holds this country by armed force, to hasten the coming of Irish freedom under the pressure of such affrays.'[4]

For the paper, 'lawlessness' damaged Ireland's cause and allowed Macpherson, the Chief Secretary, an excuse to plead justification 'for the policy of negation and repression'.[5] The proper alternative to this policy of repression the paper argued was self-government for Ireland. The paper was strongly supportive of Dominion Home Rule and, in response to the failure by Dáil Éireann to gain representation at the Paris Peace Conference, began to become more critical of the Dáil and Sinn Féin. Following Horace Plunkett's creation of the Irish Dominion League and the ongoing series of articles in *The Times* advocating Home Rule, the *Cork Examiner* professed its full support for the idea of Dominion Home Rule, declaring the achievement of an Irish Republic to be 'unattainable'.[6] It warned Sinn Féin that recent failure at the Paris Peace Conference had shown that its 'quixotic election pledges' had no hope of being fulfilled and that it risked losing the support of the Irish people:

> If a Republic be impossible and Dominion Home Rule be attainable – and everything points to the truth of these statements – a practical and keen-witted people will not long be content in pursuing the shadow and leaving the substance go by. Events are shaping themselves that Dominion Home Rule on the lines indicated by the Irish Dominion League is to be regarded as a practical possibility in the near future.[7]

In its support for Home Rule the paper utterly opposed any partition of Ireland even if the two state legislatures were united under a central parliament as proposed by *The Times*:

> No reasonable person would object to the granting of adequate guarantees within the Irish Constitution [of an Ireland with

complete Dominion Home Rule] in order to allay the
groundless fears of Ulstermen but we have yet to learn that
enlightened opinion would care to see a number of Parliaments
in a small country like this …[8]

The British Government and Irish Administration's policy of
'coercion, inaction and drift' in Ireland were the leading aspects of the
paper's coverage over the year. The paper accused the Government
regularly of being in thrall to Edward Carson and castigated
Macpherson and French for their decisions.[9] The results of the
Volunteers' activities were criticised as 'tragedies' and detrimental to
the cause of 'Irish freedom'. The coverage of this time is very much in
line with the other nationalist dailies with the basic theme being that
Ireland was being repressed and that the Irish Administration was
'governing by panic'.[10] This government by panic manifested itself in
the Irish Administration's determination to crush Sinn Féin. The
Administration, in the absence of any defined policy, decided that a
general suppression of nationalist Ireland would ease the unrest in the
country. Both Sinn Féin and the Dáil were suppressed in early
September. The *Cork Examiner* criticised the 'drastic action' unaware
that the paper itself would be suppressed five days later (see Chapter
1).[11] The paper's crime was to have published the prospectus for the
Dáil Éireann loan fund. Considering the wave of newspaper
suppressions and the proscription of the Dáil and Sinn Féin, the paper
asked: 'is this our reward for the Irish blood that was spilled in the
Great War. The victory that was to give freedom to the world has been
achieved and our share of the spoil is a return to the methods of
Arthur James Balfour'.[12]

1920 – 'A bleeding Ireland'

Following the ending of its suppression and watching the *Freeman's
Journal* (to whom the paper gave strong support) endure a similar fate
the *Cork Examiner* repeated its criticisms of the 'repressive' Irish
Administration and of the Government of Ireland Bill deploring 'the
perversity which coerces Ireland while promising self-government'.[13] It
continued these criticisms even though it admitted its wariness of doing
so 'in a country where ordinary law has given way to exigency
measures such as the Defence of the Realm Act'.[14] In common with all
newspapers in Ireland during the early months of 1920 the main
fixation of the *Cork Examiner* was the Government of Ireland Bill,
which proposed to repeal the Act of Union. When the actual text

become known the paper indicted the Bill in strong terms as 'offensive' especially the clauses that proposed 'the dismemberment of the country'.[15] A day later saying that the whole of Ireland rejected the Bill, a disgusted editorial wrote that 'the Bill as printed will settle nothing'.[16]

Of increasing concern to the paper was the intensifying violence in Ireland. The *Cork Examiner* and its editor, George Crosbie, unequivocally backed Dr Cohalan, the Bishop of Cork, who made a series of pronouncements condemning attacks on police barracks and individual policemen. The paper considered the situation in Ireland analogous to the events of 'the early eighties [1880s] when Mr Forster locked up the leaders of the Home Rule movement'. Then, as now, a 'wave of arrests and deportations' had imprisoned the elected repre-sentatives of the Irish people and left a vacuum that had created the conditions for violence. However, this should be no reason for violence, the Archbishop argued: it was wrong and 'brought us no nearer to freedom'.[17] Following the shooting dead of Tomás MacCurtain on 20 March, the *Cork Examiner*'s black-bordered editorial coincided closely with the statement of the Archbishop in deploring the 'murder of the Lord Mayor of Cork'. Suspicions were already rife that some unknown members of the Crown forces had committed the murder. This was tacitly recognised in the editorial, which utilised the words of the Archbishop to warn against reprisal attacks on the Crown forces and to remind readers that the recent 'murders' (of police) were wrong. The editorial concluded by warning that 'the cause of Ireland should not be advanced by crime'.[18]

The *Cork Examiner* continued to warn against violent attacks on Crown forces over the following months. The theme was constant: British Government in Ireland was inherently bad and was provoking the people to a massive extent but the paper argued that this was no justification for attacks on police such as the one in Kerry, which left RIC Constable Patrick Foley dead. The paper reported he had 26 wounds on his body.[19] The *Cork Examiner* took its line on such deaths almost entirely from Dr Cohalan. The paper (to a far larger degree than the *Irish Independent* or *Freeman's Journal*) infused its editorials with religious imagery, repeatedly calling violence 'crime against divine law' or 'crime against moral law'.[20] The paper, for example, spoke of the 'Angel of Death' hovering over Cork in the aftermath of the MacCurtain's death. Such imagery was not uncommon when the paper discussed violence. This was again apparent in May following the deaths of three RIC constables in Cork city and county in the preceding days. The *Cork Examiner* editorialised:

> Wilfully to take human life is murder, and the Fifth Commandment makes no exceptions, but includes all human beings in its scope. The killings of policemen cannot help Ireland's cause and those who have the country's interests most at heart have freely and frequently denounced such crime.[21]

However, the paper saw little hope of an end to violence in a 'bleeding Ireland still held in subjection by the force of British arms'.[22] This condition was exacerbated, the *Cork Examiner* believed, by Lloyd George and the British Government's insistence on applying the Government of Ireland Bill to Ireland in a policy of 'Partition, Prussianism and Promises'.[23]

In its denunciations of 'crime' the *Cork Examiner* did not apply blame towards Sinn Féin and seemed to judge the actions the results of more militant men who were being given free rein by the excesses of British rule in Ireland. This was a similar belief to many other newspapers. While the mass of Sinn Féin were seen as 'moderates', ultimate blame was seen to rest with the Irish Administration who had caused the 'country to be trampled underfoot by rampant militarism'.[24] The increasing violence was such that military chiefs were pressing for Martial Law in the south as they had lost control of much of Munster. Unable to effectively counter the IRA, military and police reprisals against civilian targets became increasingly common and reports on these reprisals began to appear with depressing regularity in the pages in the papers. The *Cork Examiner* openly blamed the Crown forces for many of these.[25] Such comments may have lead to the military raiding the offices of the paper on Academy Street, Cork, on the first day of August. Although documents were taken the machinery was not touched. The paper made no editorial comment on the event but it was, unfortunately for the *Cork Examiner*, a pointer to future intimidation of the paper and its staff.[26]

The *Cork Examiner* showed no signs that it had been cowed and continued to report on and publish photographs of reprisals from all across Munster. One reprisal in Mallow was especially large and the *Cork Examiner*'s photos were incontrovertible proof of the damage wreaked on the town by the British army.[27] Munster was now being consumed by a sustained wave of violence and Tomás MacCurtain's successor as Lord Mayor, Terence MacSwiney, had embarked on a hunger strike in protest against his arrest. More republican prisoners were on hunger strike in Cork Jail. The *Cork Examiner* compared the punishment meted out to MacSwiney and the prisoners in Cork with the inaction taken against Carson after the numerous occasions when 'he openly flouted and defied the law'.[28] This was not the first time that the paper had attacked Carson and had accused the British Government of partiality towards northern unionists. During the summer of violence in Derry, a shocked *Cork Examiner* repeatedly urged the Crown forces to protect the Catholics attacked in Derry and Belfast.[29]

The paper made repeated calls for the release of MacSwiney and the other hunger-strikers but to no avail. Following MacSwiney's death in Brixton Prison the paper carried all its columns in black borders writing that 'Terence MacSwiney may have passed away but the cause of Irish freedom still lives. It can never die'.[30] His sacrifice and those of Michael Fitzgerald and Joseph Murphy who had died in Cork Jail would 'intensify love of freedom' which existed among all Irishmen, 'whether his home is in oppressed Ireland or whether he enjoys the freedom in other lands which is denied to him at home'.[31] Although the remaining hunger strikers in Cork Jail ended their protest following a plea from Arthur Griffith the atmosphere in Cork was now extremely tense. This tension was heightened by the British army's ostentatious display of might during MacSwiney's funeral. To help calm the situation, the *Cork Examiner* advised that 'restraint and good conduct are the most fitting companions for sorrow'.[32] Soon after, the *Cork Examiner* following its own counsel editorially condemned the shooting dead by the IRA of RIC Sergeant James O' Donoghue in the city. The attack had resulted in a police reprisal that left three civilians dead and one seriously wounded. All the killings were criticised as a contradiction of the Fifth Commandment:

> To the average peace-loving citizen, this overwhelming catastrophe that has suddenly befallen the City of Cork seems more like a terrible nightmare than a real occurrence in a Christian community; yet the bodies rigid in death of the police sergeant, shot in the public street, and of the several men subsequently shot in their own houses, bear silent testimony to the reality of a great tragedy that revolts and appals.[33]

While the paper condemned these attacks unequivocally it was not immune to the deep feelings of sympathy that were expressed widely for men such as Kevin Barry who had been captured while in an ambush of Crown forces. It had called for his death sentence to be quashed. Only days before it had made the above condemnation it reported 'How Kevin Barry met his death in a most edifying manner'.[34]

The Cork paper, as with most newspapers in Munster, was operating in very dangerous circumstances. A state of open warfare existed and fighting on the streets of Cork was a regular event. The staff of the newspaper now became targets for intimidation. Notices threatening the local population and signed by the 'Black and Tans' or a group calling itself the 'Anti-Sinn Fein Society' began to appear in the newspaper over the following months.[35] These notices appeared in the paper under duress: armed men entered the paper's premises on a number of occasions and ordered their publication. Local Sinn Féin TD Liam de Róiste wrote in his diary that 'the office of the *Cork Examiner* is, I hear, in continual danger'. He detailed how armed men had forced the staff to print one of the 'Anti-Sinn Fein Society' notices a few days earlier.[36] Staff members stated that the armed men were Auxiliaries although Greenwood denied this in the House of Commons.[37]

In response to the increasing violence the military had been pressing the British Government to introduce Martial Law but had been refused. However, in November, when a party of Auxiliaries was destroyed by an IRA ambush at Kilmichael the request was finally granted. On 10 December 1920 Martial Law was proclaimed in Cork, Kerry, Limerick and Tipperary. While the military had believed that this would enable them to take control of the situation, the ensuing weeks and months saw a deepening of the conflict.[38] Less than a day after the proclamation of Martial Law a company of Auxiliaries launched an extensive arson attack on the centre of Cork. The paper reported the attack as a 'Sequel to Cork Ambush'; an IRA attack on Auxiliaries near Victoria Barracks earlier that day.[39] It expressed the shock of the general populace: 'Cork in Flames' and 'Night of Terror' ran the headlines. The Auxiliaries were blamed for the attack but even in such extraordinary circumstances the *Cork Examiner*'s reports were not sensationalistic.[40] On the morning after the attack the Archbishop of Cork issued his strongest denunciation to date of the violence in his diocese. He excommunicated anybody 'who shall take part in an ambush, or in kidnapping or otherwise shall be guilty of murder, attempted murder or arson'. The excommunication was aimed at the IRA whose methods the Archbishop had denounced throughout the year. He was supported in the editorial of the *Cork Examiner*, which agreed with the Archbishop's statement that 'ambushes are murderous'.[41]

This continued support had damaging repercussions. On Christmas Eve the offices of the *Cork Examiner* were attacked and badly damaged. The paper reported:

> A body of armed and disguised men entered the 'Examiner' office premises after 8 o' clock on Xmas Eve and caused much damage to the printing presses. Bombs, gelignite and sledgehammers were used. The raiders claimed they were acting under the orders of the Irish Republic.[42]

Even though the damage was extensive, the *Cork Examiner* missed only one issue. Apart from the support of the *Cork Examiner* for Cohalan's statement on excommunication the paper had repeatedly called for a truce in Ireland. This was undoubtedly another reason for the attempt to shut down the paper. These calls for a truce had become more insistent in the weeks following Bloody Sunday.[43] Again, it had taken its lead from a Catholic Bishop, this time the Archbishop of Tuam, Dr Gilmartin.[44] Although tentative peace moves were under way at this time, involving the Australian Archbishop of Perth, Dr Clune, as an intermediary, the IRA were very eager to dampen down any talk of truce, fearing that it would be seen as encouraging the British Government to believe that the IRA and Dáil Éireann were desperate for peace. The policies of the *Cork Examiner* were therefore unwelcome reading for the IRA. Whatever the reasons for the attack, the editorial accused the perpetrators of being 'misguided' and warned them 'that the voice of sane and moderate opinion in this country would not be stifled'.[45] These were brave words in an area where a single report or editorial could result in violent assault and intimidation from either the IRA or the Crown forces.

1921 – Martial Law

Perhaps to demonstrate that it had not been cowed the *Cork Examiner* repeated its beliefs following another spate of violence in Cork, claiming 'that armed resistance to the existing government was useless because there was no chance of success' and because of the 'evils which it would cause'.[46] Even though the paper now operated under Martial Law there seems to have been little change in the paper's reportage during the first weeks of the year. The Government of Ireland Bill was a predictable bête-noire while the decision of the Government not to publish the Strickland report into the burning of Cork was utterly condemned.[47] The paper continued to criticise the British

Government's policy of executions and called for the remission of the death sentences of six IRA men in Victoria barracks.[48] These criticisms did not go unnoticed and the censorship of reports was quickly applied by the military. The *Cork Examiner* was blunt with its readers:

> We think it right to draw to our readers attention to the fact that the 'Examiner' being published in an area where Martial Law is in force, everything which appears in this journals editorial and news columns is liable to censorship, and that this censorship has occasionally been exercised.[49]

From the British army viewpoint, one of the stated advantages of Martial Law was 'control of the press'.[50] In a Martial Law Area (MLA) the local Military Governor, Major General Peter Strickland, had the power to censor all newspaper material. By this stage the law had been extended to Clare, Kilkenny, Waterford and Wexford. General Macready later wrote that it was only in this area 'was there a semblance of accuracy and truth in the news served out to the public'.[51] Unfortunately for the newspapers and their readers, this news was now seriously circumscribed by the power of the military. The Attorney General, Denis Henry, defined these powers to the House of Commons in response to a question from Oswald Mosley. Henry's reply showed that the military governor effectively held carte blanche:

> … the press in the Martial Law Area would not be interfered with so long as nothing was published calculated to cause disaffection among his Majesty's subjects or to interfere with enforcement of martial law.[52]

This placed journalists in a doubly precarious position, Firstly, the military decided what was designed to cause 'disaffection'. Secondly, what they judged as causing 'disaffection' was often inconsistent and arbitrary. A correspondent of the *Westminster Gazette* was arrested by the military in April after he had filed a report from outside Cork Jail detailing the sombre reaction of the assembled crowd to the executions of four IRA Volunteers.[53] He was told that his report should not have described the reactions of the crowd. Other foreign correspondents were also ordered to appear before a military officer for similar 'offences'.[54] Days later, the military issued a warning to all journalists and newspapers operating in Cork that cautioned them against sending reports 'which seem in any way to reflect on the conduct of the Crown forces' although 'No charge of inaccuracy was brought against any of them'.[55] Even the phrase 'in any way reflect' effectively meant any reporting of military or police activities could be deemed by the army to be inaccurate or prejudicial of the Crown forces. The whole affair was an unsubtle attempt to block news from Cork. It was certainly seen as such by the newspapers. The reaction from the press in Ireland and England was predictably furious. The *Manchester Guardian* echoed the sentiments of many when it stated that the military order would be seen as 'a sign that we [British army] have something to hide'.[56] In effect, the military was extending some of the controls it had imposed on Irish papers over the past two years to the foreign press operating in the MLA. From February the *Freeman's Journal* and *Irish Independent* had begun attaching the appendage 'as passed by military censor' to many of their reports from the Martial Law Area.

It is probable that censorship in the MLA corresponded closely with that which had operated across all Ireland until August 1919 although in the absence of records the exact nature of the censorship cannot be fully ascertained. Even before the south came under the direct control of the military the *Cork Examiner* carried little from the *Irish Bulletin* preferring to rely on its own correspondents. Similarly, official reports coming from Dublin Castle were often ignored. The paper also relatively rarely reported on the activities of the Dáil 'counter state' such as the Dáil courts. It is likely that even without Martial Law the *Cork Examiner* would have continued with this policy. As regards its reporting of the news what was always a relatively staid and cautious newspaper (compared to the national dailies, for example) was now seriously hampered in its reporting of events within the MLA. Its reporting suffered with more reliance, from now, on Dublin Castle's official reports and press agency news items.[57] Despite the determination of George Crosbie and the staff, another suppression hung like a sword above it and all other papers in the MLA. General Strickland, the Officer Commanding the Cork area, noted in April that the attitude of the press in the MLA had, 'thanks to firm control', greatly improved. The papers were too fearful to publish anything which may have caused offence to the Crown forces.[58] As the political and military situation had worsened since the introduction of Martial Law it is clear that newspapers were not being allowed to report freely and were in fact strictly constrained in what they could publish.

Unsurprisingly, the *Cork Examiner* was not the only paper being censored at this time in the MLA. The national dailies carry reports of censorship of others such as the *Enniscorthy Echo, Kilkenny People, Leinster Leader, Limerick Leader, Munster News* and *Wexford People*. Indeed, the *Wexford People* complained that 'all reports appearing in its columns have been censored by the military'. In the case of the *Kilkenny People*, the local O/C of the British army informed the editor that, before publication, each issue would have to be submitted to him for censorship.[59] The army O/C in the Enniscorthy area, apart from censoring the *Enniscorthy Echo*, had also ordered it to print extracts from *The Irish Times* and *Weekly Summary*.[60] Unquestionably, the policy of military censorship was widespread in the Martial Law Area and the problems faced by the papers above give some idea of the pressures afflicting the *Cork Examiner*. What is known is that events such as the execution of IRA member Patrick Casey by the military in Cork Barracks were censored. The reason given by Attorney General Denis Henry to the House of Commons was that this was done 'in the interest of peace' in the region. Henry refused to answer a question from Tory MP Lord Cecil as to 'How reporting of the execution in London or America could add to the disturbances in Cork'.[61] Another facet of Martial Law was that newspapers could be prohibited from being sold in the MLA. This happened to the *Freeman's Journal* and its allied newspapers in early June following General Strickland's judgement that an article on roadblocking and trenching by the IRA was prejudicial to the operation of Martial Law.[62]

The Truce

The paper continued to criticise British actions – especially denouncing the dismemberment of Ireland that would result if the 'Partition Act' were enforced. It also condemned Crown reprisals but was restricted in what it could say by Martial Law. The only hope for Ireland now, the paper argued, was a truce. It praised the 'patriotism' of the IRA Volunteers such as the men executed in Mountjoy Jail but wrote that their deaths were futile:

> ...even the most extreme of the extremists must acknowledge that superiority in wealth, arms, organisation and equipment makes a barrier that ardour, no matter how intense, can hope to surmount.[63]

Criticisms of the actions of the IRA were now joined by attacks on Sinn Féin and de Valera. Saint Patrick's Day was used as the occasion to warn de Valera as well as James Craig that 'there is a large and growing class in Ireland which neither of them may be said to represent'.[64] This 'growing class' was supposedly moderate Irish opinion which could, the paper believed, form a bridge 'over which North and South may unitedly march'.[65] Like other nationalist papers the *Cork Examiner* welcomed the alliance between Sinn Féin and Nationalists in the northern elections. It was hoped that their joint success would go a long way towards 'undermining partition'.[66] When the hoped-for results failed to materialise a dispirited editorial blamed Unionists for 'wholesale gerrymandering of the electorate, intimidation, personation and so on'.[67] The criticisms of the IRA and the calls for a truce upset many republicans. Seán Hayes spoke against the paper and 'its policy of moderation' during a Dáil Éireann meeting in March.[68] But there were no more IRA attacks on the paper. Tragedy touched the paper two months later when four *Cork Examiner* employees were attacked in an ambush (see Chapter 2). One of the group, Stephen Dorman, was targeted by the attackers as he was a known member of the IRA. He died the next day.[69]

A truce had been the concern of the Cork paper throughout the conflict and its calls became more insistent as slight signs of hope emerged in the bloodiest phase of the war. Lord Derby's entry into the country (widely rumoured to be acting as an intermediary for the British Government) and the meeting of de Valera and Craig in May heightened these hopes. While the paper desired a truce it was vague about what form a settlement should take. Unlike many others the Cork paper issued no great proposals for a settlement. It proposed only that Ireland should have 'self-government', preferably Dominion Home Rule and most definitely that any settlement should not include partition. However, the ultimate form of settlement, the paper believed, could only be decided upon after the much sought-after truce.

When this truce arrived in July, the *Cork Examiner* expressed hope that the issue of partition and Northern Ireland could be overcome and resolved. It pressed a case for peace, which included a form of autonomy for the Northern Parliament led by James Craig:

> Under a scheme of Dominion Home Rule for all Ireland it is conceivable that Sir James Craig could still retain his local parliament and at the same time not be divorced from membership of the empire which in the case of the Dominions is a voluntary tie.[70]

The *Cork Examiner* proposed such a scheme on the basis that

Northern objections were 'not insurmountable' and that southern unionists had:

> ... already shown by their attendance at the Mansion House that they have no doubts or mental reservations as to the toleration of the majority under any form of government that Ireland may secure.[71]

The paper also believed that Eamon de Valera had expressed the notion that such a measure was not incompatible with Irish freedom. It congratulated de Valera for his part in arranging the truce and urged him and Craig as well as the British Government to compromise.[72] The basis of liberty the paper editorialised was the protection and acceptance of minorities and reminded its readers, as well as the proposed negotiators, that peace-talks would:

> ... necessitate compromise and concessions all round, and that it is only by fostering and developing goodwill and meeting difficulties in a spirit that will permit of adjustments and the accommodation of conflicting views that an agreed peace can be secured.[73]

This statement succinctly reflected the ethos of a paper that had, through a period of horrific violence, Martial Law and intimidation, refused to compromise its convictions. Despite the constrictions placed on the paper it never wavered in its argument that the British Government had a duty to grant Ireland's demands for Home Rule. These convictions also included a belief that all violence was wrong and that partition was the worst possible solution to the violence in Ireland. We now turn to one of Ireland's other main papers, *The Irish Times,* a paper politically opposed to the aims of the *Cork Examiner* and the other nationalist papers discussed so far.

6

THE IRISH TIMES

The Irish Times was anxious about the emergence of the Sinn Féin party and the coverage the paper gave to the opening of the first Dáil reflected this. Owned by the industrialist Sir John Arnott and his family, it was historically a conservative and unionist paper, considered in Ireland and Britain as the premier Irish unionist paper and the paper that was seen as representing the unionist population outside of Ulster.

1919 – 'Cloud-cuckoo Land'

The Irish Times' editorial treatment of the first Dáil was the most critical of any of the Irish papers. Its editorial 'Cloud-Cuckoo Land' accused Sinn Féin of embarrassing itself and the nation and predicted that the movement must now 'end in ridicule or disaster'.[1] According to the paper Ireland was 'one of the most favoured countries in the world' and it advised the Irish people to turn their attentions towards the Dublin Chamber of Commerce rather than the Mansion House (that is to say Dáil Éireann). Here they could witness the success of the Irish economy.[2] 'Already', the paper claimed, 'popular opinion was beginning to rally to the side of the forces of order, sanity and law'.[3] Little coverage was given to the shooting dead of two RIC men at Soloheadbeg bar a denunciation of the 'murder'.

Surprisingly little editorial space was devoted to the increasing unrest in Ireland until the latter months of 1919. Reports of the shootings of policemen were carried under headings such as 'cold-blooded crime', 'outrage' and 'murder' and were given substantial space.[4] Events such as the November looting of shops in Cork city centre by Crown forces received minimal and perfunctory comment.[5] One event that did arouse the ire of *The Irish Times* was the attack on the Lord Lieutenant, in December which the paper claimed was the culmination of the 'campaign of murder in Ireland'.[6] It then used the coverage of the attack to launch a sideswipe at critics of the Government whom the paper claimed 'advocated – without defining – a milder and more general policy'. Explaining its stance, the editorial continued to say that the Irish Administration was 'engaged in a grim conflict with a far-reaching conspiracy of crime'.[7] Indeed, the paper seemed to push the reach of this conspiracy as far as the general public from whom the Government was 'getting no support'.[8] This attack in many respects marks the ending of the initial phase of the IRA campaign. The attempt on the life of the Lord Lieutenant signalled that the IRA, which had initially confined itself to arms raids and occasional attacks on police throughout 1919, was now more confident of escalating its campaign against the Crown forces. *The Irish Times*, perhaps for the first time, began to recognise both the inherent danger Sinn Féin and the Dáil posed to the Union and the level to which the conflict was escalating.

1920 – From coercion to Dominion Home Rule

Two great themes dominated *The Irish Times* during 1920: the Government of Ireland Bill and the increasing violence in the country (which *The Irish Times* believed was manifested most gruesomely by the sustained attacks on the RIC). The paper devoted most of its editorial space to the proposed Government of Ireland Bill during the first quarter of 1920, consistently warning against what it called the 'peril of partition'. In early January it warned southern unionists of the need for immediate action 'against proposals that threaten them with every variety of ruin' anticipating that the opportunity for effective opposition 'would have vanished' once the Bill reached a second reading.[9] *The Irish Times* devoted more attention to the Bill than even the *Freeman's Journal* and *Irish Independent*. *The Irish Times* also realised earlier than the other two that the Bill was destined to pass through the British Parliament. The paper's clear abhorrence of the Bill was the equal of that of the nationalist dailies and it again warned in late January that 'no bad bill ever had a better prospect of reaching the statute books'.[10] If this did occur *The Irish Times* had no doubts about the results: 'It is clearly established that if partition is enforced it will be permanent and the British Government will have presented a vitally important area of the United Kingdom to an implacable foe.'[11]

Yet *The Irish Times* was fighting on a number of fronts, against what it perceived as a 'murder campaign' being carried out by the

IRA, against the proposed partition of the country and against any settlement of the Irish question through Home Rule, even for an united Ireland. The paper wavered between support for and disillusionment with the Irish Administration and the Crown forces in Ireland and it was deeply wounded at Edward Carson and the northern unionists' willingness to leave southern unionists stranded in a 'republican' state. Carson had informed a deputation of the Irish Unionist Alliance in early March that he would accept the terms proposed in the Bill. He expressed his sympathy for what the paper called the 'betrayed Loyalists of the South' but made it clear that the southern unionists could expect no practical support from northern unionists. In unusually dramatic language the paper condemned Carson: 'When the ghost of a murdered community stands in Westminster Sir Edward Carson will be able to say with a sound conscience – "Thou canst say that I did it. Never shake thy gory locks at me".'[12]

The Irish Times continued to attack Carson over the following days, bitterly claiming the decision was 'a final breach of the Solemn League and Covenant'.[13] The paper had little doubt that the proposed Council of Ireland, the supposed guarantor of eventual Irish unity would forever remain 'a fleshless, bloodless skeleton'.[14] For this reason, the Bill was 'fatal' to southern unionism, which would be cast adrift outside the Empire after the nationalists, and especially Sinn Féin had transformed the 26 counties into an independent republican state. The prospect of being divorced from the Empire was horrifying.[15] One editorial in March depicted the leaders of Sinn Féin as 'Peter Pans – the boys that will never grow up'. What historians have described as the 'counter state' initiated by Sinn Féin was compared to children 'prattling on the nursery floor'. The paper continued that the world at large would ask the question that 'thoughtful Irishmen could not evade':

> Can a people still in the nursery, mentally and morally be allowed to govern itself, either in much or in little? If the thoughtful Irishman replies: 'This play-acting is only the work of a few youthful irresponsibles', the world will say: You give the children a majority of your suffrage: You place them in control of your municipal affairs.[16]

The increasing violence and general unrest within Ireland was the other dominant concern of *The Irish Times* in the first half of 1920.

The paper clearly supported the actions of Dublin Castle when introducing measures the other national papers called coercive. The theme of the paper was that the duty of the Government was to maintain law and order, and that duty must be fulfilled, the paper urged, 'by all the means at its command'.[17] Following a statement by the Irish Bishops in late January criticising the Irish Administration *The Irish Times* leapt to its defence: 'We do not believe that the Irish Government has made no mistakes but we see – and every reasonable Irishman sees – that it is doing its best to grapple with formidable forces of disorder and crime.'[18]

This was a marked contrast to the stated positions of the *Irish Independent* and the *Freeman's Journal*, who placed the bulk of the blame for the state of unrest on the Irish Administration. *The Irish Times* blamed the 'terrorism in Ireland' for the current state of anarchy where 'the life of a policeman is a thing of no account'.[19] Whereas the other papers were deeply annoyed by the motor permit regulations (see Chapters 3 and 4) and the Curfew Order in the Dublin area (from midnight to 5 a.m., later extended), *The Irish Times* termed them an 'effort to remedy a disgraceful set of affairs' rather than an attack on civil liberties.[20]

In March, the paper urged that the full weight of the law be thrown against 'these bands of desperate men' that were devastating the country. *The Irish Times* displayed fewer qualms about what others called coercion and it believed fully in the courage and loyalty of the Government's servants. However, it doubted the 'power of initiative and organisation and the intellectual ability to grasp the nature of the vital issues' among the leaders of these Government servants.[21] Dublin Castle must have seemed at this time to be one of the few friends an increasingly anxious southern unionist population possessed. It was now becoming apparent that they were to be abandoned by northern unionists and by the British Parliament. As such, the Irish Administration's failures in the face of increasing violence were very disheartening. When Macpherson commented in the House of Commons that the Irish Administration would continue to use whatever means necessary to maintain law and order, the paper admonished him with the judgement that 'there is no law and order to maintain'.[22] *The Irish Times* was adamant that the RIC should re-occupy the barracks it had recently abandoned. It knew that the RIC could not do this alone and that the British army would have to aid in the 'provision of security for the police'. If this was not done 'everything will go'.[23] This proved to be an accurate assessment of events on the ground as large sections of the countryside were increasingly under effective republican control as Sinn Féin and the Dáil courts filled the vacuum left by the absence of the police (see Chapter 2).

This 'anarchy' was used as further evidence as to the dangers of the Home Rule Bill. Aggravation of the current anarchic state of Ireland would only result from the Government's 'Partition Bill' warned one editorial. This anarchy would not be cured by the 'gift of self-government' and in fact was 'proof of the unfitness for self-government'.[24] In another article the paper pleaded with the formulators of the proposed Home Rule Bill, the British Government: 'Ireland consists of two anti-pathetic communities that cannot be given unrestricted freedom because one would attack the other, and cannot be given restricted freedom because they refuse it.'[25]

For *The Irish Times*, the solution was therefore clear – the Union, as it currently existed, was the best of all possible worlds and had to be maintained. To achieve this, the paper repeatedly counselled, it would be necessary for the violence of the 'assassins' to be met head on. In this vein, following the suspected RIC shooting of Tomás MacCurtain in Cork *The Irish Times* published a strong defence of the police. It praised the work they had to undertake and the manner in which they had done so over a period of immense trial. It totally refuted 'the monstrous suspicion' that MacCurtain had been 'killed by agents of the Government': 'It is no business of ours to lecture our contemporaries, but we must say we are appalled by the utter lack of any sense of responsibility of some Irish newspapers which are inflaming, in effect, public opinion against the forces of the Crown.'[26]

Even though all the evidence pointed to the involvement of Cork-based RIC men in the killing of MacCurtain *The Irish Times* refused to accept the result of the inquest into his death. Such a crime, the paper argued, had 'no motive' and was 'absolutely out of keeping with the magnificent character and traditions of the Royal Irish Constabulary'.[27] The paper accused nationalist Ireland, including the general public, of putting unfair and colossal pressure on the police and charged the British Government with failing to relieve this pressure:

> The Royal Irish Constabulary are scattered in little parties throughout large areas where every man's hand is against them. Socially, they are the victims of a cruel boycott. Day and night they live in a state of nearly intolerable strain and almost daily

their ranks are thinned by murder.[28]

While *The Irish Times* unreservedly condemned the attacks on the Crown forces as the 'most lamentable' feature of the state of Ireland the paper declared they 'are not the most significant'. What was even more damaging to the Union was the Dáil Éireann counter state that had been derided by *The Irish Times* previously and especially the Dáil courts:

> The most serious feature is the gradual suppression of British Authority by Republican Authority in all the matters that concern the general government of Ireland. Sinn Fein courts are elbowing the Four Courts and the County Courts into a brief-less desuetude. County Councils and other bodies are giving their allegiance to Dail Eireann.[29]

However, a major shift in opinion was under way within *The Irish Times* at this time. The violence which the paper had urged the Crown forces to meet 'head-on' was intensifying, not abating. While still having no sympathy with the 'terrorism' of the 'Volunteers' *The Irish Times* now judged the British Government's persistence in pushing the hated Government of Ireland Bill through parliament as a major contributory factor to the violence and political upheaval in Ireland, commenting that 'the present Home Rule Bill is a serious obstacle in the path of national peace'.[30] The paper was fearful that civil war was the inevitable outcome of the current wave of violence. In the wake of severe fighting in Derry *The Irish Times* judged that Ireland was 'on the brink' of 'a triangular war that no side could win' between the Crown forces, armed unionism in the northeast and Sinn Féin.[31]

It was clear to *The Irish Times* that the Bill had no support whatsoever outside the section of unionism within the northeast and the paper indicted the British Government for its part in so deeply antagonising public opinion throughout Ireland. By the summer of 1920 *The Irish Times* had become convinced that the issue in Ireland was 'between any tolerable form of government and no government at all'. It was certain that 'it will be no government at all if the present Home Rule Bill becomes law'.[32] That this attitude now corresponded with the vast bulk of southern unionist opinion was evident from the resolution passed by the Council of the Dublin Chamber of Commerce, which called for 'a measure of complete self government for Ireland'.[33] The majority of this Council was unionist and the decision greatly affected *The Irish Times*: 'It is a startling resolution: two years ago – one year ago – it would have been impossible … and of the men who sign this demand the majority are Unionists.'[34]

This was followed, in early August, by the British Government's Restoration of Order in Ireland Act (ROIA) whose terms became known in the weeks before it was passed by Parliament. It was a defining moment for *The Irish Times*, which stated that the Bill was a 'confession of the complete failure of British authority in Ireland'. The majority of public opinion in Ireland, the paper stated, had moved consistently towards Dáil Éireann and would not be won over by the ROIA.[35]

The changed outlook of the paper can be gauged from a meeting between the editor of *The Irish Times*, John Healy, along with the editor of the *Freeman's Journal* and Captain Harrington, the Secretary of the Dominion Home Rule Group with the Under Secretary, John Anderson. According to Anderson: '*The Irish Times* editor was most anxious. He said the PM's declaration and his martial law was hopeless and futile and the worst possible step. Only a big frank generous appeal could meet the situation now.'[36]

The Irish Times demonstrated its new attitude by supporting what it now believed was the only way to bring peace to Ireland, Dominion Home Rule and a revocation of the Act of Union. The paper and the unionists had been forced into this by the provisions of the Government of Ireland Bill which *The Irish Times* believed would have one of two results: an independent republic outside the Empire or a Crown colony government of a country never at peace. Dominion Home Rule at least kept the link with the Empire and gave unionists a measure of power over their futures. Consequently, in early August, the paper publicly proclaimed its support for full Dominion Home Rule for the whole island.[37] The editorial was, as Mark Sturgis confided in his diary, 'an amazing evidence of change that the premier Irish "Unionist" paper should come out with it'.[38]

The editorial had actually been composed by Cecil Fforde, a member of the Irish Bar, Counsel to the Irish Administration and a prominent southern unionist. 'Fforde wrote it mostly in Wylie's room', detailed Sturgis.[39] William Wylie, prominent legal adviser to the Irish Administration and another Dublin Castle official convinced of the need to end coercion and create a settlement in Ireland, had not only played a part in the new approach of *The Irish Times*, days earlier he had convinced Jeremiah McVeagh of the *Freeman's Journal* to write a detailed article proposing Dominion Home Rule (see Chapter 3).

Contrary to the actions of the British Cabinet, many of the officials of the Irish Administration in Dublin Castle sensed that coercion in the form of the ROIA allied to the Government of Ireland Bill as a settlement were predestined to fail. Wylie seems to have taken this initiative himself but with the backing of Anderson, officials such as Andy Cope and Fforde soon began to seek means of organising a truce. Mark Sturgis' diaries are filled with a multitude of peace moves and attempts at creating a truce (usually involving Cope). *The Irish Times* would have been aware of the thoughts of figures within the Irish Administration such as Wylie who judged a settlement in Ireland along the lines of Dominion Home Rule as the only viable way of making peace in Ireland. This may well have been another contributory factor to *The Irish Times*' change of policy.

The paper gave the reasons for its Dominion Home Rule demands in an editorial soon after this meeting and following the resolution passed by the 'Unionist Anti-Partition League'. The League called for a settlement that would give Ireland complete control of her affairs while remaining in the Empire, essentially asking for Dominion Home Rule. *The Irish Times* saw this as the only possible solution that would meet the hopes of the majority of public sentiment in Ireland: 'The essential facts today are that Unionist Ulster's acceptance of the Partition Bill has scrapped the Act of Union and that British Law, being no longer supported by the sanctions of public opinion has ceased to operate in this country.'[40]

The paper urged the British Government to listen to the voice of a community that, the paper reminded the Government, was the only section of society in Ireland, north and south, which had never threatened to, or actually taken up arms against the Crown forces in Ireland. Tinkering with the Bill in the hope of making it more amenable to public opinion in Ireland was futile, *The Irish Times* cautioned the Government. Such changes as reducing the south's imperial levy were of no benefit it stated as 'the country rejects the Bill on principle rather than in its details'.[41]

However, the Bill was passed into law in December 1920 despite being 'despised by the mass of the Irish people'.[42] Some hope was displayed by the paper that some late changes to the proposed Council of Ireland would alleviate the worst effects of partition and perhaps even bring unity. These changes made the Council a second chamber with some powers of veto over legislation enacted in the two Parliaments. This change was introduced into the Bill by southern unionist peers under Lord Midleton, whom the paper praised as 'proving the value of southern unionist brains and character as a national asset'.[43] Another vital change, the paper hoped, was the creation of an upper house in both states designed to protect minorities, which was 'a gain of, perhaps, even greater importance for the Nationalist minority in the North than for the Unionist minority in the South'.[44]

Although holding major reservations and despite its previous resistance, *The Irish Times* regarded the Act as 'a fait accompli'. As the British Government had determined to follow this path, it was, the paper argued, the only tool with which to repair the dire situation in Ireland. To help in this end the paper called on the South to 'escape the tyranny of crime' but placed a special onus on Edward Carson whom the paper claimed had 'heavy responsibilities not merely to Belfast and Londonderry, but to Dublin and Cork'. The editorial continued 'Success in the North – especially success in winning the confidence and co-operation of the Roman Catholic – must half [sic] the difficulties of a settlement in the South'.[45] The editorial writers did however realise that the omens for either occurrence were not encouraging.

'The tyranny of crime' continued to preoccupy the paper. There was no change in the paper's reportage of IRA violence from 1919. Deaths of policemen and soldiers were always termed 'murder' and Dublin Castle official reports formed the mainstay of the paper's news on the activities of the IRA, especially when General Macready arranged for such reports to be disseminated more widely by military sources in April 1920.[46] The violence had by now reached such a level, in part *The Irish Times* believed, because the British Government was engaged in the pretence that 'if you call war "disorder" it ceases to be war'. This meant that the police had absorbed, almost single-handedly, the IRA campaign and as they were clearly failing to meet the challenge – they had now to be supported by the army. The paper conceded that the need for an 'army of occupation' implied 'the failure of law' but countered that 'its work of protection and vigilance is a condition precedent to the restoration of law'.[47] The RIC had 'suffered as severely as if it held a front line trench in France' the paper claimed.[48] The paper believed that what was intensifying this strain on the police was the 'murder conspiracy' that was at war with the Crown forces but that 'refused to recognise the laws of war'.[49] *The Irish Times* wrote that this was especially disastrous for southern Ireland and that its population's attempts to defeat the Government of Ireland Bill were being subverted by the violence in Ireland. Following the events of Bloody Sunday the paper warned:

> Today the House of Commons is wholly out of sympathy with Ireland and arguments based on political conciliation and settlement make no appeal to it. Its sympathies are entirely with the widows and orphans of its loyal servants murdered foully by Irish hands and it is beginning to feel that a country that can make itself a slave to such an unholy terror is unfit for any form of self government.[50]

Nonetheless, the paper maintained throughout the latter half of the year that the 'incurably fanatical element in Irish life is very small'.[51] *The Irish Times* was sure that 'the vast majority of Irishmen' wanted an end to violence. Ending all attacks on the Crown forces would mean a consequent end to reprisals and repression. This goal could be met by freeing Ireland's 'moral force' from the fear of terror by which the IRA supposedly won much of its support: 'We do not believe that the mass of the Sinn Fein party approves of murder; we are convinced that the bulk of the Irish people detest it'.[52] Reprisals by Crown forces were also condemned in the editorial as 'wholly wrong' but the paper did not believe that these were anything other than a symptom of the pressure under which these forces operated. The paper claimed, without evidence, that the Irish Administration was trying to stop reprisals but the paper warned they could not be truly ended 'until the last vestige of provocation for them shall disappear'.[53] As the year came to a close the paper called on the churches to bring forth their moral influence. Following the Archbishop of Cork's excommunication of IRA members and of anyone who aided them *The Irish Times* called for a similar announcement throughout all Irish dioceses: 'A general censure of excommunication upon the crime of murder would be of tremendous appeal to the national consciousness'.[54]

1921 – Peace and the 'New Unionism'

The Government of Ireland Bill, which had dominated the pages of *The Irish Times* during 1920, had now come into law and was being put into operation by British and Irish civil servants through 1921.[55] As the 'Partition Act' was now on the statute books *The Irish Times* urged the people of 'Southern Ireland' to make the best of the situation. The paper argued that if the population resolved to work the

Act and if a climate of trust could be cultivated between the two jurisdictions in Ireland partition would soon give way to unity. Obstructing the hopes of *The Irish Times* was the still-rising tempo of violence that had continued steadily throughout 1920 to reach a crescendo in 1921. As the year progressed the paper criticised the British Government for continuing to implement the provisions of the Act. The paper stressed its belief that a political settlement was impossible 'until law and order has been restored'. Once again the paper called for a 'national demand for a stoppage of murder and lawlessness' with the Churches, newspapers and commercial groups to the fore.[56] Republican violence and the necessity of its end were to be the outstanding concern of *The Irish Times* until the truce in July.

The critics of the Government in both Ireland and Britain were censured for both failing to provide this 'national demand' and for their criticisms of the British Government. The 'responsibilities of British Governments for these conditions may be large' accepted *The Irish Times* but the question had become academic. Only a 'complete end to the campaign of murder' would restore peace to Ireland. What caused *The Irish Times* most frustration was what it believed to be a blinkered concentration on the activities of the Crown forces by critics of the Government:

> These are the facts and if the Government's critics would discuss them fairly, some real progress might be made towards peace in Ireland. They prefer however, from Mr Asquith down, to concentrate their whole attacks on the forces of the Crown and to ignore almost completely the wickedness and peril of the campaign of crime.[57]

The Irish Times, which had a consistently fierce antipathy towards English critics of the Government, additionally accused these critics of ignoring the fact that 'the Republican movement refuses to mitigate its impossible claim', that of an independent republic: 'The British Government is bound to protect the lives of innocent citizens and owes to the whole Empire the duty of fighting the Republican claim'.[58]

The Auxiliaries, who were attracting most of this criticism, were defended in strong terms by *The Irish Times* despite the mounting evidence of their campaign of terror: 'It is wicked and ridiculous to suggest that police work in Ireland has produced a sudden degeneration in men who fought bravely and honourably in every area of the Great War.'[59] Such loyalty to a quasi-military force that was operating far outside the norms of policing was a result of a natural inclination to support the forces of the Crown and also a reliance on and acceptance of the official news reports emanating out of Dublin Castle. The paper was also trapped by its belief that nearly all reports of police reprisals were false or motivated purely by a hatred of the RIC and the Auxiliaries. This topic is one area where *The Irish Times* abandoned its normal integrity, refusing to look to the story beyond the official reports.

This acceptance of official reports meant that *The Irish Times* was more suspect about placing blame in incidences of death other than deaths among the Crown forces. For example, while the paper did condemn the deaths of civilians such as the Sinn Féin Lord Mayor of Limerick, George Clancy and two of his colleagues as 'murder', the paper claimed the deaths were 'mysterious' when the evidence pointed to the involvement of Crown forces.[60] Throughout this period *The Irish Times* was far less willing to place the blame for the violent activities of which sections of the Crown forces were guilty. The issue of reprisals did not arouse the anger or the print space seen in the nationalist papers and in many English and international papers. The criticism of these attacks was muted, especially in regard to the paper's condemnation of attacks on the Crown forces. The paper did admit 'that at Cork, Trim and other places discipline had failed and self control been thrown to the winds' but it was very reticent to blame the Crown forces in most of the cases of reprisals.[61] This reticence could be seen in December 1920, following the burning of Cork city centre by the Auxiliaries. An *The Irish Times* special correspondent gave a detailed account of what he uncovered on visiting the city:

> ... Patrick Street business premises from Merchant to Cook Street are all gone, the eastern side of the northern section of Cook Street has been demolished, while establishments in Oliver Plunkett Street, Winthrop Street, Morgan Street, Merchant Street, Maylor Street and Caroline Street have also been wiped out. It was a terrible as well as a complete destruction.[62]

The correspondent listed the destruction to five acres of the city, including the City Hall. The paper made no effort to maintain that the arson attack was anything other than a reprisal but the editorial accompanying the above report, while condemning reprisals, warned that they 'are the direct outcome of murder'.[63] That was the standpoint that *The Irish Times* maintained throughout the conflict and that was also advanced by Administration figures such as Greenwood and the British Government – incidents of reprisals were the inevitable result of prolonged provocation.

The Government of Ireland Act, which had been passed into law in December 1920, came into actual operation on 19 April 1921. *The Irish Times* despondently called for the attendant elections set for May to be postponed as the country was too violent and the elections would only 'provoke the fiercest passions', especially in the newly instituted Northern Ireland. To this new state *The Irish Times* urged goodwill and advocated a policy of rapprochement between the two jurisdictions as the only means by which partition would be defeated. To achieve this, *The Irish Times* proposed a 'New Unionism'. By this the paper meant a united Ireland in partnership with the British people and the Empire: 'The first essential of such a unity is a settlement of the quarrel between North and South. It was in the spirit of the new Unionism that Sir James Craig met Mr de Valera'.[64]

In this spirit, *The Irish Times* accepted the results of the Northern elections which saw the Unionists take a large majority. *The Irish Times* rebutted the tendency in the nationalist press to 'belittle the Northern Parliament, to predict its speedy failure, to talk almost as if its existence could be ignored'. The paper argued this was futile because the Parliament was 'a fait accompli of the most solid kind' and that working with the new Parliament 'was the only approach to the goal of a peaceful and united Ireland'.[65] It offered its analysis of the challenge facing southern Ireland's attempts to end partition:

> For many years Irish Nationalism has carried its case to the Imperial parliament at Westminster. Henceforth it must carry that case to the Northern Parliament at Belfast. This is, perhaps, the most radical change in the whole history of Irish politics and it is a change that no wise Irishman need regret.[66]

Furthermore, the Parliament 'was an experiment in self-government':

> ... the South has been protesting for a hundred years that Irishmen are fit to govern themselves. The North has decided that it can govern itself under the new Act. Southern Irish men, however sceptical of that confidence, can have no patriotic reason for wishing the success a failure.[67]

These were all reasons, the paper stated, to foster and support good relations with the Northern Parliament. Yet as negotiations aimed at creating a truce continued, evidence of future good relations with the Northern Parliament were not forthcoming. Eamon de Valera made public his plans to consult the leaders of the 'minority' in Ireland and these included Sir James Craig. Such a move ignored Craig's constitutional standing as Northern Ireland leader. As *The Irish Times* noted, the decision was 'not a very hopeful indication of Dail Eireann's mind'.[68] Furthermore, the comments of leading Unionists in the North had given no indication of a wish for unity within any foreseeable timeframe. Craig had recently told an election meeting that he challenged 'any authority, whether it be the British Government or De Valera, to take away from us a Parliament once it is rooted in Ulster soil'.[69]

The Irish Times naturally celebrated the truce that soon followed, arguing that the wording of the statement from Downing Street preceding the draft publication of the truce details itself was highly significant for future negotiations in that it read that on the appointed day 'hostilities' would cease. According to the paper, the use of the word 'hostilities' to describe the conflict appeared 'to concede the belligerent status of the Irish Republican Army'.[70] The editorial writers realised that the truce would greatly help final peace negotiations and furthermore: 'Its psychological effect will be incalculable, and however our desires may cheat us, the nation will not exchange it lightly for a new state of war'.[71]

On the day of the truce the editorial wrote that the country was 'irradiated not only with sunshine but with hope'.[72] Amidst the hopes the paper realised that there remained the real potential for a disastrous destabilisation of the current hopeful political climate; a northeast whose Parliament 'remained irreconcilable with the avowed aims of the Republican Party'.[73] Nevertheless, in the heady days of the nascent truce the tone of the paper's editorials was hopeful, best signified by its maxim that 'pessimism would be a crime against Ireland'.[74]

The Irish Times had responded dramatically to the changes it had covered over the previous thirty months. It continued to remain utterly opposed to the aims of Dáil Éireann and the IRA yet it had witnessed the extraordinary events that had occurred in Ireland and responded accordingly. From the first appearance of the Bill for the Better Government of Ireland in February 1920 the paper had realised that the Bill would not satisfy the vast majority of opinion in Ireland and changed from opposing to supporting Dominion Home Rule within a few months of the Bill's publication. The paper made some shrewd assertions of the situation in Ireland. Although it was furious and saddened at the decision of Carson, Craig and northern Unionists to seek a six-county northern state, thereby damaging hopes of unity between the two proposed parliaments, *The Irish Times* wished no ill-will towards the northern state. It was one of the few commentators to quickly realise that the new Parliament in Northern Ireland was not to be a temporary feature of the Irish political landscape. Next we must turn to another paper which had also been a long-term opponent of Irish Home Rule, *The Times*.

7

THE TIMES

English papers reporting from and on Ireland during these years were to have a profound effect on the situation in Ireland. By publicising the violence of the Crown forces they made the situation in Ireland an international talking point and a scandal in England. *The Times*, at the time perhaps the most influential paper among political circles in England, was to play a vital role in this process. The paper had been a traditional opponent of Irish aspirations towards Home Rule and had a long history of enmity towards leaders of Nationalism in Ireland, such as Daniel O'Connell and Charles Stewart Parnell. In 1914 *The Times* criticised the Home Rule Bill and editorialised: 'We have consistently opposed the principle of Home Rule for Ireland and continue to do so'.[1] However in the post-war world there existed a sense that substantial changes were necessary in the political map of Europe if the brutal carnage of the recently ended Great War was not to be repeated. The Paris Peace Conference and US President Woodrow Wilson's fourteen points were the most visible manifestations of this process.

1919 – A settlement for Ireland
The Times was not aloof from such momentous events and the historian of *The Times* (writing in 1952 for the paper's own official history book) noted that in 1919: 'Conditions were then ripe for a reversal of the antipathetic attitude towards Ireland' maintained by the previous three editors.[2] This willingness to treat Irish claims for Home Rule more generously was furthered by the appointment of Henry Wickham Steed as editor of the paper in February 1919. Steed, who replaced Geoffrey Dawson, had attended the Paris Peace negotiations and seen at first hand the attempts of de Valera, Griffith, Plunkett and the Sinn Féin leaders to pressurise the American delegation into allowing an Irish representation.

Outside of the international changes in the post-war world there were a couple of other powerful influences for *The Times*. One influence, especially powerful for Lord Northcliffe, the owner of *The Times*, was his recently developed but deeply entrenched hatred of Lloyd George. Northcliffe had been an integral part of the war effort during 1914–1918 and he was a leading figure in the huge British propaganda effort. But the issue of how to treat the defeated Germany led to a spectacular falling-out with his former friend, Lloyd George. Northcliffe believed the Prime Minister to be to be too lenient on the Germans and from 1919 onwards Northcliffe was willing use his papers to attack the Government at every opportunity. Besides his hatred of the Prime Minister there was another hugely powerful motivation for Northcliffe and also Steed. It was their anxiety that the so-called 'Irish question' could threaten the close relationship between Britain and the US. Throughout 1919 *The Times* printed a number of American issues and editorials that reflected the owner and editor's belief in America as the 'future of humanity'. Northcliffe was a frequent visitor to America and believed fervently in a close relationship between the USA and Britain. He was especially fearful of the growing isolationist trend in America that culminated in the United States' absence from the League of Nations.

Both viewed the political power of Irish-Americans in the US political and electoral system as a guarantee that the Irish question would soon come to dominate US foreign relations. This, they feared, could result in American pressure being applied to Britain in an effort to secure Irish independence, an occurrence 'that would not be tolerated by the British people'. The only outcome of such a situation would be a rupture in the close relationship between Britain and the United States. Given the persistence of the Anglo-American Alliance, the so-called 'special relationship' since the Second World War, it may be hard for us today to imagine that many leading commentators and politicians on both sides of the Atlantic feared that the emergence of the US as a world power would lead, in the near future, to inevitable diplomatic rancour between the US and Britain. More excitable commentators even foresaw the possibility of wars over trade, shipping routes, oil, and so on. It was in this atmosphere that Steed resolved 'on international grounds to press forward a measure of self-determination for Ireland'.[3]

This anxiety was obvious in editorials throughout 1919. In April the paper claimed that 'the Irish imbroglio is having an ill effect on the relations of Great Britain with the Dominions and with the United States'.[4] Only weeks earlier the US House of Representatives had voted 216–45 in favour of a motion that the Paris Peace Conference should favourably consider Ireland's claims to self-determination.[5] While the Paris Conference afforded no recognition to Irish claims, the vote was an indication of how powerful an issue Ireland could become in US politics and a justification of the fears held by Steed and Northcliffe. De Valera's visit to America during 1919 and 1920 heightened these fears and the Washington correspondent reported: 'Mr. de Valera's appearance in New York is likely to start the transatlantic Irish pot boiling with a vengeance'.[6] By this time also the American Commission investigating conditions in Ireland had arrived in the country (see below).

These political moves pushed the paper to produce a series of articles reflecting on the situation in Ireland. Beginning on the last day of June 1919 the articles were heavily influenced by R.J. Herbert Shaw. Shaw had served as an assistant Press Censor to Lord Decies in 1916 and had also been on the staff of Lord French. He had therefore gained quite a depth of experience in Irish current affairs. He also shared Steed's belief that the issue of Ireland should be resolved so as not to endanger relations between Britain and the USA. Interestingly, Shaw had shown a draft of what he considered a viable Irish settlement to his superiors in the Irish Administration and then to the British Cabinet. His ideas were rejected.[7] His proposed settlement – while vague in detail – supported Irish 'self-government' and clearly opposed partition as a means of settling what he termed the 'Anglo-Irish controversy'. He also proposed that it was essential: 'in the interests of the British Empire and particularly so in its relation to the United States, that the Irish question should be concentrated in Ireland, and world interest focussed on Irish bickerings rather than Anglo-Irish relations.'[8] What resulted were some of the most significant of all reports and proposals by a newspaper reporting on Ireland during the conflict.[9]

Despite being composed by writers with a strong working knowledge of Ireland, the articles made some misjudgements of the situation in the country. Sinn Féin and the Dáil were castigated within the series as a 'disconcerting failure' with Sinn Féin apparently showing signs of rupture. The writers also claimed, without evidence, that there was 'a slowly growing discontent with the policy of abstention from Westminster'.[10] Contemplating a settlement the paper conceded that 'the Union is doomed' because 'the Southern Irishman rejects its advantages and passionately prefers his own more primitive methods'.[11] Attention was then focused on what should replace the Union. 'The grant of full independence to Ireland under whatever name' was definitely ruled out: 'Great Britain cannot and will not concede that demand'. The paper's solution was a settlement based on self-government for Ireland. However, this did not constitute full Dominion Home Rule similar to that enjoyed by Canada, South Africa and Australia. While the writers agreed that there was a widespread conviction in Ireland that Sinn Féin would gladly swap their calls for a Republic in exchange for Dominion Home Rule, *The Times'* reporters were more wary, commenting: 'It is more than likely Dominion Home Rule has hitherto had a very precise meaning in Ireland. It differs from the Republican demand in that it retains the common link of the Crown, but in little less.'[12]

If full Dominion Home Rule were granted, Ireland would still be linked in 'common citizenship of the Empire' under the Crown as the head of state but the paper convincingly argued that 'the catch cry of modern Ireland sets that tie at naught'. What the paper essentially suggested was a form of quasi-Dominion Home Rule with closer links between Britain and Ireland than between Britain and its other Dominions with the stated aim of preventing Ireland using its new-found freedom to divorce itself completely from Britain.[13] Partition was also declared unfeasible on the basis that it would not satisfy nationalists, would isolate southern unionists as well as northern nationalists and create a basis for further conflict between north and south:

> If it is found essential that in the interests of the United Kingdom, that Ulster should, with absolute safeguards for her liberty and protection remain a part of Ireland, Great Britain would be justified in insisting that a settlement of the Irish question should take that form.[14]

These reports were generally well received by the Irish and English press but the reaction from the British Government to the series was reserved. Ulster Unionists reacted angrily. Carson made an impassioned Twelfth of July speech where he threatened once again to 'call out the Ulster Volunteers'.[15] This speech was widely criticised in English as well as Irish newspapers. *The Times* wrote:

> No good purpose could be served by an attempt to conceal the

extreme disappointment with which Sir Edward Carson's speech in Belfast has been read by all moderate men, Unionist and Nationalist outside the North-East corner of Ireland.[16]

Perhaps stung by the cool response of the British Government to its articles *The Times* continued to be extremely critical of Government policy towards Ireland over the following month, claiming that the absence of what the paper called a 'constructive policy' was a danger to Britain nationally and internationally. Such was the frustration felt by *The Times* that the paper boldly proclaimed in late July that 'if the Government will not make the first move then others must'.[17] Responding to its own challenge *The Times* published a far more detailed plan, written by Steed and Shaw, for a settlement in Ireland. In a lengthy editorial the writers firstly detailed how they viewed the current situation in Ireland:

> The position is that the Home Rule book is on the Statute Book. It cannot be enforced in its present form. Opinion in Ireland has turned almost unanimously against it. Ulster could only be brought within its provisions by direct coercion ... Sinn Fein will have none of it.[18]

According to the paper, the remedy to this situation consisted of two state legislatures: one for the nine counties of Ulster and the other comprising the rest of Ireland. Steed had clearly taken heed of the furious reaction from Carson following the paper's previous suggestions for a settlement. Any attempt to force northern unionists into an all-Ireland settlement would meet with such resistance that a settlement would be doomed. A nine-county Ulster was chosen, over a four- or six-county Ulster, in the belief that 'a powerful Nationalist minority' in the whole province 'would give protection against disregard for minority rights and interests'. Steed and Shaw also tried to overcome the predictable reaction from nationalists and southern unionists to the creation of the two state legislatures. These states would not be divorced but would be linked under an all-Ireland Parliament with equal representation for each jurisdiction. Upon these states 'there should be bestowed full powers of legislation in all matters affecting their internal affairs'. The Irish Parliament would not have the right to raise an army or navy. More importantly each state legislature could veto any act passed by the all-Ireland Parliament.[19]

Overall, the Irish press was opposed to the planned settlement. The idea of partition was abhorrent to all. The *Freeman's Journal*, *Irish*

Independent and *Cork Examiner* criticised the plan, especially the two separate legislatures. The *Cork Examiner's* London correspondent suggested that Northcliffe had decided that the Irish question 'was to be the question of the hour' and he wanted his paper in at the beginning so it could claim credit for making it so.[20] *The Irish Times* was more open to the plan as long as the proposed all-Ireland Parliament functioned as proposed by *The Times* (something about which it had considerable doubts).[21] Once again, there was no substantial response to the proposals from Lloyd George and the British Government. Carson also dismissed the plan. Ulster Unionists were determined on obtaining a more manageable (from their point of view) six-county state. Fewer counties meant fewer Catholics.

The Times continued to press for a settlement in Ireland throughout 1919 and increasingly castigated Lloyd George and the British Government on whom it laid responsibility for the increasing violence in Ireland:

> For having allowed Ireland to come to this pass, the Prime Minister and his colleagues must have the chief blame. They have given no sign that they wished well to Ireland, yet signs that would have opened a door of hope would have been easy to give.[22]

This criticism came directly from Steed, who placed no restrictions on his editorial writers and composed many of the editorials himself.[23] In October the paper again pressed a settlement 'based on the essential unity of Ireland'.[24] By the end of the year the criticism of British actions in Ireland had reached a new level. Editorials had deplored the increasing coercion in Ireland throughout 1919 as 'the very bankruptcy of statesmanship' and in early December *The Times* expressed its dismay at the stance of the Irish Administration and the British Cabinet more succinctly:

> There is a strong prima-facie evidence of a powerful conspiracy against the prospects of an Irish peace … Our fear is this: that the Irish Executive is being used, whether with the connivance of members of the Cabinet or not, in order to arouse in Ireland a state of feeling, if not a state of rebellion, in which settlement may become impossible … The time has come for the Government immediately to announce their Irish policy. Every day that passes darkens suspicion and not in Ireland alone.[25]

This was followed within days with a similar attack on what the paper described as a policy that was 'irreconcilable' with an Irish settlement. *The Times* was now giving capacious coverage to Irish events and in December published another major series on 'The State of Ireland' which continued on the same vein as before, even going so far as to criticise General Frederick Shaw personally (the GOC of the British army in Ireland until the arrival of Nevil Macready in April 1920). The paper claimed the position of Commander in Chief of the army was the most important in the current situation in Ireland and that the post required 'a man possessing sympathy and breadth of vision'. These qualities *The Times* special correspondent lamented 'are not generally attributed to Sir Frederick Shaw'.[26]

Throughout 1919 *The Times* continually absolved Sinn Féin and by extension the Dáil from any involvement in the increasing violence in Ireland.[27] Following the death of Detective Patrick Smyth (of the G. Division, DMP, dealing with intelligence and not to be confused with DC Gerard Smyth shot in Cork during 1920) *The Times* commented on the state of Ireland: 'We do not attribute these outrages to Sinn Fein nor do we regard Sinn Fein as a moral perversion'.[28] Furthermore, *The Times* claimed in the aftermath of a night of looting and destruction of property carried out by British soldiers in Fermoy that British policy was playing into the hands of the 'assassins'. *The Times* claimed that the increasing number of 'outrages' were the result of 'local secret societies' operating in areas where '… the crust of civilisation is thin and the evil deeds of the Land War are a living tradition' (the correspondent judged the crust of civilisation to be especially thin in Clare and Tipperary).[29] That is not to say that *The Times* did not condemn those responsible as 'murderers' and their deeds as 'seditious' but the reporters of *The Times* refused to place the blame for these events on Sinn Féin and the Dáil. As we have seen, this belief was paralleled by other papers both nationalist and unionist. There was a widespread conviction that a schism existed within Sinn Féin, the 'popular movement', between moderates and extremists with the extremists being 'more noisy than numerous'.

This viewpoint was more advanced than that of the Irish Administration which tended 'to treat the various aspects of separatism and republicanism as one undifferentiated mass and to regard them as a monolithic 'Sinn Fein movement'.[30] The decision to proscribe Sinn Féin throughout all Ireland was seen by the paper as futile and an action that would only result in 'more adherents for the republican party'.[31] Continuing the 'State of Ireland' series of articles, the special correspondent assessed the results of the Sinn Féin and Dáil Éireann suppression and found the Irish Administration guilty of increasing the unrest in Ireland: 'Many Sinn Feiners would agree that at present owing to the restrictions placed on the actions of accredited leaders, a regrettable deal of power has fallen to the secret societies –or society.'[32]

The correspondent also placed blame on Sinn Féin 'for breaking down the police system' but reckoned that this was mostly achieved through social boycott and not violence.[33] Even the attack on the Lord Lieutenant, which caused such a sensation, was used to highlight the desperate need for a settlement in Ireland. *The Times* was highly critical of the 'perversity of mind' behind the attack, which was compared to the infamous Phoenix Park murders. However, the paper also warned that, despite the fact that: 'there can be found Irishmen so fanatical as to perpetrate murder and so infatuated as to counsel rebellion, does not absolve the people of this country from the paramount obligation of meeting the just demands of the Irish race.'[34]

Contrary to the view espoused by *The Irish Times*, *The Times* editorial held that those who considered coercion was the correct policy in Ireland were wrong. Indeed, throughout the previous months the paper had, on numerous occasions, accused the Irish Administration of actively seeking to provoke violence in Ireland in order to justify a military response. Coercion had failed and it was time for a settlement, argued *The Times*. The paper ended the year calling again for a settlement based on an all-Ireland basis with a nine-county Ulster that 'would prove a powerful force working in the direction of eventual union'.[35]

1920 – The State of Ireland

The paper's obsession with Ireland deepened further throughout 1920 and the Government of Ireland Bill was a main preoccupation. As details of the Bill became more widely known *The Times* was initially non-committal but Steed became worried as opinion in Ireland was mostly antagonistic and the Washington correspondent reported home that opinion in America was not well disposed to the planned scheme. When the text of the Bill was introduced before the House of Commons in late February *The Times* expressed a mixture of hope and disappointment, although not surprise. Walter Long, the Chairman of the Committee framing the Bill visited Steed in January 1920. The two men discussed the Bill at length and Long informed Steed that Bill would resemble *The Times*' proposals of the previous July. So far so good, but Long also apparently told Steed that Lloyd

George would perhaps be unsupportive of a settlement proposed by the paper due to the Prime Minister's ongoing feud with Northcliffe.[36] The Bill differed from *The Times'* proposals in that it proposed to create a six-county northern state, a point which upset the paper as it seemed to threaten hopes of any possible future union and would thus be rejected by nationalists. This disappointment was tempered by the fact that the Bill could be yet 'greatly improved' on its passage through parliament and that a starting point for a settlement had finally been reached.[37] As we have seen the reaction from nationalists and southern unionists to the Bill was intensely negative. The Council of Ireland, which was substantially less powerful than the All-Ireland Parliament proposed by *The Times*, was seen by them as a mere sop to their fears about partition. Recognising this, *The Times* made a call to Carson and northern Unionists. Having secured such a strong position from the Government, 'the most favourable that Ulster is ever likely to obtain', the paper stated that Unionists should now undertake 'active cooperation in the administration of all-Ireland matters': 'This, then, is the opportunity of Ulster Unionism to prove that path which its insistence has indicated to a compliant Government leads, not to an irreconcilable division of Ireland but towards an Irish peace.'[38]

When the Ulster Unionist Council decided to accept the proposals contained in the Bill the paper expressed disapproval. *The Times* had consistently called on Lloyd George and the Cabinet to declare their Irish policy. It was now clear for all to see. The paper editorialised:

> Unfortunately ... the Bill, as presented to Parliament, bears, on its face, evidence of painstaking adjustment to the susceptibilities of Sir Edward Carson and his followers. It is obvious that the Government ... have been prepared to jeopardize every chance of conciliating nationalist opinion by the prodigality of their provision for Ulster Unionism.[39]

Carson who had now become a regular critic of *The Times* wrote a letter to the *Morning Post* attacking Northcliffe and the paper for its editorials over the previous weeks and months.[40] Criticised by northern Unionists and practically ignored by Lloyd George, the paper remained hopeful that the Government of Ireland Bill would mark a step on the road to settlement, not the settlement itself. However, it was forced to take its focus away from events at

Westminster. *The Times* had been warning for months that the situation in Ireland was worsening and that 'an evil and futile system of Irish Government' was encouraging extremism among the Irish public.[41] Proof came with the deaths of Tomás MacCurtain and Alan Bell. *The Times* was shocked by the fact that the suspicion in Ireland was that the forces of the Crown were involved in killing MacCurtain and strongly criticised the Dáil and the *Freeman's Journal* for proposing this. *The Times* Dublin correspondent, Maurice Healy, wrote: 'I need not enlarge on the state of mind which this outrageous assumption indicates or on the dangers of its further development'.[42] After the shooting dead of Resident Magistrate Alan Bell *The Times* now concluded that: 'so bitter is the sentiment against the spirit and the methods of the present Government of Ireland that vast numbers of Irishmen have begun to accept with sullen acquiescence the existence of open war upon the forces of the Crown.'[43]

The overriding aim of *The Times* was now to end this state of 'open war'. Almost daily, long columns, reports and editorials on Ireland filled the paper. As well as the Irish Administration, Sinn Féin also came in for direct criticism. Following a night of IRA attacks on police barracks nationwide the paper editorialised that:

> We have always discriminated between Sinn Feiners of the type of Messrs. de Valera and Arthur Griffith and the men who perpetrate assassinations under a plea of war, though the apparent equanimity with which the moderate section of Sinn Fein have suffered the pass without public condemnation the flagrant misdeeds which are now done in the name of Irish liberty has made that discrimination far more difficult than we should have wished.[44]

While the paper still fell short of accusing figures such as de Valera and Griffith from instigating the violence it stated that a large portion of the 'responsibility for the present appalling condition in Ireland lies at their door'.[45] Despite the more regular criticisms of Sinn Féin, the paper was still unconvinced of the policies of the British Government in Ireland, deriding the claims advanced by Lord Lieutenant French and later by Greenwood that there existed an IRA force of some 200,000 men. *The Times* was able to report that a Downing Street conference on Ireland attended by the new GOC Nevil Macready concluded that there 'are not more than two thousand terrorists in Ireland'.[46]

The paper continued to maintain the necessity of a settlement like the one it had proposed the previous July. But unlike 1919, when the situation in Ireland had not yet spiralled out of control, *The Times* now had to sit and watch while the British Government carried the Government of Ireland Bill into the autumn, a move the paper considered should be 'profoundly deplored' as it left the political vacuum in Ireland unfilled.[47] *The Times* lambasted the Government's attempt to fill this vacuum with the Restoration of Order in Ireland Act (ROIA). Its editorial claimed that the Act 'confesses the complete collapse of the Irish legal system'. It continued: 'We do not believe that this Bill offers any remedy for the situation in Ireland'.[48] While *The Times*' historian has commented on the thunder of the leading articles of the paper much of which 'came from the pen of the Editor', a sense of helplessness had pervaded *The Times*' editorials over the previous months.[49] In August it had again called on Lloyd George to say that the Government of Ireland Bill 'was not the last word in British statesmanship'.[50] Nonetheless, by the month's end it was forced to admit that the Government had chosen to follow a course very much at variance to what it had advocated: 'We can do no more, save to assure the Irish people that a great body of public opinion in this country shares its anxiety, and regards the cause of it with deep regret and no small measure of shame.'[51]

Reprisals, which were now emerging as a major issue in England and in which the evidence against the Crown forces was strong, began to feature regularly in the paper's reports.[52] Following the large reprisal at Balbriggan the paper accused the Government of a 'perilous silence' on the issue of reprisals and more definitely of: 'Recognising that they have failed to wean Ireland away from Sinn Fein by their proposals for self-government, ministers have sought an alternative policy in rivalling the methods of the Irish "Republican Army". Their agents are the "Black and Tans"'.[53] *The Times* was not willing to find the Crown forces guilty on every charge which was levelled against them but it found enough evidence to condemn the Crown forces on very many occasions writing that 'the reprisals are an act of war, and of a very ugly war too'.[54]

While its attempts at influencing a political settlement in Ireland were in limbo, *The Times* was now criticising the Government and British actions in Ireland with a directness that would have seen an Irish newspaper printing similar material suppressed or attacked by Crown forces. Sympathetic coverage had been afforded to the hunger-striking Terence MacSwiney throughout the previous months. While MacSwiney was slowly starving to death in Brixton Prison the editorial writers of *The Times* were clearly moved by a man who 'by the very quality of his courage has appealed directly and most dramatically to the mercy of a strong and generous people'.[55] Following his death the paper defended its pleas for clemency and dismissed the rumours that MacSwiney was being 'fed surreptitiously' by his friends. The editorial declared that had MacSwiney been guilty of any violent crime they would not have called for clemency but 'the offences carried against him were not sufficiently grave ... to carry the law to its strictly logical conclusion'.[56]

The Times' reportage was attracting much disapproval from readers and politicians in England, some of whom also personally criticised Steed and Northcliffe. General Macready wrote that 'considerable irritation was felt among the troops of Ireland by the publication in *The Times* of extracts from the *Irish Bulletin*'.[57] Northcliffe was given an armed guard of plainclothes police as enraged readers had berated him and even personally threatened him. One letter to the paper's office came attached to a photograph of Northcliffe with a bullet hole through the head.[58] Subscriptions to *The Times* were cancelled and circulation began to fall. The offices of *The Times* (as well as the Northcliffe-owned *Daily Mail*) were now given police protection in fear of an attack by loyalists who now considered the paper traitorous or, less likely, republicans who disliked the paper's insistent demands for an Irish settlement involving two legislatures.[59]

November witnessed a terrible increase in violence throughout Ireland. Stirring attacks on reprisals again featured in the paper; on each occasion the editorials utterly condemned attacks on police and soldiers but proceeded to say that in no instance could these attacks be seen as justification or excuse for reprisals.[60] *The Times* still fretted upon what foreign opinion thought of British actions in Ireland, especially those of the Dominions and the United States.[61] While the paper reacted with complete shock to the events of Bloody Sunday (reporting on the 'circumstances of revolting brutality' in which the fourteen officers died), very little coverage was given to the deaths in Croke Park. It continued that the only answer to the 'murders' of the British officers was 'the sternest and most unremitting vindication of the law' adding that 'the injury that Sinn Fein has wrought, not only to its own reputation but to the cause of Ireland is incalculable'.[62] In spite of this, the paper also argued that this law needed to be beyond reproach as:

> ... an Army already perilously undisciplined, and a police force
> avowedly beyond control have defiled, by heinous acts, the
> reputation of England; while the Government, who are the
> trustees of that reputation, are not free from suspicion of
> dishonourable connivance.[63]

Following the ambush of a party of Auxiliaries at Kilmichael, (see
Chapter 1) *The Times* warned, in a line that has been much quoted, that
'British wrath is, indeed growing, hot at the latest outrages in Ireland'.
The paper had printed the official report that the bodies of the
Auxiliaries had been mutilated with axes but made no mention of this
claim in the editorial condemning the ambush.[64] Incensed by the
ambush the editorial advised that it 'is the paramount duty of the
Government to fight and crush such enemies'. However, the paper felt
it necessary to counsel against reprisals in the same paragraph, writing
that 'vindictiveness is a sign of weakness'.[65] The paper had no illusions
that such incidents were common and many reports on IRA attacks
concluded with statements such as 'reprisals are feared'. Following the
burning of Cork city centre and City Hall the paper tacitly blamed the
Crown forces, in spite of the adamant official claims that republicans
had committed the arson attack. *The Times* did not summarily dismiss
the Government's claims that its forces were innocent and the paper
hoped against hope over the following months that the Strickland
report would offer even a partial acquittal to the Crown forces but was
forced to admit the guilt of the Crown forces with the Cabinet's refusal
to publish the report. It was, an editorial concluded, 'equivalent to a
confession'.[66] Such was the situation that existed in Ireland at the end
of 1920 that *The Times*, which condemned the coercion of the Irish
Administration, welcomed the introduction of Martial Law in four
Munster counties. This was not the result of a bellicose reversal of
attitude from the paper but a sense of relief that from now on the all
of the various Crown forces in the area would be 'subordinate to
responsible military commanders'. This, the paper hoped, would end
'the mob-justice' of reprisals.[67]

1921 – Making peace

The Times' editorial best summed up the general attitude of the House
of Commons to the Government of Ireland Bill, writing that on its
passage through Parliament the Act was 'treated with an indifference

wholly out of keeping with its great and far-reaching importance'.[68]
The paper maintained its attempts to promote a peace in Ireland into
1921 and the reporting of events in Ireland did not change over the
year. For its news the paper still concentrated on its own reporters and
while it printed official reports and occasionally *Irish Bulletin* reports
these were secondary to their own journalists' work. *The Times* pressed
its case for a truce and a settlement based on a close relationship
between the two legislatures in Ireland most effectively in its editorials.

Surveying the political situation in Ireland during January *The
Times* concluded that Ireland was in a state of deadlock.[69] Editorials
now urged the Government to take notice of 'the strength of the new
spirit which animates the Irish People'.[70] The paper denounced the
'campaign of murder' but it was reprisals that continued to cause Steed
and his fellow editorial writers most distress. The editorial despaired
of the Government and its backing of reprisals in Ireland:

> ... in no circumstances, however grave, was it pardonable for
> them to institute a force of irregulars under conditions which
> would have strained the discipline of even the most tried
> personnel and launch it upon the monstrous understanding that
> it was to be a law upon to itself ... British processes of justice,
> which for centuries have commanded the admiration of the
> world, have been supplanted by those of lynch law.[71]

In an editorial most probably composed by Steed (perhaps with the
help of Shaw who was still with the paper as its 'Irish expert') the
Government's increasingly coercive measures were deplored as so
misguided that the 'logical end could only be the extermination of the
last Sinn Feiner'.[72] It warned that this was causing grave international
repercussions for the Empire, which could continue far into the
future. The only solution was a settlement in Ireland:

> The Irish in Ireland are but a fraction of the Irish race, and that
> race is a distinctive and integral factor in modern civilisation. The
> Irish of the Dominions present an Irish problem to the Dominion
> Governments. The many millions of Irishmen in the United States
> have a created a very living question for every American politician
> ... If the growth of nationalism throughout the world menaces
> our Imperial fabric; if our natural friendship with the United
> States is imperilled by hostile propaganda and hostile conspiracies,
> where shall we find the root of the malady more certainly than in
> the cancer of the unsolved Irish problem?[73]

Steed had written to Churchill in December stressing these points. He appealed for a constitutional settlement before anti-British feeling in the United States was intensified by the conflict in Ireland.[74] While relations between Lloyd George and *The Times* as well as Northcliffe continued to be unfriendly (indeed practically non-existent), it would be an error to conclude that *The Times*' reportage of events in Ireland was completely motivated by a personal animus towards the Prime Minister, a claim that had been made by Lloyd George and others on numerous occasions. In a letter to a friend Steed wrote that the persistent Government attacks would fail 'as all their attacks have been based on the false assumption that our policy was inspired by personal rancour'.[75] Steed was undoubtedly sincere in his beliefs.

As we have seen Northcliffe's position was more complicated. Northcliffe believed the Prime Minister had been too soft on Germany after the First World War. Northcliffe's other paper, the *Daily Mail*, had been running a consistent campaign against the Germans throughout the negotiations and ratification of the Peace Treaty in 1919. Each day it warned its readers about the Germans under the repeated banner headline: 'They will cheat you'.[76] This had infuriated Lloyd George. Northcliffe who had been at the centre of power during the First World War was also frustrated at being sidelined in the years after. He certainly held a grudge against the Prime Minister, telling a friend how he despised Lloyd George's 'big head on a little body'.[77] While he may not have been as worried as Steed about the wrongs of Crown violence in Ireland there is no doubt that he was sincere in his belief that the ongoing turmoil in Ireland was potentially disastrous for the Empire and Anglo-American relations. At this time Northcliffe was publicly calling for a truce in Ireland. In a review of the situation in Ireland written for the journal *The Nineteenth Century and After*, he claimed the Government had made a grave error in proscribing Sinn Féin in 1919 and again advanced a proposed settlement very similar to that of *The Times* in July 1919.[78] This settlement he wrote 'could only be reached by a truce'.[79]

The Times' continual criticisms of the Crown forces not only irked the Prime Minister but also General Macready. During March he had written directly to Steed to complain about the paper's attitude and to 'expose the unreliability of some of your correspondents in Ireland'. Steed repudiated Macready's letter, defending his journalists who had risked their lives during the First World War and who were now performing a similar duty in Ireland: 'Though they naturally went with feelings of loyalty and admiration for the Forces of the Crown, they returned filled with loathing at the manner in which operations in Ireland are conducted on both sides.'[80]

In a tone similar to his earlier letter to Churchill, Steed continued to impress his view on Macready that a settlement 'by negotiation' was vital – otherwise the situation in Ireland would not only create grave difficulties with the US but 'would ruin the Empire'.[81] This may sound like hyperbole but the South African Prime Minister, Jan Smuts, expressed the same fears to Lloyd George only months later:

> I need not enlarge to you on the importance of the Irish question to the Empire as a whole. The present situation is an unmeasured calamity; it is in negation of all the principles of government which we have professed as the basis of Empire, and it must more and more tend to poison both our Empire [sic] relations and our foreign relations.[82]

Steed's worries about the Empire's relations with the US were only deepened by the publication in March of the *Interim Report of the American Commission on Conditions in Ireland*. Its conclusions damned the British Government:

> We find that the Irish people are deprived of the protection of British law, to which they would be entitled as subjects of the British King. They are also deprived of the moral protection granted by international law, to which they would be entitled as belligerents. They are at the mercy of Imperial British forces which, acting contrary to both law and to all standards of human contact, have instituted in Ireland a 'terror'...[83]

Claims of partisanship may have been made against the Commission but it was not so biased that its findings could be merely dismissed. After all, its conclusions were similar to reports and editorials in many of the English papers, including *The Times*. A Committee of 150 people had overseen the work of the Commission and its membership had comprised figures from both the main US political parties, senators, congressmen, governors, church leaders of various creeds, labour leaders and nationally prominent figures from a range of professions.[84] Although the US President, Warren Harding, was content to view Ireland as a British domestic problem, the work of the American Commission was a further spur to Steed as it clearly showed how the Irish conflict could influence American opinion.

Closer to home, persistent criticism of the paper by the British Government did not turn the paper from its course but a deep frustration was now evident in the paper's editorials. *The Times'* hopes for a settlement 'by negotiation', it wrote, were being hampered not only by the Government but also Sinn Féin. Moderate opinion in Ireland, which the paper declared wanted a truce, was being sidelined:

> The criminal insanity of the present leaders of the Irish people tend only to hold in check the practical expression of that desire and to accredit anew the fatal and discredited Irish policy of the Government. Surely it is time for reasonable and patriotic men in both countries to call a halt.[85]

The paper reiterated that it supported its own proposals of July 1919 as they were designed to promote unity in Ireland. The Government of Ireland Act 'fell far short of what we outlined nearly two years ago' and it 'has divided Ireland into two states almost entirely independent of each other'. The result of this lack of statesmanship was 'the present state of warfare'.[86] This violence was at such a high pitch that *The Times* counselled that the May elections in Ireland should be abandoned.[87] A truce leading to negotiations was now the only way forward, the paper argued, and it continually urged Lloyd George to 'follow the open road of statesmanship'. *The Times* argued: 'The Republican demand is symbolic, and the vast majority of those whom Mr de Valera has bidden to vote "for the legitimacy of a republic" will in reality give their suffrages for complete local autonomy'.[88]

Steed's frustration with the lack of progress in Ireland was exacerbated by internal divisions at *The Times*. Northcliffe's previous strong support for Steed began to waver amid the lack of progress in arranging a settlement in Ireland. Northcliffe was under pressure from his fellow proprietor, John Walter, who was particularly troubled by the criticism that the paper was receiving from the Government and who was beginning to pressurise Northcliffe for a change in the paper's policy on Ireland. Northcliffe transferred this pressure to Steed. The editor asked for some more time to continue his Irish policy. He was given one month.[89]

Fortunately for Steed, he saw some hope of a breakthrough in King George's trip to Belfast to the new Northern Parliament. The King was to open the Parliament with a speech. These speeches were routinely written by the Government but Steed realised that a speech from the King in which he made a call for peace in Ireland would have a profound effect. It would put great pressure on the British Government and Lloyd George to proclaim their plans for a truce in Ireland openly. Steed met with the King's private secretary Lord Stamfordham and begged him to speak with the King and to ask him to use this opportunity to make a speech that could help foster a peaceful settlement, 'to encourage his people to call a truce to their quarrels'.[90] On Stamfordham's advice, and in the face of the poor relations between *The Times* and the Prime Minister, Steed also met with Sir Edward Grigg, one of Lloyd George's private secretaries. Through Stamfordham, Steed's intercession with the King was successful. King George recognised the potential inherent in his speech and rejected the first draft proffered by the Cabinet. In a flurry of activity a number of drafts were created with the final wording of the speech prepared only hours before the King left to travel to Belfast. This final draft was created by the Cabinet with the active participation of South African Prime Minister, Jan Smuts.[91] Steed had also promised Stamfordham that he would use *The Times* to 'go bail' for the King, in effect setting the scene for the King's speech in his editorials.

Two days before the speech, in an editorial written by Steed and Shaw, *The Times* advised that the King's journey to Belfast was not to be taken as another example of the British Government's partiality towards northern Unionists. The editorial stated that the King would have gone to Ireland 'with equal readiness and pleasure to inaugurate a Southern Irish Parliament, or to discharge the greater function of opening a united Parliament in Ireland'.[92]

On the day of the King's speech and aware that he would make a call for peace, *The Times* launched a stinging editorial attack on the Government. Their policy was accused of promising 'naught but a prospect of continued repression'.[93] The speech which followed later that day was a clear call for an Irish settlement calling on Irishmen 'to join in making for the land which they love a new era of peace, contentment and good-will'. Influence from *The Times* could clearly be seen in the speech which contained a number of ideas commonly expressed in Steed's editorials. The King told his audience 'The eyes of the whole Empire are on Ireland today' and stressed the vital need for peace in Ireland.[94] On the next day the speech was welcomed by all sides while *The Times*, eager to capitalise on the moment, urged the Government to follow the 'high courage' of King George and to begin a policy of reconciliation.[95] In the circumstances, the speech was recognised by participants and commentators as a sign that the

British Government was ready to enter into proper negotiations. A day after the speech, Lloyd George issued an invitation to de Valera to confer in London with a view to a truce. The behind-the-scenes efforts to arrange an end to the fighting justified these hopes and following a series of negotiations between all sides a truce was signed on 9 July 1921. It came into effect two days later.

One recurring motif across the newspaper's coverage of the truce was that of an end to a conflict between nations. Lloyd George's often-repeated declaration that 'you do not declare war on rebels' had been totally negated. *The Times* explicitly expressed this mindset in every aspect of its reportage. The paper's editorials spoke of a truce between two nations and of the problems which British and Irish statesmen would face in creating a permanent peace. The paper also grasped the fundamental importance to the British Empire and to relations with the United States of a settlement in Ireland. At this time, Britain's imperial gains were being threatened by armed rebellion in Mesopotamia and political moves for independence in Egypt. Furthermore, since the Amritsar massacre of 1919, India was becoming increasingly restless. The nature of the settlement in Ireland would have much wider repercussions. *The Times* warned that unless a settlement could be produced Ireland would continue 'to envenom Anglo-American relations'. One editorial stated that: 'Seldom has British statesmanship been confronted by a graver task. Upon its success there depend almost incalculable benefits to the Empire and the nation'.[96]

The dangers to Ireland were also acknowledged and *The Times* judged what a period of peace could do to the public mood: 'Should Mr de Valera require further sacrifices from the people of Ireland for the sake of the difference between an Irish Republic and a status virtually equivalent to that of the Dominions, his hold upon them might, in the long run be severely tested'.[97]

Of more immediate danger, was once again the northeast or for *The Times*, Belfast, which had witnessed violent and fatal rioting in the days following the truce. The paper warned northern Unionists that any attempts to destabilise the peace negotiations would 'discredit their cause in this country' and that the actions of any of the protagonists would not alter 'the determination of this country to do full justice to Ireland'.[98] *The Times* and its editor Henry Wickham Steed had played an important and courageous role over the previous 30 months in getting Britain and Ireland to this stage.

Conclusions

The approach of the British Government to the press in Ireland during the years 1919–1921 was a blend of heavy-handed censorship, intimidation and propaganda. This approach failed. Censoring and suppressing newspapers did nothing but antagonise an already critical press. The propaganda failure arose because the efforts to improve British propaganda were not taken until republican propaganda had established a foothold in the consciousness of the public and the newspaper press. Republican propaganda had already shown itself to be highly adept at favourably portraying the republican position and more importantly at attacking British actions. This meant that British attempts were almost always by definition reactionary, never proactive.

In some ways the successful British propaganda against the Germans in the First World War may have rebounded against them during the Irish War of Independence. Allegations of 'Prussianism' made in English newspapers against the Crown forces in Ireland and comparisons with the Germans' treatment of the Belgians were very damaging to the British Government's policy. Such reports led many British newspapers and influential sections of British society to view British rule in Ireland as inherently wrong. After all, the British and Irish public had been told during the Great War that they were fighting for the defence of small nations. In those years, 'Britain had defined the war against Germany as a struggle between civilisation and barbarism, morality and militarism'.[1] After four years of brutal carnage with casualties on a daily scale often far greater than all the casualties of the conflict in Ireland a sense of war-weariness was also conspicuous with the British public. The British Government took the line that reprisals were the inevitable result of Irish attacks on Crown forces but this defence was quickly and totally dismissed by the press in England. The *Manchester Guardian* spoke for the vast majority of the newspaper press when it condemned the Government's approval for reprisals:

166

Conclusions

This is exactly what the German Commanders in Belgium said when they put a dozen innocent people against a wall and shot them, because someone not in uniform had sniped a German soldier. It is exactly what the Russian Anti-Semites always said by way of excuse for a pogrom, and the Turks in excuse for a massacre of Armenians. Some other Jew, some other Armenian had always done something atrocious.[2]

Added to this was the feverish work of statesmen all over Europe involved in the settlement of disputes and the creation of new countries. The largest manifestation of this phenomenon, the Paris Peace Conference 'saw parliamentary democracy enthroned across Europe'[3] and many sections of British opinion now judged the time right to give Ireland its own parliament within the Empire. *The Times* advocated a form of Dominion settlement in 1919 and many other papers followed. Elements within the Liberal Party supported a policy of Home Rule and figures such as former Prime Minister Herbert Asquith lent their support to the widely based 'Peace with Ireland Committee'. This potent combination of opinion is what any British propaganda system had to influence. It was an almost futile task whose difficulty was exacerbated by the reaction of the British Government. Many within the Irish Administration seemed shocked that their policies in Ireland were the subject of such vigorous criticisms but the only advice Greenwood could offer to Bonar Law was: 'Do not believe the *Manchester Guardian, Daily News, Westminster Gazette* or the *Daily Herald.*'[4] Pretending criticism does not exist was not an effective political or propaganda technique. The Government made this same mistake in 1921 when it refused to publish the Strickland Report on the burning of Cork city centre. The report condemned the Auxiliary force but this had already happened in the press generally and the dumping of the report was in direct opposition to Basil Clarke's hopes of a viable news-based propaganda system.

This situation was further exacerbated by the relationship between the British Government and sections of the British press. C. P. Scott, the editor of the *Manchester Guardian*, who had been a long-time supporter of Lloyd George was bitterly disappointed at the results of the Paris Peace Conference and also repulsed by British policy in Ireland. In 1919 Lloyd George had apparently told a colleague of Scott's that he could easily 'govern Ireland with the sword'.[5] If the *Guardian*'s criticisms can be seen as resulting from a genuine dislike at the course of events in Ireland, there were others who were willing to use Ireland as a stick with which to attack the Government. Owner of *The Times* and the *Daily Mail*, Lord Northcliffe deplored what he considered Lloyd George's pro-German policy and his failure to form a settlement in Ireland. The two men had a falling-out which resulted in the Northcliffe papers becoming critics of Lloyd George and his Government. Northcliffe's brother, Lord Rothermere, owner of the *Daily Mirror* and *Sunday Pictorial*, followed his sibling's lead. Therefore, political chess at the highest levels of British society erected a huge barrier to the aims and success of Clarke and the PIB. Moreover, the divisions between the military and PIB were too great to overcome the gargantuan propaganda task they encountered. It was only in May 1921 that it was finally agreed on the Chief Secretary's insistence that all 'articles written by Military Officers or from military sources should be sent by Major Marians to Mr Clarke'.[6] The lateness of this decision shows to what extent the history of British attempts at propaganda during the period from the first Dáil up to the truce was one of internecine conflict.

Another great dilemma for any British propaganda system was the comparisons made between the activities of the Crown forces and those of the IRA. Many commentators believed and reported that there existed a division between 'moderates and extremists' within Sinn Féin and that the actions of the IRA were the result of the imprisonment of the elected leaders and supposed moderates such as de Valera and Griffith. This was portrayed as leaving a vacuum filled by 'secret societies' or impassioned but misguided young men. This view was especially apparent until the middle of 1920 and was of great frustration to military men like Macready. Contrastingly, the Crown forces were, from the beginning, linked inextricably with the British Government and Irish Administration and the violent reprisals, murders and arson carried out by sections of the Crown forces were seen as a coherent part of Government policy. The Irish nationalist dailies and many English papers held this view. This viewpoint was enhanced by the performances of Lloyd George and Greenwood in the House of Commons. Lloyd George constantly offered a defence and tacit approval to reprisals while Greenwood's sole tactic consisted of denying incontrovertible proof of reprisals. As a result, when the press became more cognisant of the degree of convergence between the IRA and Sinn Féin the violence of the IRA was depicted as regrettable and wrong but the inevitable result of British repression and misgovernment.

Conclusions

The *Irish Bulletin* brilliantly exploited this difference in reaction to the violence of the Crown forces and the IRA. Every opportunity afforded by reprisals to reveal British atrocities was accepted and prominently displayed. Graphic headlines such as 'War on Women and Children', 'Dying Irish prisoners Beaten in English Prisons' and 'Economic Destruction of Ireland' were regularly published and repeated. The British campaign was portrayed as a war against the Irish nation: a nation administered by Dáil Éireann and its court system. The *Irish Bulletin* also contained long articles about particular incidents that provided a more embellished addition to the matter-of-fact approach of listing the Crown force's 'atrocities'. This matter-of-fact style was very similar to Basil Clarke's proposed idea of 'propaganda by news'. Reports of British actions were often based upon captured army or police documentation and these reports forced many newspapers in Ireland and England to confront the issues raised by the *Irish Bulletin*. This was also replayed in Europe where the success of the *Irish Bulletin* as a supplement to the work of Irish diplomats resulted in a change in attitude to events in Ireland. In the words of French journalist Sylvain Briollay, French newspapers 'ceased to pin their faith to accuracy of Reuters' version of events in Ireland'.[7]

In Ireland the Dáil and the court system, which it generated, were not only designed as a counter state to win the confidence and allegiance of the Irish people but as an exercise in propaganda showing the failure and futility of British rule in Ireland. The two Governments came into direct competition and Dublin Castle was found wanting. Arthur Mitchell has written about the public perception of the competitors:

> The Sinn Féin leaders were Irish; those in Dublin were not. The leaders of Dáil Éireann were young fresh personalities seeking to carve out a new age for their country. Dublin Castle was staffed by stuffy middle-aged Englishmen, some with dubious pasts and most with no knowledge of the country, who pontificated on law and order while reluctantly moving toward a minimum grant of national autonomy.[8]

Whether the perceptions were true or not matters less than the fact that they existed and were widely held. This is certainly how the Irish Administration was presented in the pages of the *Cork Examiner*, *Freeman's Journal* and *Irish Independent*. While *The Irish Times* wrote of the honest but dour civil servants doing an impossible job in intolerable conditions, the nationalist press derided and harangued the Administration as worthless. Almost every day saw a new demand from these papers for the resignations of Macpherson and his replacement Greenwood as well as those of Lord Lieutenant French and General Nevil Macready, the 'soldier-dictator of Ireland'. Even *The Irish Times* became more critical of the Irish Administration and British policy in Ireland as events progressed, if for different reasons. As a whole the Irish papers displayed more foresight than an Irish Administration whose policies were increasingly estranging itself from the Irish populace.

What the newspapers strongly convey are the conflicting beliefs and emotions aroused by the events in Ireland, both political and military. Most papers cannot be seen as slavish followers of the Dáil, the British Government or either propaganda campaign. How successful was this propaganda? Irish newspapers were not influenced to any great extent by the *Irish Bulletin*, while republican newspaper propaganda in Ireland was severely constrained, indeed practically non-existent. Outside of *The Irish Times* and a few other unionist papers, no Irish paper was won over or even vaguely convinced by the PIB and British propaganda. In Ireland, British propaganda was not only a failure but counter-productive. For most Irish papers the overriding influence was fear of intimidation and attack. That – not propaganda – was the greatest influence. The other great influence common to all nationalist papers was a belief that British rule in Ireland had run its course. It had to cease. Many newspapers in Ireland had already made their minds up, irrespective of newspaper propaganda. They needed to be convinced of the means, not of the end. Republican propaganda in Ireland was propaganda through actions, though the Dáil, its courts and the IRA. Nothing succeeds like success. These endeavours convinced newspapers and the public that self-government or independence was not a pipe dream but possible, natural and near to fruition. Although the nationalist press may have, to varying degrees, been uncomfortable with IRA violence, they all agreed that responsibility for the violence in Ireland lay with the British Government. But even papers such as the *Freeman's Journal* and the *Irish Independent*, which by 1920 were very supportive of Sinn Féin, repeatedly called for Dominion Home Rule and never once called for the republic that the Dáil and IRA were ostensibly pledged to fight for. In saying that, they demanded that Ireland receive full Home Rule similar to the other Dominions and total control of its own affairs. Nothing less was acceptable to them. The *Cork Examiner*, also, demanded complete Home Rule for Ireland. *The Irish Times* realised by 1920 that only a full measure of Dominion Home Rule could end the violence in Ireland. Although the newspapers wanted Ireland to have full control of its own affairs, a republic was thought to be too unlikely. De Valera's insistent calls for a republic and the synchronised republican propaganda on this issue were thought of as a bargaining position.

In England the republicans' propaganda campaign was propaganda through words. The *Irish Bulletin* was an undoubted masterpiece of this type of propaganda because it was so often seen to be accurate. It may have inflated IRA ambushes from small skirmishes into large-scale military engagements but when it came to accounts of reprisals and violence by the Crown forces, it was rarely shown to be wrong or deliberately lying. Its greatest successes came in England because it played upon the campaign of reprisals and intimidation of the Irish public, a campaign which 'touched a very sensitive area in the make-up of Englishmen themselves'.[9] Despite its success, we should be wary of great claims of success made on the behalf of propaganda schemes. Republican propaganda superbly exploited these fears but it did not create them. It was not newspaper propaganda which created the conditions in which most of the newspaper press in England would oppose the Government. While English nationalist imperialist papers such as the *Morning Post* revelled in the colonial adventures of British troops, other more widely read and influential British papers across all spectrums of opinion recognised not only the dangers to the reputation of the British Government and the Empire but also the inherent wrongs of reprisals and of the dangers of the quick-fix solution of partition. If anything, reporters, in the aftermath of the huge propaganda campaigns of the First World War, were very suspicious of anything that could be construed as propaganda.

Independent of republican propaganda, English newspapers decided that the British campaign in Ireland was not only damaging to Britain's good name in the world but also morally wrong. Why they made this decision is beyond the scope of this book. Certainly the brutality of the First World War was a factor. The propaganda of that war said it was a war to end wars, a war to free small countries. Now, directly after that cataclysm Britain was faced with a decision as to what to do in Ireland. Ireland was a small country. It wanted independence. Was Britain to fight a war to prevent Ireland's independence? Most of the press were disgusted that this was the route seemingly being taken by the British Government. Was what was happening in Ireland simply the normal brutalisation and repression of colonial dissent? Normally hidden from view, it was now being played out on the pages of English newspapers and across the world daily. Was this why the English press was so shocked and appalled by the British Government's tactics in Ireland? It can be said that there was much more to the English press reaction than claims that they were the dupes of republican propaganda, as Lloyd George and his Government so tirelessly and tiresomely claimed. In 1919 the English press had still been more worried about the Empire's reputation than the state of Ireland. They initially ignored republican claims of reprisals and intimidation. It was only after reporters from the English press had visited Ireland and seen conditions for themselves that they began to attack the British Government and the actions of the Crown forces. They were appalled at the violence and intimidation being routinely administered by the police and army. *The Times*, for example, had pushed a policy of Home Rule for Ireland since 1919. Although Steed would become convinced of the immorality of British actions in Ireland, the position of the newspaper initially owed far more to its owner's belief that the events in Ireland were ruinous to Britain's reputation and prestige in both the Empire and the United States. Other English papers seem to have undergone a similar process of change. It was after this, in the middle of 1920, that the *Irish Bulletin* became a source of news for English newspapers.

The issue of violence aroused diverging responses from the press. All the papers expressed their disgust at the catalogue of 'dastardly crimes' and 'shocking murders' that were perpetrated by the IRA in 1919. The *Irish Independent* and *Freeman's Journal* never quite shook off their uneasiness with the IRA campaign but from early 1920 regarded the violence as an inevitable consequence of British actions and policy. This was also mirrored to an extent by *The Times* which continued to attack republican violence but from late 1920 concentrated more and more on the activities of the Crown forces in Ireland, especially the Auxiliaries and Black and Tans. As expected, *The Irish Times* was completely hostile to the IRA and continued throughout the War of Independence to claim that there could be no peace until 'the murder campaign' of the IRA removed the cause of Crown reprisals. The paper, which was disgusted by the provisions of the Government of Ireland Bill, was supportive of the Irish

Administration's coercive attempts to defeat the IRA. If the nationalist papers could be accused of ignoring aspects of the IRA's campaign then the counterclaim could be levelled at *The Irish Times* that the paper's acceptance of 'official reports' from Dublin Castle meant that the paper refused to acknowledge the guilt of Crown forces in many acts of reprisals, an issue to which the paper gave far less coverage than other newspapers. One paper that could not be accused of ignoring any violence was the *Cork Examiner*. Motivated by strong religious beliefs, the editor of the paper was a consistent opponent of violence as 'a violation of the Divine Law' and this position was maintained throughout the whole conflict. But this paper also judged the British Government as the root cause of the violence in Ireland.

The British Government's attempts to end this violence, the 'Government of Ireland Bill', aroused contempt from all sides. The nationalist papers disparaged what they called the 'Bill for the partition and plunder of Ireland', viewing the legislation as a bribe to Ulster Unionists led by Edward Carson for their support of the Government. If the contempt of the nationalist papers can be seen as the genuine feeling of the mass of the nationalist population in Ireland, then *The Irish Times* can be seen as mirroring that of the unionist population outside of the northeast of Ulster. *The Irish Times* underwent a remarkable change in August 1920 when it came out in support of Dominion Home Rule for Ireland. While the nationalist papers professed their disgust at partition, *The Irish Times'* pages make clear that the paper viewed partition and what it called the 'Bill for the further unrest of Ireland' as a life-or-death issue: life or death for a unionist community that had been betrayed by unionists in the soon to exist six-county state. That paper's conversion to Dominion Home Rule marked its acceptance that the old order had passed and that the Union of Great Britain and Ireland was dead. Once the Bill became law *The Irish Times* resolved to work the Act as best as possible to retain the link with the Empire. This was similar to the attitude of *The Times*, which, initially frustrated that its own proposals for a settlement in Ireland had been ignored, decided that it too would support the Act, even with its many flaws. The nationalist papers continued to treat the Act as a temporary measure and not a genuine solution. While the study of newspaper coverage is not the study of public opinion, with regard to the issue of the Government of Ireland Act, the newspapers accurately portrayed the opinions of differing sections of the country and especially nationalist Ireland's blinkered response to the possibility, then reality, of partition.

The history of the tangled relationships between the press, the competing Governments and the opposing armies during the Irish War of Independence tell us much about the Ireland of the time. There were elements on both sides that held the idea of a free press in contempt. But with regard to the War of Independence it was only a constant and integral factor in the tactics of one side, that of the British Government and the Crown forces. Ultimately, how the press is treated is one barometer of how free a society is. Does the manner in which the British Government responded to the Irish press reveal that its rule relied mostly on the fact that it possessed more guns than anyone else? This book concentrates on only one aspect of the War of Independence but at the very least the decisions of the Irish Administration to suppress a long list of newspapers illustrates in how little regard the implementers of British rule in Ireland held a vital aspect of Irish society and democracy. Remember, in 1919 many commentators judged the press in Ireland, nationalist as well as unionist, to be unsympathetic to Sinn Féin. Despite this hostility, that party had won a huge mandate in the 1918 general elections. This meant that in the following years even a paper hostile to Sinn Féin would have to report on the party and its doings. It was the story. But the mere fact that Irish newspapers began to cover the newly installed Dáil and Sinn Féin resulted in an increasingly tight censorship and a wave of newspaper suppressions. The intent of the British Government and its Irish Administration was to prevent republicans from appearing at all in the newspapers. They may have been voted in by the will of the people but they were not going to be allowed to speak to those people.

Over the following years as the British Government responded in piecemeal and incoherent fashion to events in Ireland: the one constant was the increasing brutality with which the newspapers and their staff were treated. The progression was from censorship to suppression to court martial, culminating in threat, violent assault and arson attacks on newspaper offices throughout the country. Even Macready, who was generally opposed to the policy of reprisals (the great majority of reprisals were carried out by the various sections of the police), thought it natural that the Irish newspapers' criticisms of the Crown forces would result in attacks on these newspapers. The intimidation administered by the Crown forces and to a lesser degree by the IRA to the press at different times demonstrated that both sides believed there was a war on in Ireland. As such, the flow of news and opinion needed to be controlled, influenced and stopped, if necessary. Macready was particularly upset at the effect of negative press reports on his soldiers, hankering after the type of press control seen in the recently ended Great War. This was impossible in the Ireland of the time. While the Irish newspapers could be suppressed via DORA and later the ROIA, the fact that the British Government was unwilling to admit to a war in Ireland, allied to the fact that to introduce something akin to Crown Colony Government in Ireland would arouse international indignation, meant that – unlike during the Great War – journalists from England and further abroad were relatively free to report from the 'front lines' and beyond.

How influential was the press? The British Government ignored the insistent calls of the Irish and British papers for the Government of Ireland Bill to be scrapped. This shows the limits of press and public power in the face of a determined Government. However, in other ways, the press was enormously influential. The issue of reprisals by Crown forces dominated the coverage of so many newspapers and the actions of the Crown forces were constantly scrutinised. If the press had been prevented from reporting from Ireland it seems likely that the Crown forces would have had a much freer hand to commit atrocities and reprisals as they did in later independence and anti-colonial struggles.[10] This is not to accuse the British army of being uniquely malevolent but armies, when given free rein, fight to win, to cause as many casualties and as much disruption as possible to enemy forces while trying to minimise their own losses. The logical (from the military viewpoint) response to the IRA's guerrilla warfare and the tacit support of much of the populace would have been to greatly increase the number of troops and to brutalise areas and people which seemed to offer assistance to the IRA. Instead, a police force supplemented with a dangerously uncontrolled paramilitary wing and given licence to commit wanton violence by Lloyd George's wink-and-elbow language of deceit was never going to be in a position to end IRA attacks. All it achieved was to match the IRA in increasingly ferocious violence while repulsing the Irish public and journalists from across Ireland and abroad. The republicans adjusted far better to the conditions in Ireland. The Dáil and the IRA, despite the bravery of many of its volunteers and the support of majority of the populace, could never have defeated the Crown forces militarily. Collins and Mulcahy, to name just two republican leaders, intuitively grasped this fact and took advantage of whatever means they could to advance the cause of Irish independence. As Collins said in December 1920: 'It is too much to expect that Irish physical force could combat successfully English physical force for any length of time if the directors of the latter could get a free hand for ruthlessness'.[11]

On the other side, Macready, French and Greenwood wanted to wish away the negative press coverage, although the nature of the conflict made this impossible. Field Marshal Sir Henry Wilson made constant demands to Lloyd George that the Prime Minister abandon the use of the Auxiliaries, use the army and get the English public on the side of the Government. 'If you get England on your side', he implored the Prime Minister, 'there is nothing you can't do'.[12] If this happened, Wilson believed, the Crown forces would have a free hand in Ireland to suppress the IRA and any resistance by whatever means possible. 'If these men [Sinn Féin and the IRA] ought to be murdered, then the Government ought to murder them', he told Lloyd George.[13] Bernard Law Montgomery who served as Brigade Major in Cork during this time made the same point in a letter written in 1923. He discussed the problems of the British army during the War of Independence:

> To win this sort of war you must be ruthless. Oliver Cromwell, or the Germans, would have settled it in a very short time. Nowadays public opinion precludes such methods, the nation would never allow it, and the politicians would lose their jobs if they sanctioned it.[14]

Public opinion in England was being influenced by the newspapers and they would not have condoned any increased coercion by the British Government. The inevitable result of Wilson's demand for a freer hand would have been a marked increase in violence against the general public. As an example, the burning and looting of Cork city centre as well an increasing civilian death toll followed immediately after the introduction of Martial Law. Thomas Mockaitis, when writing of the often violent British counter-insurgency campaigns throughout its colonies, wrote that the 'absence of intense media coverage removed yet another inducement to moderation'.[15] In 1920, as the violence in Ireland dominated the news columns, British forces in Mesopotamia (today's Iraq) quelled a rebellion there in a quick and ruthless manner. Even gas-shells were used and some 9,000 Iraqis were killed. The following year there was a sustained bombing campaign against the Kurdish north of the country.[16] There was no public outcry. While this may have had a lot to do with racial attitudes common across all of Europe at the time, the fact that no information was forthcoming about the situation in the country was a definite factor in preventing the Mesopotamian campaign becoming a controversial issue. *The Times* and other papers were aware that some appalling violence was occurring in that country but they regularly lamented that they could not obtain independent verification of the facts and that the British Government was keeping a very tight rein on the news from Mesopotamia.

However, the British Government never got the mass support that Wilson hankered after. One reason was that the mass of people in Britain simply did not care about events in Ireland. A second reason was Lloyd George's insistence that events in Ireland were not a war. As he famously said 'you do not declare war on rebels'. Trapped by his belief in that statement, he gave his support to the disastrous half-measure of the Auxiliaries and Black and Tans. A further reason was the reaction of the British newspapers. Throughout the war, Greenwood and members of the British Government had defended themselves by saying that if only the British people were 'on the spot' in Ireland they would understand why the Government and its forces acted as it did. That defence missed the point completely. There were quite a few British people on the spot in Ireland – journalists who were often shocked by what they saw. Many of these also criticised IRA violence but they judged the failure to give Ireland a form of Home Rule and the lawlessness of the Crown forces to be an indefensible blot on the reputation of the British Empire. Newspapers which had cooperated so closely with the British Government's propaganda during the First World War, now refused to trust the official Government news from Ireland. The *Liverpool Post* expressed the general press wariness succinctly:

> Official propaganda and official provision of news are an undesirable survival of war conditions of which there is no justification even in the present disturbed condition of Ireland ... News does not become any more convincing because it is official.[17]

The First World War was a war on a massive scale and it had threatened Britain and the Empire with ruin. This was not the case with Ireland and journalists from many of the English newspapers now began to travel to and report from Ireland with a freedom they had not enjoyed during that war. For many of these English reporters, it was not only this freedom that was important. Among these reporters there existed a palpable sense that their profession must be redeemed as a crusader for truth and justice. In some ways Ireland was a battleground of a different kind, a battleground whereby these the newspapers could make amends for having been so completely incorporated into the massive propaganda campaign of the British Government during the First World War.[18]

They were mirrored in their zeal by the Irish press. The bravery of Irish journalists at this time should not be dismissed. Some of these reporters (Michael Knightly of the *Irish Independent*, for example) had very strong ties with republicanism but that is not true of the majority of Irish reporters and newspapers. Despite the violence of the Crown forces against newspapers and the suppression of so many papers, the Irish press tried to report the truth, as they saw it, on conditions in Ireland. Inevitably, they did not have a free hand and all the Irish newspapers made it clear that self-censorship was a vital, perhaps the most vital, component in their survival. Yet, the Irish newspapers still printed enough material critical of the British Government and the Crown forces to suffer violent attack, censorship and intimidation over the years of the War of Independence. Of course, it was not only the Crown forces who were upset by the newspaper coverage of events. The Cork IRA displayed a similar attitude when they tried to silence the *Cork Examiner*. The IRA attacked a number of other newspapers and many republicans were exasperated by newspapers supporting Home Rule for Ireland rather than an outright republic. These attacks show that republicans were not immune to the virus of press intimidation. This tendency to silence critical opinion would be exacerbated after the Treaty and during the Civil War.

Ultimately, this uneasy relationship between press and the enemy sides meant that during the years 1919–1921 the newspapers became not just a chronicler of events but a participant and sometimes a central protagonist. Both the British Government and Dáil Éireann attempted to control and influence the press during these years and it is a testament to the determination and bravery of so many of the newspapers and their journalists that they continued to work and report amid the storm of suppression, censorship, intimidation, propaganda and violence.

ENDNOTES

Chapter 1 – Dublin Castle and the Crown forces

1. Glandon, Virginia, *Arthur Griffith and the Advanced Nationalist Press,* 1900–1922, (Peter Lang, New York, 1985), p. 159. See also pp. 147–52 for a brief description of DORA and the radical nationalist press during the First World War.
2. The 'Mosquito Press' was the generic name given to 'small and difficult to kill' republican newspapers that were forever engaged in written battles with the Censor and Dublin Castle. See Hogan, David, *The Four Glorious Years*, (Irish Press, Dublin, 1953), pp. 39–40. Hogan was Gallagher's pseudonym.
3. Colonial Office (CO) 904 167 – file number 416, Jan/1919 (Press Censorship Reports).
4. CO 904 167 (417): Jan/1919.
5. CO 904 167 (545): Mar/1919.
6. CO 904 167 (446): Jan/1919.
7. *Freeman's Journal (FJ)*, 05/Apr/1919.
8. CO 904/167 (415): Decies, French said, 'was admirably suited to the job'.
9. Hogan, *Glorious Years*, pp. 41–2. Decies was the chairperson of a lobby group that campaigned against income tax.
10. Ibid.
11. Briollay, Sylvain, *Insurrection in Ireland*, (Talbot Press, Dublin, 1922), p. 81. This book was originally published in French and consists entirely of articles that appeared in *Revue de Paris* and *Le Correspondant*.
12. Sinn Féin propaganda in Ireland was severely hampered by the suppressions. See Chapter Two.
13. These were Cornelius O'Mahony & E. Keane; editors of the *Kerry News* and *Kilkenny People* respectively. O' Mahony had refused to recognise the court.

14. *Irish Independent,* (II) 18/Sep/1919.
15. *The Times, (TT)* 22/Sep/1919.
16. *II,* 23/Sep/1919.
17. *II,* 25/Sep/1919: See also the interim report of the *American Commission on Conditions in Ireland,* 1921: Appendix C. This gives a list of some fifty newspapers suppressed over the previous two to three years.
18. *Cork Examiner (CE),* 22/Sep/1919: The paper had been suppressed under the Criminal Law and Procedure Act 1887.
19. *Manchester Guardian* (MG), 22/Sep/1919.
20. *TT,* 27/Sep/1919: Letter.
21. *FJ,* 29/Nov/1919.
22. *Evening Telegraph,* 16/Dec/1919: Copy of warrant. These recruits later became known as the 'Black and Tans'.
23. *The Irish Times (IT),* 16/Dec/1919.
24. *Evening Telegraph,* 24/Dec/1919.
25. *Evening Telegraph* and *Daily News,* 17/Dec/1919: *The Daily News* was the paper of Hugh Martin, author of *Insurrection in Ireland* and one of the most famous war correspondents in Britain.
26. *Evening Telegraph,* 17/Dec/1919.
27. *Westminster Gazette,* 17/Dec/1919.
28. *The Times'* Washington Correspondent wrote that the suppression had provoked a harsh response among American newspapers and politicians. See issue of 20/Dec/1919.
29. *Evening Telegraph,* 17/Dec/1919 & 17/Jan/1920: see also the *Cork Examiner,* 10/Jan/1920. It carried a report on the editor of the *Catholic Herald,* Charles Diamond. Diamond later received a short prison sentence but the paper continued printing.
30. The one area from which support was not forthcoming was Dublin. No comment in support of the *Freeman's Journal* came from *The Irish Times* or the *Irish Independent.* It was a feature of these years that the three competitors remained hostile to each other, no matter the travails suffered by the other papers.
31. *CE,* 31/Dec/1919: The paper printed Patrick Hooper's (editor of the *Freeman's Journal*) letter to newspapers across Britain and Ireland. Many others printed the letter in full or in part.
32. For example., see *Freeman's Journal,* 06/Apr/1920: Underneath the banner headline 'Provocation, Provocation, Provocation' was a photograph of 'distinguished American, Canadian and Irish journalists being held up at the point of bayonet and searched for arms'.
33. *II,* 07/April/1920: Reprinted from *Daily Express.* In the same interview

French claimed: 'I am fed up and wish someone would relieve me of my job' a comment gleefully taken up by all the newspapers.

34. *FJ*, 30/April/1920: See also *Irish Independent* and *The Irish Times*.
35. Macready, Sir Nevil, *Annals of an Active Life, Volume 2*, (Hutchinson, London, 1924), pp. 454–5. Kenworthy was a Liberal MP for Central Hull and a vocal opponent of British policies in Ireland.
36. Ibid., p. 456.
37. This 'small office' was to remain until the withdrawal of British troops and remained separate from the soon to be created Public Information Branch (PIB).
38. *IT*, 08/May/1920.
39. *II*, 03/May/1920 & 17/May/1920: Report – 'Mailed fist and Iron Heel for Ireland'.
40. *Freeman's Journal*, 12/May/1920: see also 30/Apr/1920.
41. *Freeman's Journal*, 12/May/1920: The *Morning Post* was the most fervent of Government supporters (with regard to military action in Ireland) among the English papers. It was seen by the Irish press as an apologist for reprisals and coercion, and was correspondingly hated. It was also deeply anti-Irish.
42. *FJ*, 06/May/1920: The paper reported that Sir Auckland Geddes had 'taken personal control of anti-Irish propaganda in America'.
43. Taylor remained as Joint Under Secretary but the Colonial Office Papers and the diaries of Mark Sturgis show he was clearly subservient to Anderson and wielded little power or influence in Dublin Castle in the succeeding years.
44. McColgan John, *British Policy and the Irish Administration*, 1920–22, (George Allen & Unwin, London, 1983), p. 15. See also Wheeler–Bennett, John W., *John Anderson, Viscount Waverley*, Macmillan, London, 1962), Chapter 3.
45. *FJ*, 21/Oct/1920.
46. CO 904 188: Macready to Anderson, 11/Oct/1920.
47. *FJ*, 28/Aug/1920: See also *Irish Independent, Cork Examiner* etc.
48. Ibid.
49. Hopkinson, Michael, *The Last Days of Dublin Castle: the diaries of Mark Sturgis*, (Irish Academic Press, Dublin, 1999), p. 44.
50. *FJ*, 02/Oct/1920: See also *Irish Independent*.
51. Jones, Diary, p. 46. Despite instructions to the contrary, Griffith was later arrested after Bloody Sunday on the orders of General Boyd in what a furious Lloyd George called 'a piece of impertinence'.
52. CO 904 168: Macready to Sturgis. See also his letter to Anderson of

11/Oct/1920: CO 904 188.

53. CO 904 168 (62), Dublin Castle Statement, 02/Oct/1920.

54. Macready, *Annals*, p. 476. See also his letter to Anderson of 12/Oct/1920: CO 904 188.

55. *FJ*, 21/Oct/1920: See also report 16/Sep/1920. It stated that the men were murdered because they had tendered their resignations from the RIC.

56. *FJ*, 27/Oct/1920: See also report of 30/Sep/1920.

57. *FJ*, 25/Oct/1920.

58. *FJ*, 06/Nov/1920. See also report of 25/Oct/1920. Quirke's name first appeared in the *Freeman's Journal* during the court report on the opening day of the trial – 25/Nov/1920.

59. *MG*, 29/Dec/1920. *The Times* accused the Government of 'penalising honest opinion'.

60. See for example *Connaught Tribune, Limerick Leader, Birmingham Post, Sheffield Mail* etc.

61. *CE*, 29/Dec/1920.

62. *FJ*, 31/Dec/1920.

63. Townshend, Charles, *The British Campaign in Ireland, 1919–1921*, (OUP, Oxford, 1975), p. 159. See Sturgis' diary for this time. See also UK Parliamentary Archive: LG/F/19/3/1 Greenwood to Lloyd George, 06/Jan/1921.

64. Macready, *Annals*, p. 476.

65. Ibid., p. 475.

66. CO 904 188: Anderson to Macready, 07/Mar/1921.

67. List compiled from various newspapers and books. Journalists were also arrested in many of these raids. One well-publicised arrest was that of Australian journalist, Sydney Loch, who was detained without charge for three days in Dublin Castle during April 1921. IRA attacks on newspapers are discussed in Chapter 2.

68. Sheehan, William, *British Voices from the Irish War of Independence 1918–1921*, (The Collins Press, Cork, 2005), p. 156.

69. Ibid.

70. *FJ*, 09/Nov/1920: Editorial – 'The Sword is Mightier…'

71. Oram, Hugh, *The Newspaper Book*, (MO Books, Dublin, 1983), pp. 145–6.

72. *FJ*, 09/Nov/1920: Editorial – 'The Sword is Mightier…'

73. *TT*, 03/Nov/1920: The paper also reported that Black and Tans had threatened the populace of Tralee 'with reprisals of a nature not yet heard of in Ireland'. For a study of the violence in Kerry during these months, see Dwyer, T. Ryle, *Tans, Terror and Troubles: Kerry's real fighting story,*

1913–1923, (Mercier Press, Cork, 2001), pp. 208–65.

74. Borgonovo, John, *Spies, Informers and the 'Anti-Sinn Féin Society'*, (Irish Academic Press, Dublin, 2007), pp. 8–9. Borgonovo's book is a superb study of the intelligence war in Cork city and especially insightful when explaining the role of a British reprisal campaign against the IRA in the city, which often used the alias of the 'Anti-Sinn Fein Society'.

75. *II*, 07/Dec/1920: Collins wrote to the paper to warn the public against believing the rumours of peace negotiations that were currently circulating. The *Irish Bulletin* of 09/Dec/1920 printed his second letter in full. It was an expansion of the theme of the first letter. See Chapter 2.

76. Martin, Hugh, *Ireland in Insurrection*, (O'Connor, London, 1921), pp. 137–51. See also the *Daily News* and the daily press in the first weeks of November. See also Gleason, James, *Bloody Sunday*, (Peter Davies, London, 1962), p. 174.

77. *II*, 04/Dec/1920: A meeting of these bodies took place in the Gresham Hotel in Dublin. A resolution of protest was adopted against the 'outrages committed by the British Government in Ireland against the press': see University College Dublin (UCD) P80/14.

78. *TT*, 08/Nov/1920: Editorial – 'The Condition of Ireland'.

79. *FJ*, 09/Oct/1920: Report – 'Nobody Loves Them'. According to the paper, on the reverse of the threatening letter, a member of the police wrote 'Your own regular RIC police burnt Balbriggan' – signed 'A Britisher'.

80. Ibid.

81. CO 904 188 (595): Macready to Anderson, 11/Oct/1920.

82. *FJ*, 30/Nov/1920 and 01/Dec/1920: see also *II*, 30/Nov/1920.

83. CO 904 188 (595): 11/Oct/1920, Macready to Anderson.

84. Jones, Thomas, *Whitehall Diary - volume III*, (OUP, London, 1971). P. 26: (23/July/1920).

85. Farrar, Martin J., *News from the Front: War correspondents on the Western Front 1914–1918*, (Sutton, Gloucestershire, 1999), p. 13.

86. CO 904 168 (903 – 904): Clarke to Cope, 04/Apr/1921.

87. See Townshend, *Campaign*, p. 100, see also pp. 95–105.

88. Hopkinson, *Sturgis*, p. 88 & p. 206. Sturgis called the *Weekly Summary* 'BT's Weekly'. A typed note attached to the collection of the *Weekly Summary* in University College Cork (UCC) also names Basil Thomson as editor. Thomson was Director of Home Office Intelligence at this time and was therefore involved with police intelligence in Ireland. Hugh Martin wrote that the paper was 'edited in the office at Dublin Castle of Major-General Sir Henry Tudor'.

89. *FJ*, 08/Sep/1920: Editorial – 'Making Ireland a Hell' and Report. See also *Weekly Summary* – Vol. 3, 27/Aug/1920.

90. E.g., the *Morning Post* claimed in April 1921 that the 'Irish psychology is so puzzling that it understands only severe repression', see 11/Apr/1921. Such nonsense, masquerading as insight, regularly appeared in the paper. It was, as D.G. Boyce wrote, one of the only English papers which 'condoned reprisals at any price' (the *National Review* was the other). It was therefore perfect material for inclusion in the *Weekly Summary*. See Boyce, D.G., *Englishmen and Irish Troubles*, (Jonathon Cape, London, 1972), p. 81. This superb study of English public opinion concerning Ireland over this period provides much detailed information on the attitude of the English papers and wider public opinion towards events in Ireland.

91. See *Weekly Summary*, 8 & 15/Oct/1920. By the start of 1921, the level of bad publicity heaped on the publication had forced the editors to tone down the support for reprisals. From that time the paper concentrated on quoting articles supportive of the RIC or attacking Sinn Féin and the IRA.

92. *Irish Bulletin* (IB), 09/Nov/1920.

93. Martin, *Insurrection*, pp. 191–2.

94. E.g., see *Cork Examiner*, 25/Nov/1920: Greenwood, defending the *Weekly Summary* from the assertion of Joseph Devlin that each edition was 'an incitement to assassination of civilians in Ireland', stated that publication of the paper would continue.

95. Callwell, C.E., *Field-Marshal Sir Henry Wilson: His Life and Diaries*, (Cassell, London, 1927), 23/Sep/1920.

96. Boyce, *Englishmen*, p. 51.

97. *MG* & *TT*, 22/Sep/1920.

98. *FJ*, 25/Sep/1920.

99. Further confirmation of Macready's attitude can be seen in Mark Sturgis' diary for 19/Aug/1920 in which Sturgis describes Macready as expressing the exact sentiments he expressed in his interview. See Hopkinson, *Sturgis*, p. 25. Macready, unlike Tudor, was not a supporter of the policy of reprisals (especially undisciplined and unofficial reprisals) but he was so concerned with deflecting criticism away from his troops that he was blind to other considerations, such as the political and publicity effects of his comments.

100. *II*, 30/Sep/1920: See the *Daily News, Manchester Guardian, Westminster Gazette*, the *Star* and *The Times* for similar viewpoints.

101. *TT*, 27/Sep/1920.

102. The Germans had responded to the naturally uncooperative attitude of the Belgians during the 1914 invasion by killing civilians, destroying property and increasingly random violence. See, e.g., *Daily News*, *Manchester Guardian* and the *Star* for 29/Sep/1920.

103. Sturgis noted in his diaries, 'Macready got properly wigged by both L.G. and Winston for his interviews'. Hopkinson, *Sturgis*, p. 70.

104. Ayerst, David, *Biography of a Newspaper: the Manchester Guardian*, (Guardian Newspapers, London, 1971), p. 421. A decade earlier Clarke had been on the staff of the newspaper.

105. *FJ*, 09/Sep/1920.

106. *FJ*, 14/Sep/1920.

107. CO 904 168 (766): Clarke to Trimble (Editor of *Armagh Guardian*), 17/Feb/1921.

108. CO 904 168 (842): Clarke to Cope, 10/Mar/1921. This passage has also been quoted by others, most recently in Murphy, Brian P., *The Origins and Organisation of British Propaganda in Ireland*, (Aubane Historical Society, Cork, 2006). This is a very interesting short study of the British propaganda attempts during 1920. I agree with Murphy's thesis that the work of the PIB should lead us to be very careful in how we, today, use these official reports for research purposes. However, with regard to the above quotation from Clarke I think it is a mistake to take it at face value and deem the PIB as having the ability to control or greatly influence what the papers reported at that time. Murphy speaks of the 'British propaganda machine' having perfected itself by late 1920. I would argue that Murphy is wrong in this regard and that the evidence shows that the newspaper press, at that time, was very suspicious of Clarke and his work with predictable exceptions such as the *Morning Post* and other committed Government supporters.

109. *MG*, 28/Dec/1920.

110. Oram, *Newspaper Book*, p. 142.

111. General Peter Strickland resisted this task but was ordered to compile the report. Like Macready, he was not a supporter of the Auxillaries and police reprisals.

112. *TT*, 21/Mar/1921.

113. Hopkinson, *Sturgis*, pp. 48–9. See also Boyce, *Englishmen*, p. 89. The large-scale reprisal occurred on 29/Sep/1920 after the IRA had temporarily captured the local military barracks on the previous day.

114. See Townshend, *Campaign*. This work, one of the most important ever published about the War of Independence, provides the best study of relations between the military, police and Castle. Sturgis was also bitterly

critical of the lack of a unity of command seeing the administration as 'a great, sprawling, jealous hydra-headed monster spending much of its time using one of its heads to abuse one or other of the others'.

115. CO 904 168 (832 – 835): The above structure was created from a lengthy memo from Clarke to Anderson, 18/Apr/1921.

116. Some of the successful articles are in the Colonial Office files.

117. CO 904 168 (832 – 835).

118. Ibid.

119. CO 904 188 (732) - (Sir John Anderson papers): Macready to Anderson 28/March/1921.

120. CO 904 188 (741): Anderson to Macready 29/March/1921.

121. CO 904 188 (693 – 694): Macready to Anderson 07/Mar/1921.

122. CO 904 188 (722 – 723): Macready to Anderson 28/Mar/1921.

123. Macready, *Annals*, p. 465.

124. CO 904 168 (833): Memo to Anderson.

125. *Freeman's Journal*, 04/Nov/1920.

126. CO 904 168 (1178).

127. Macready, *Annals*, p. 465.

128. Seedorf, Martin, 'Defending Reprisals: Hamar Greenwood and the 'Troubles', 1920–1921', *Éire-Ireland xxv: 4*, 1990, pp. 85–6.

129. *II*, 05/Nov/1920. Editorial – 'Amazing Chief Secretary'.

130. Ibid.

131. *TT*, 29/Dec/1920. See also *The Report of the Labour Commission to Ireland, 1921*.

132. Ibid.

133. UK Parliamentary Archives – LG/F/36/2/16: Macready to Miss Stevenson 11/Feb/1921.

134. Hopkinson, *Sturgis*, p. 124.

135. *TT*, 26/Oct/1920.

136. See for example *The Times* and *Daily News* during this time. For MacSwiney family statement see CO 904 168.

137. On 27/Oct/1920 the *Irish Independent* and *Freeman's Journal* carried supportive and sympathetic quotes from newspapers in America and Europe.

138. See English press of 26/Nov/1920.

139. *II*, 27/Nov/1920. This newsreel is not the only fake from the period. A search of the British Pathé website for newsreel footage in Ireland from these years yields a number of reels which were 'staged' by Crown forces for the benefit of watching cameramen. See www.britishpathe.com.

140. *II*, 26/Feb/1921.

141. See also Sturgis, *Dublin Castle*, p. 73. On 16 November he reported meeting Pollard and Garro-Jones 'fresh back from their Kerry Battle'. Jones was heading to England to place the photograph. Sturgis gave no indication that he knew of the ruse being perpetrated.

142. Pollard, H.B.C., *The Secret Societies of Ireland: their rise and progress* (Philip Allan, London, 1922), pp. 238–56. Pollard's book is riddled with bad history and false reasoning. In an attempt to give the book a rational scientific veneer, his writing, especially when he pours forth on the 'psychology of crime', is a bizarre blend of blind prejudice, psycho-analysis and criminal psychology. Unhappily, such prejudices still exist, albeit in a modified form, among some elements of British Conservative thought, erupting occasionally in the columns of the modern right-wing nationalist papers or staining the writings of self-confessed Conservative historians.

143. CO 904 168: Memo to Clark 10/Nov/1920.

144. CO 904 168 (466): 02/Nov/1920.

145. CO 904 168 (November file).

146. CO 904 168.

147. CO 904/168 (1036–1083).

148. *FJ*, 10/Jun/1921: see also the II.

149. Ibid.

150. *IB,* 01/July/1921.

151. See the press in the days after the attack.

152. CO 904 168.

153. *IT*, 28/Mar/1921.

154. CO 904 188 (732–737): Macready to Anderson, 28/Mar/1921.

155. *IT*, 29/Mar/1921.

156. See the three papers for 29 & 30/Mar/1920.

157. *IB,*Vol. 4, No. 59, 01/Apr/1921.

158. Hopkinson, *Sturgis*, p. 151. See also CO 904 188 (742): Anderson to Macready, 29/Mar/1921.

159. Boyce, *Englishmen*, p. 91.

160. Martin, *Insurrection*, pp. 10–11. Philip Gibbs, Great War journalist and friend of Hugh Martin, wrote this preface. In 1919 Gibbs had resigned from Lloyd George's paper, the *Daily Chronicle* in protest against the Prime Minister's policy in Ireland.

161. CO 904 188 (698): Anderson to Macready, 08/Mar/1921.

162. Gleason, *Sunday*, p. 75.

163. *IT*, 01/Dec/1920: Report – 'The Murdered Cadets'.

164. Ibid.

165. For a detailed study of the Kilmichael Ambush see Peter Hart's ground-breaking study of the IRA in Cork: Hart, Peter, *The IRA and its Enemies*, (OUP, Oxford, 1998). Nowhere in the PIB's official report was a 'false surrender' mentioned, a point on which there has been much controversy in recent years. There are two opposing views of how the ambush concluded: either the surviving Auxiliaries were executed after surrendering, or they made a false surrender leading to the deaths of two of the IRA party. They were then shot dead during renewed fighting. Hart's research led him to conclude that some of the Auxiliaries were executed. This issue need not detain us here as the false surrender and above controversy were not a part of the original official report of the ambush and did not feature in newspaper accounts from the time. It became an issue after the War of Independence. For an opposing view to Hart, see Murphy, *Propaganda*, pp. 62–80.

166. *TT*, 02/Dec/1920.

167. *II*, 02/Dec/1920.

168. Hopkinson, *Sturgis*, p. 93.

169. O'Farrell, Padraic, *Who's Who in the Irish War of Independence and Civil War: 1916–1923*, (Lilliput Press, Dublin, 1997), p. 86. The doctor's name was William Pearson.

170. CO 904 168 (191).

171. CO 904/168 (184–1845): Memo from Darling to Clarke, 22/Nov/1920.

172. Gleeson, *Sunday*, pp. 151–3. Gleeson concluded that the press statement was 'typical of the insulting way in which the Auxiliaries and the Authorities were treating the Irish people and misleading the people of Britain'.

173. See for example *The Times* and *Freeman's Journal* of 24/Nov/1920. For the results of the military inquiry see *Irish Independent*, 30/Nov/1920. See also *Irish Bulletin* 22/Apr/1921 which disputed the official report. Brian Murphy writes that the PIB also released a faked photo of the guardroom in which the men were held and from which they supposedly tried to break free. See Murphy, *Propaganda*, p. 59.

174. CO 904 188 (564–568): JAG to Greenwood, 06/Apr/1921. Typically, this memo bypassed Basil Clarke and the PIB.

175. Ibid.

176. CO 904 188 (891): Anderson to Macready, 08/Mar/1921.

177. CO 904 168 (521): Clarke to Loughnane, 22/Sep/1920.

Endnotes

Chapter 2 – Dáil Éireann and the IRA

1. Laffan, Michael, *The Resurrection of Ireland*, (CUP, Cambridge, 1999), p. 265. This book is indispensable for anyone studying or interested in Sinn Féin during these years. One paper, Aodh de Blacam's *Young Ireland*, survived but its circulation was tiny.

2. For an examination of Dáil propaganda in Europe and America see Mitchell, Arthur, *Revolutionary Government in Ireland*, (Gill & Macmillan, Dublin, 1995). See also Fanning, R., Kennedy, M., Keogh, D. and O' Halpin, E. (eds), *Documents on Irish Foreign Policy; volume 1, 1919–1922*, (Royal Irish Academy, Dublin, 1998). This collection of foreign policy documents provides an insight into the production of republican propaganda on the continent and also details where to find the relevant documentary sources.

3. Costello, Francis, *The Irish Revolution and its Aftermath. 1916-1923*, (Irish Academic Press, Dublin, 2003), p. 37. Sinn Féin won 73 out of 105 seats. The IPP won 6 seats. As Costello notes, the results of the election did not necessarily imply a vote for violent revolt against British rule.

4. See CELT – The Corpus of Electronic Texts: http://www.ucc.ie/celt/published/E900013/index.html.

5. For a detailed study of the Dáil Éireann submission to the Paris Peace Conference and of republican propaganda in England and Europe see Inoue, Keiko, 'Sinn Féin and Dáil Propaganda', (Unpublished MPhil, University College Dublin, 1995).

6. NAI DE 2/269: Dáil Éireann Report on foreign affairs, 19/Aug/1919.

7. Ibid.

8. NAI DE 2/269: Dáil Éireann report on foreign affairs, 27/Aug/1919.

9. NAI DE 4/1/3: Dáil Éireann report on foreign affairs, 25/Jun/1920.

10. Briollay, *Rebellion*, pp. 52–3.

11. *II*, 04/Sep/1920.

12. *FJ*, 05/Oct/1920: The *Freeman's Journal* printed the whole front page.

13. NAI DFA Early Series, Paris 1921, 15/Jul/1921: O' Kelly to Robert Brennan.

14. Mitchell, *Government*, p. 19.

15. Houses of the Oireachtas: Notice of Motion for Daily Paper, 02/Apr/1919.

16. UCD P80/14: Report on Fitzgerald's visit to London, 01/Jan/1920.

17. NAI 1125/1, George Gavan Duffy Papers, 22/Jun/1919.

18. McKenna, Kathleen, 'The *Irish Bulletin*', (*Capuchin Annual*, 1970), p. 505.

19. Ibid., pp. 505–6.

20. Keogh, Dermot, *The Vatican, the Bishops and Irish Politics, 1919–1939*, (CUP, Cambridge, 1986), p. 33.

21. UCD P150/1370: Meeting of Cabinet, 07/Nov/1919.

22. BMH WS 643: Kathleen Napoli McKenna.

23. BMH WS 643: Kathleen Napoli McKenna. For a study of Gallagher see Walker, Graham, 'The Irish Dr Goebbels': Frank Gallagher and republican propaganda', (*Journal of Contemporary History*, Vol. 27, No. 1, January 1992). Even with the title's very strange comparison of Joseph Goebbels and Frank Gallagher this article contains many insights on his wider career.

24. *IB*, 26/Jan/1920.

25. *IB*, 20/Dec/1920.

26. Street, C.J.C., *Ireland in 1921*, (Philip Allan, London, 1922), p. 05. This book and another book he published under the pseudonym I.O. (*Ireland in 1920*) were both published and paid for by the British Government.

27. *IB*, 20/Dec/1920.

28. *IB*, 21/Dec/1920: a number of witnesses testified to seeing both men tortured by Auxiliaries. For some more information on the two men see www.clarelibrary.ie/eolas/claremuseum.

29. See Ryan, Louise, 'Drunken Tans': representations of sex and violence in the Anglo-Irish War 1919–1921, (*Feminist Review*, No. 66, 2000). There is no figure on how common such occurrences were, except to say that such attacks on woman were probably vastly under-reported. The *Irish Bulletin* was the only publication I have seen to openly report rape and assault during raids by the Crown forces on domestic homes. See also Benton, Sarah, 'Women Disarmed: the militarization of politics in Ireland, 1913–1923', (*Feminist Review*, No. 50, 1995). Both authors agree that such attacks occurred. Ryan concludes that there is sufficient evidence for a reassessment of how women may have been more routinely intimidated in 'heavily militarized areas of the country' than has been suggested in most historical accounts of the period.

30. Ibid. There were a number of articles detailing attacks on women during this month. See for example *Irish Bulletin*, 08/Apr/1921 – 'Patriot Women and their Punishment'.

31. *Sunday Independent*, 13/Apr/1947.

32. McCarthy, Cal, *Cumann na mBan and the Irish Revolution*, (The Collins Press, Cork, 2007), pp. 150–1.

33. McKenna, *Bulletin*, p. 523.

34. Ibid. pp. 523–4.

35. Bennett, Richard, *The Black and Tans*, (Barnes and Noble, New York, 1995), pp. 187–8. Bennett is the only source to name Darling as the editor

of the bogus *Irish Bulletins*. There is no reason to doubt Bennett on this issue as his book on the War of Independence contains much detailed information. It also fits with what we know about Darling's work at this time. C.J.C. Street also mentioned the episode and wrote that the forged editions were created by an officer 'on the staff of the chief of police'. See Street, 1921, p. 303.

36. *IB*, 29/Mar/1921.
37. Fake *Irish Bulletin* Vol. 4, No. 56, 30/Mar/1921.
38. Fake *Irish Bulletin* Vol. 4, No. 57, 31/Mar/192: see also the following days.
39. *IB*, 07/Apr/1921.
40. *Daily News* (DN), 05/Apr/1921.
41. Military Archives: CD/131/5/3.
42. UCD P80/14: Report on Propaganda, 07/May/1921. It is unsure for how long publication of the fake version continued. It seems to have lasted for at least two months.
43. *II*, 04/Apr/1921: Report from *Daily News*, 02/Apr/1921.
44. UCD P/150/1379: de Valera to Director of Publicity, 02/Apr/1921.
45. *II*, 04/Apr/1921.
46. *II*, 05/Apr/1921: Editorial – 'Loaded Dice'. The *Irish Independent* compared the incident with the forgery of *Pravda*, the Bolshevik newspaper in Russia. Apparently, the British Home Office was involved in the production of forged issues of this paper which were then smuggled into Russia and passed off as the original.
47. *IB*, 07/Apr/1921.
48. *DN*, 05/Apr/1920. See also *Irish Independent* and *Freeman's Journal* of this day.
49. NAI DE 4/8/8: Dáil Éireann Report on Propaganda, 18/Jan/1921.
50. UCD P80/14: Dáil Éireann Report on Propaganda, 10/Mar/1921.
51. UCD P80/14: Dáil Éireann Report on Propaganda, 07/May/1921.
52. NAI DE 4/4/2: Department of Publicity Report – History and Progress, August 1921.
53. Houses of the Oireachtas: Departmental Report – Department of Propaganda, 25/Jan/1921.
54. Ibid.
55. Ibid.
56. UCD P80/14: Dáil Éireann Report on Propaganda, 10/Mar/1921.
57. NAI DE 2/10: Dáil Éireann Report on Propaganda Department, June 1920.
58. BMH WS 779: Robert Brennan, p. 593 of his annotated version of '*Allegiance*'.

59. UCD P150/1379: de Valera to Director of Publicity, 17/May/1921.

60. UCD P150/1379: de Valera to Collins, 19/Mar/1921.

61. Houses of the Oireachtas: Departmental Reports – Publicity, 10/May/1921.

62. UCD P150/1379: de Valera to Director of Publicity, 11/Apr/1921.

63. Military Archives: CD/6/9/16 (K & L): List of *Irish Bulletin* recipients.

64. Inoue, Keiko, 'Propaganda II: propaganda of Dáil Éireann, 1919–1921' in Augusteijn, Joost, *The Irish Revolution*, 1913–1923, (Palgrave, Hampshire, 2002), p. 97.

65. UCD P7/A/5: O'Hegarty to Mulcahy, 18/Mar/1921.

66. UCD P7/A/45: General Order 23.

67. UCD P7/A/5: O'Hegarty to Mulcahy, 18/Mar/1921.

68. UCD P80/22: Gallagher to Béaslaí, 15/Jul/1921.

69. UCD P80/22: Assistant Chief of Staff to Béaslaí, July 1921.

70 UCD P150/1371: Meeting of Cabinet, 18/Nov/1921.

71. Bew, Paul, 'Moderate Nationalism and the Irish Revolution, 1916–1923', (*The Historical Journal,* Vol. 42, No. 3, 1999), p. 742.

72. Jones, *Diary*, pp. 24–5, (01/Jul/1920): The letter had been sent to the Irish Committee chaired by Walter Long that was in the process of formulating the Government of Ireland Bill.

73. For example the *Daily News* reported that 'Sinn Fein law has a sanction that no other law in Ireland has had for generations'. See Laffan, *Resurrection*, p. 316.

74. Kotsonouris, Mary, *Retreat from Revolution: the Dáil Courts 1920–1924*, (Irish Academic Press, Dublin, 1994), p. 41. The *Cork Examiner* was one regional newspaper that did not give much space to the proceedings of the courts. The operation of the courts was largely disrupted in 1921 with the increased violence and the operation of Martial Law across the south.

75. Figgis, Darrell, *Recollections of the Irish War*, (Ernest Benn Ltd, London, 1927), p. 282.

76. *IT,* 13/Mar/1920.

77. *IT,* 01/May/1920.

78. NAI DE 2/527: Collins to Bishop Fogarty, 20/Sep/1920.

79. This film followed on from another in April 1919 called the Sinn Féin review. This film chronicled 'events of Sinn Féin interest since 1916' and was shown in various parts of Ireland. See Laffan, *Resurrection*, p. 264 and *Irish Independent*, 17/Apr/1919.

80. Coogan, Tim Pat, *Michael Collins*, (Arrow, London, 1991), p. 117. 'G–Man' was the term used for members of the G Division of the DMP, which dealt in intelligence matters. Collins initially targeted the members of G

Division because he realised that if the intelligence section of the police were shattered they would prove ineffective in the face of a more sustained IRA onslaught.

81. Figgis, *Recollections*, pp. 262–3. See Laffan, *Resurrection*, p. 291 for RIC reports from around Ireland bemoaning the effects of the boycott on police morale. See also Abbott, Richard, *Police Casualties in Ireland: 1919–1922*, (Mercier Press, Cork, 2000), p. 66. This boycott intensified in the following years and for 1920 Abbott lists 1,647 resignations from the RIC.
82. Valiulis, Mary Ann, *Portrait of a Revolutionary*, (Irish Academic Press, Dublin, 1992), p. 57.
83. UCD P7/A/18: Mulcahy to Brugha, 14/May/1921.
84. UCD P7/A/45: General Order 26.
85. NLI MSS 739: 22/Jun/1921: General Order No. 26 – It must be recognised that at this time in the conflict IRA command unity had been fractured to a large degree and it is improbable that an outlying brigade in Cork could have succeeded in going through (or wished to) the entire chain of command. In addition local commanders involved in areas of heavy fighting gave little thought to propaganda and often felt hampered by GHQ. See Barry, Tom, *Guerrilla Days in Ireland*, (Anvil Books, Dublin, 1991).
86. Valiulis, *Revolutionary*, pp. 69–70. Many IRA prisoners were shot 'while trying to escape' and Lynch felt that his method of reprisal would end this practice.
87. Houses of the Oireachtas: Private Motion, 11/Mar/1921.
88. Lindsay's chauffeur was also executed by the IRA.
89. CO 904 168 (427). See also Bennett, *Tans*, pp. 191–2.
90. *TT*, 19/Apr/1921.
91. UCD P7/A/16: Letter to Mulcahy, 14/Feb/1921. The unnamed Commandant blamed a local woman for an ambush by Crown forces on his Brigade. They had only barely escaped.
92. Valiulis, *Revolutionary*, p. 68.
93. UCD P7/A/16: General Order 17.
94. UCD P7/A/45: General Order 23.
95. Ibid.
96. UCD P80/18: Childers to Minister of Defence, 22/Jun/1921.
97. Ibid.
98. *TT*, 02/Jul/1920.
99. Townshend, Charles, *Political Violence in Ireland*, (Oxford University Press, Oxford, 1983), p. 360.

100. UCD P/150/1379: O'Brien to Childers, 19/Mar/1921.

101. NLI MSS 8,427: O'Brien to Fitzgerald, 04/Sep/1920.

102. Houses of the Oireachtas: Departmental Report – Department of Propaganda, 25/Jan/1921.

103. Houses of the Oireachtas: Motions – Propaganda in England, 17/Sep/1920. The motion was withdrawn.

104. A report was released in 1921 by some British MPs, including Edward Carson, on 'Intercourse between Bolshevism and Sinn Fein'. It attempted to portray Sinn Féin as being part of an international Bolshevist conspiracy. It largely failed to make any impression on the newspapers.

105. *TT*, 31/Jul/1920.

106. Thomas Ashe led one of the few outbreaks of rebellion outside Dublin in 1916. Until his capture, he carried out a short but successful guerrilla campaign in Meath. Following his capture he refused to recognise the court and undertook a hunger strike while being imprisoned. He died after a botched attempt to force-feed him resulted in severe lung damage.

107. Sweeney, George, 'Irish Hunger Strikes and the Cult of Self Sacrifice', (*Journal of Contemporary History*, Vol. 28, No. 3, July 1993), p. 426.

108. On 28 October around 30,000 people filed by the coffin of MacSwiney as he lay in the Roman Catholic Cathedral in Southwark. See Costello, Francis, *Enduring the Most*, (Brandon, Dingle, 1995), pp. 226–7.

109. *MG*, 29/Oct/1920.

110. Costello, *Enduring*, p. 232. See also *Manchester Guardian*, 01/Nov/1920.

111. Newsinger, John, '"I bring not Peace but a Sword": the religious motif in the Irish War of Independence', (*Journal of Contemporary History*, Vol. 13, No. 3, July 1978), p. 623.

112. *FJ* and *II*, 13/May/1920: Gleeson had gone on hunger strike with the rest of the republican prisoners in Mountjoy in April (see Chapter 3) and although the strike was called off, Gleeson did not recover.

113. *Westminster Gazette*, 30/Oct/1920: see also Griffith in the *Manchester Guardian* of the same day.

114. Doherty, M.A., 'Kevin Barry and the Anglo-Irish propaganda war', (*Irish Historical Studies*, Vol. xxxii, No. 126, November 2000), p. 231. Another article worth reading is Ainsworth, John, 'Kevin Barry, the Incident at Monk's Bakery and the making of an Irish Republican Legend', (*History*, No. 87, 2002).

115. Breen, Dan, *My Fight for Irish Freedom*, (Anvil Books, Dublin, 1981), pp. 93–4.

116. Hart, Peter, *Enemies*, p. 103.

117. Borgonovo, John, *Spies*, p. 93.

118. L.M. Cullen makes reference to objections made to Eason's newsagents 'by Sinn Fein groups in a number of places to English papers' but there is little evidence of a concerted campaign of IRA seizures of English newspapers. See Cullen, L. M., *Eason & Son – A History*, (Eason & Son, Dublin, 1989), p. 208.

119. Houses of the Oireachtas: Debate on Reports – Propaganda Department, 11/Mar/1921.

120. Ibid.

121. UCD P80/22: Béaslaí to Gallagher, 12/Nov/1921.

122. CO 904 168: Dublin Castle statements to press. There is one report of a newsagent receiving a threatening letter from republicans during January 1921.

123. UCD P7A/16: GHQ Report – the only incident related to newspapers was the capture and burning of a shipment of British newspapers (mostly *News of the World*) near Dun Laoghaire in April.

124. House of Commons Debates: 20/Oct/1920 – Vol. 133 Col 935–936.

125. *CE*, 24/May/1921.

126. Kenneally, Ian, 'Reports from a bleeding Ireland': the *Cork Examiner* during the Irish War of Independence', (*Journal of the Cork Historical and Archaeological Society*, 108, 2003), p. 100.

127. Hart, *Enemies*, p. 299. Hart gives the *Cork Examiner* of 24/May/1921 as his source but the paper only reported the incident and its sadness at the death of Dorman. No mention was made of any IRA demands although it is likely that the IRA had tried to levy funds from the paper as it had done with other Cork businesses.

128. Borgonovo, *Spies*, pp. 83–5.

129. There is small amount of correspondence in the Colonial Office files (Dublin Castle-intercepted telegrams) between foreign journalists and Arthur Griffith trying to arrange meetings in Ireland. Here is one from a Mr Gibbons, the Paris Representative of the *Chicago Tribune*: 'I have decided to send Mr Seldes of our London Office to Ireland to keep our American readers informed impartially on the Irish situation. He goes with letters to Unionist leaders, and I am asking that he be accorded such facilities from the Nationalists, Sinn Fein and Independent element in Ireland.' CO 904/203/175 (Griffith), 25/Oct/1919.

130. Bennett, *Tans*, pp. 100–1.

131. O'Malley, Ernie, *On Another Man's Wound*, (Anvil Books, Dublin 2002), p. 235.

132. See the *Freeman's Journal* and *Irish Independent*, 17/Sep/1920. See also *Freeman's Journal* 20/Sep/1920.

133. Briollay, *Rebellion*, p. 84.

134. BMH WS 834: Michael Knightly.

135. The detective in Question was Gerard Smyth. See Dwyer, T. Ryle, *Michael Collins – the man who won the war*, (Mercier Press, Cork, 1990), p. 88.

136. *II*, 23/Apr/1921: Report of interview with *Philadelphia Public Ledger*, 02/Apr/1921.

137. *II*, 30/Nov/1920: letter from Sweetman. See also edition of 02/Dec/1920.

138. *II*, 06/Dec/1920: Report – 'Negotiations for an Irish Peace'.

139. Ibid.

140. *II*, 07/Dec/1920: letter from Collins.

141. See for example *II*, 07/Dec/1920. See also the letter from Paidín O'Keefe dismissing O'Flanagan's statement as 'simply a statement of personal opinion' in the *Irish Independent*, 08/Dec/1920. O'Keefe was the General Secretary of Sinn Féin.

142. Hopkinson, Michael, *The Irish War of Independence*, (Gill & Macmillan, Dublin, 2002), p. 183. For the various secret negotiations that took place with the aim of arranging a truce see Chapter 19 of Hopkinson's book.

143. UCD P/150: de Valera to Director of Publicity, 24/Apr/1921.

144. UCD P150/1379: de Valera to Director of Publicity, 23/Mar/1921: to maintain consistency I will continue to call it the Department of Propaganda.

145. Boyle, Andrew, *The Riddle of Erskine Childers*, (Hutchinson, London, 1977), p. 257.

146. See Irish newspapers for 01/Apr/1921.

147. Ibid.

148. See http://www.ucc.ie/celt/published/E900015/index.html: this is a transcript of de Valera's interview with Dr Zehnder of the Swiss paper *Neue Zeitung*, 03/May/1921.

149. BMH WS 725: Desmond Ryan.

150. Trinity College Dublin (TCD) MSS 7811: Diaries of Erskine Childers.

151. UCD P80/14: press cuttings.

152. McKenna, *Bulletin*, p. 517.

153. Hopkinson, *Sturgis*, p. 70. Mark Sturgis gives a very short account of meeting Moyston in November 1920 who was trying to arrange an interview with the Under Secretary, John Anderson.

154. UCD P80/14: DE Report on Propaganda 18/Jan/1921.

155. *DN,* 11/Nov/1920.
156. TCD MSS 10050: Gallagher to Cecilia Saunders, 13/Nov/1921.
157. CO 804/168 (577): Clarke to Foulkes, 10/Aug/1921.

Chapter 3 – The Freeman's Journal

1. Laffan, *Resurrection of Ireland*, p. 160.
2. Its Linotype warehouse, containing dozens of Linotypes, on Prince's Street was totally destroyed. The Linotype was the principal machine used in the composition of text for newspapers and the replacement of the destroyed machines would have necessitated a massive financial outlay.
3. *FJ*, 22/January/1919.
4. Ibid.
5. Ibid.
6. *FJ*, 24/June/1919.
7. *FJ*, 25/June/1919.
8. The idea of using partition as a means of engineering a settlement in Ireland had first come to the fore in the years before the First World War, during the run-up to the 1912 Home Rule Bill.
9. *FJ*, 18/October/1919.
10. This shortage was commented upon at length by Irish and British newspapers and used to justify the series of price rises that practically all newspapers undertook around this time. The paper admitted on 10/Mar/1920 that it was losing money because of the present price of paper.
11. *II*, 18/September/1919. A liquidator was appointed to the *Freeman's Journal* on 17/September/1919. None of the above was printed in the *Freeman's Journal* itself.
12. Lester left the paper during the Civil War to join the newly formed Irish diplomatic corps and in a dazzling career, eventually became Secretary General of the League of Nations.
13. For a précis of Allen's career see Oram, *Newspaper Book*, pp.133–6. Allen joined the paper in late 1919 or early 1920.
14. Ryan left a short account of his time at the *Freeman's Journal* in his memoirs. See Ryan, Desmond, *Remembering Sion*, (Arthur Barker, London, 1934), pp. 256–81.
15. Felix M. Larkin gives the circulation of the paper at this time as about 35,000 copies per day. Despite the huge and increasing demand for daily newspapers the production capacity of the *Freeman's Journal* was badly hampered by the financial problems it had suffered in previous decades and the destruction of its property during the 1916 Rising. The figure of

35,000 copies was the maximum production capacity of the paper's printing equipment and suggests a public demand greater than this. The new owners would surely have sought to remedy the production problems and increase circulation. See Larkin, Felix M., 'A Great Daily Organ': the *Freeman's Journal*, 1763–1924', (*History Ireland*, Vol. 14, No. 3, May/June 2006).

16. Ryan, *Sion*, p. 260.
17. The *Freeman's Journal* called the motor permit 'an attack on the civil liberties of ordinary people'.
18. *FJ*, 28/November/1919: See also *The Times* in Chapter 7.
19. Ibid.
20. *Evening Telegraph* 20/Dec/1919.
21. Ibid.
22. Ryan, *Sion*, p. 260.
23. *FJ*, 19/January/1920.
24. *FJ*, 28/Jan/1920: Editorial – 'The Attack on the Freeman'.
25. *FJ*, 30/Jan/1920.
26. *FJ*, 18/Feb/1920: Report on Catholics in a proposed six-county 'Orange State'.
27. *FJ*, 20/Feb/1920: Editorial – 'How to defeat Partition'.
28. Ibid.
29. *FJ*, 28/Feb/1920.
30. Ibid.
31. Ibid.
32. *FJ*, 04/Feb/1920: The German Plot was an attempt to break Sinn Féin in May 1918. Many leaders of the party including de Valera and Griffith were arrested.
33. *FJ*, 06/Feb/1920: Von Bissing was the Head of the German forces in Belgium during the First World War.
34. *FJ*, 10/Feb/1920.
35. *FJ*, 14/February/1920.
36. *FJ*, 22/March/1920: Editorial – 'The Murder of the Lord Mayor of Cork'.
37. Ibid.
38. Ibid.
39. *FJ*, 11/March/1920.
40. Dwyer, *Squad*, p. 70.
41. Macready, *Annals*, pp. 475–6.
42. *FJ*, 03/April/1920.
43. *FJ*, 17/April/1920.

44. *FJ*, 13/April/1920: See also report of 14/April/1920.
45. *FJ*, 15/April/1920.
46. *FJ*, 15/April/1920: Editorial. The editorial asked if this was 'political revenge'.
47. *FJ*, 30/April/1920: Editorial. See also previous days report on the 'Arklow Shooting' and Macready, *Annals*, p. 476. The *FJ* had published the official report of the incident in full, as acknowledged by Macready, but had also printed a report from its one of its own reporters which differed from the official report in a number of aspects.
48. The paper even brought a small compensation claim which had been brought against it before the Dáil Éireann Arbitration Court – See *FJ*, 09/Aug/1920.
49. *FJ*, July/05/1921.
50. This was an ongoing facet of the paper's reportage at this time.
51. *FJ*, 17/June/1920: Report – 'The Source of the Sewer – England's Lying Propaganda against Ireland'.
52. *FJ*, 10/July/1920.
53. Dwyer, *Tans*, p. 213. Dwyer also writes that Collins later arranged for Mee and two of the other constables to take part in a speaking tour of America.
54. *FJ*, 10/July/1920.
55. After the 'mutiny' Constable Mee drew up an account of Smyth's speech which repeated the claims against Smyth. It was signed as accurate by the other thirteen constables who resigned. See Ryle Dwyer, *Collins*, pp.87–8. For a copy of this account see the interview given by one of the constables, John McNamara, to the American Commission on Ireland. McNamara states that 25 constables originally refused Smyth's orders. Of these, fourteen, all unmarried men without children, offered their resignations: *American Commission Interim Report*, pp. 68–71 & 131–5.
56. *TT*, 19/Jul/1920: See also report on 30/Jul/1920.
57. *FJ*, 14/July/1920.
58. Hopkinson, *Sturgis*, pp. 11–13.
59. Greenwood led the intense condemnation in the House of Commons from such predictable figures as Carson and Bonar Law as well as supporters of the Government amongst the English press. *The Irish Times* also made an editorial criticism of the coverage of Bell and Smyth. See also Abbott, *Police Casualties*, pp. 96–104. While the author does not delve into the furore surrounding the newspaper coverage, he believes that Smyth was shot, like Bell, for the damage he was capable of causing to the IRA. In this instance, Abbott argues, Smyth wanted to introduce

radical changes into police strategy, which could have made them a more efficient and formidable foe. This may have been so but it does seem likely that Smyth's speech was correctly reported.

60. Hopkinson, *Sturgis*, p. 13.
61. *FJ*, 27/July/1920.
62. Ibid.
63. Hopkinson, *Sturgis*, pp. 15–18.
64. Ibid. p.15.
65. See especially, *The Times*, *Daily News*, *Westminster Gazette* and *Daily Mail*.
66. *IT*, 04/August/1920.
67. Jones, *Diary*, p. 34. (04/Aug/1920).
68. CO 904/188 (483), John Anderson note, undated (the memo can be dated with certainty to the week covering the very last days of July and early days of August by a reference Anderson makes to a *Freeman's Journal* editorial).
69. See O'Leary, Cornelius and Maume, Patrick, *Controversial Issues in Anglo-Irish Relations, 1910–1921*, (Four Courts Press, Dublin, 2004), pp. 101–2.
70. Taylor, A.J.P. (Ed), *Lloyd George – Twelve Essays*, (Hamish Hamilton, London, 1971), pp. 151–2. Birkenhead, Long and Balfour were especially hostile to the idea.
71. The mindset of the military chiefs at this stage was best summed up by Field Marshal Henry Wilson. In his diary (26/Nov/1920) he noted that Jeudwine (GOC of the 5th Division in Ireland) had told him: 'We had now got to the same position as in the war with the Boches in 1915. A stalemate, with rising morale on our side and dropping morale on the rebel side.'
72. CO 904/188 (483).
73. See also the *II*, 18/Aug/1920. The *Irish Independent*, which had no representative present at the meeting between the editors of the *Freeman's Journal*, *The Irish Times* and John Anderson, reported with glee on the *Freeman's* embarrassment and 'the great fiasco'.
74. Coroner's inquests had resulted in judgments highly damaging to the Crown forces, most famously in the case of Tomás MacCurtain.
75. *FJ*, 04/August/1920.
76. *FJ*, 17/August/1920: Editorial – 'Which shall Dominate Us?'
77. *FJ*, 28/Aug/1920: See also Chapter 1.
78. Ibid.
79. *FJ*, 30/Aug/1920: Editorial – 'The Government of Ireland'.
80. *FJ*, 29/Sep/1920: Report. The report was an acknowledged reprint from the *Irish Bulletin* and the *Freeman's Journal* stressed that these were 'not

alleged' but actual attacks. See the paper for the following day for the report on Black and Tan activities. The Black and Tan force doctored the posters to read one hundred and one 'police murders'.

81. *FJ*, 01/October/1920.
82. *FJ*, 09/Nov/1920: Editorial – 'The Sword is mightier...'
83. BMH WS 725: Desmond Ryan: *FJ*, 23/Sep/1920: report – 'Another Terrible Crime'. It seems that the Crown forces shot John Lynch because they believed him to be Cork IRA leader Liam Lynch.
84. *FJ*, 27/October/1920.
85. *FJ*, 30/Oct/1920.
86. *FJ*, 02/Nov/1920.
87. *FJ*, 01/Nov/1920: Dillon had used this famous phrase against Prime Minster Asquith in the House of Commons in 1916.
88. *FJ*, 22/Nov/1920: Amritsar refers to the British army's 1919 massacre of 379 Indians attending a public meeting in the Northern Indian city of Amritsar. Hundreds more were badly injured. The commander of the soldiers, General Dyer, was dismissed from the army after an inquiry but Conservative backers in the House of Commons presented him with a jewelled sword bearing the legend 'saviour of the Punjab'. 'Dyerism' was another epithet regularly applied by the nationalist papers to British policy in Ireland.
89. Ibid.
90. Ibid.
91. Ibid.
92. *FJ*, 25/Nov/1920: The court martial was undertaken against the *Freeman's Journal*, its Proprietors and its editor. The *Freeman's Journal* published a full report of proceedings each day.
93. Healy left the IPP to join William O Brien's All for Ireland League in 1910. Nationalist Party MP Joseph Devlin also robustly defended the paper in the House of Commons.
94. *Freeman's Journal*, 26/Nov/1920: See also the previous day's edition.
95. See *FJ* 25/Nov/1920 – 27/Dec/1920.
96. *Manchester Guardian*, 29/Dec/1920.
97. *FJ*, 07/Dec/1920.
98. *FJ*, 08/Dec/1920: Report p. 5.
99. *FJ*, 07/Dec/1920.
100. Ibid. Counsel for the *Freeman's Journal* immediately directed a writ of Habeas Corpus to the Governor of Mountjoy Jail and Hooper was released on 10/Dec/1920 but only into police custody where he remained for almost a week. Edwards and Fitzgerald were not released

as sentence on the first of the charges was promulgated that afternoon.

101. *FJ*, 11/Nov/1920: Report – See also issues of 08/Nov/1920 and 10/Nov/1920. The Crown case seemed confusing to all involved especially due to the fact that the editor and the owner of an independent newspaper were, in the words of Fforde, being 'prosecuted as soldiers'. The sentences were to run concurrently. See Chapter One for the reaction of other newspapers.

102. These attacks occurred on 29/Nov/1920, 25/Dec/1920 and 30/Dec/1920.

103. *FJ*, 13/Dec/1920.

104. *FJ*, 24/Dec/1920: Editorial – 'The Christmas Box'.

105. *FJ*, 07/Jan/1921: On the day of the men's release 'a delegation of prominent newspapermen' was to meet with Lloyd George to campaign against the sentences. See also Chapter One.

106. *FJ*, 19/Feb/1921.

107. *FJ*, 05/Feb/1921.

108. *FJ*, 01/Mar/1921.

109. *FJ*, 15/Mar/1921.

110. Ibid: Editorial – 'Futile Terrorism'.

111. *FJ*, 20/Dec/1920.

112. *FJ*, 08/Mar/1921: See also following days.

113. *FJ*, 17/Mar/1921.

114. *FJ*, 30/Apr/1921: see also *Daily News* 30/Apr/1921 and 01/May/1921.

115. Ibid: see also *Daily News*, 02/May/1921.

116. *FJ*, 22/Mar/1921: See also *Manchester Guardian*, 21/Mar/1921.

117. *FJ*, 15/Feb/1921.

118. *FJ*, 31/Jan/1921.

119. *FJ*, 24/May/1921: For a study of the Sinn Féin election campaign in the North see Laffan, *Resurrection*, pp. 332–45.

120. *FJ*, 28/May/1921: See also previous day's edition.

121. Laffan, *Resurrection*, p. 341.

122. Hopkinson, *Sturgis*, pp. 172–3.

123. Larkin, *History Ireland*, p.49. See also Hopkinson, *Sturgis*, p. 186 & pp. 194–200. Another journalist who became active as an intermediary at this time was Carl Ackermann of the *Philadelphia Public Ledger*. Ackermann had very close links with the head of British intelligence, Basil Thomson. A note in the annotated copy of Robert Brennan's *Allegiance* in the Bureau of Military History accuses the journalist of being a British agent. According to Brennan, Collins also held this suspicion but de Valera disagreed. See BMH WS 779: Robert Brennan.

124. Hopkinson, *Sturgis*, p. 197.

125. *FJ*, 06/Jul/1921.

126. *FJ*, 12/Jul/1921.

127. *FJ*, 12/Jul/1921: Editorial – 'The Foretaste'. The *Freeman's Journal*, which had been printing a daily casualty list from early January 1921, gave a combined casualty list for the year so far of 1,086 dead and 1,311 wounded. This was broken down as 379 members of the Crown forces killed and 555 wounded and a total of 707 IRA members and civilians killed and 756 wounded.

Chapter 4 – The Irish Independent

1. For a study of W.M. Murphy and the early days of the *Irish Independent* see Farrell, Brian (ed.), *Communications and Community in Ireland*, (Mercier Press, Cork, 1984).

2. *II*, 22/January/1919.

3. *II*, 16/May/1919: Report – The Bishop urged the Irish people 'to maintain their true Catholic spirit' and not to support violence.

4. *II*, 11/Apr/1919: Report – 'Assembly of Dáil Éireann members at Mansion House'. See also editions of 09/Apr/1919 and 10/Apr/1919.

5. *II*, 20/Sep/1919.

6. *II*, 03/Jul/1919: See Editorial obituary for W. M. Murphy on 07/Jul/1919.

7. *II*, 30/Aug/1919.

8. *II*, 09/Sep/1919.

9. *II*, 26/Nov/1919.

10. By 1920 it is estimated that the 'total sales of morning dailies in the Irish market probably exceeded half a million copies'. See Cullen, *Eason*, p. 307.

11. The *Irish Independent* reported eagerly on its competitor's financial difficulties also publishing a highly unfavourable history of the *Freeman's Journal* on 28/Oct/1919 which accused the paper of 'posturing as a Nationalist organ'.

12. Oram, *Newspaper Book*, pp. 139–40.

13. Gleeson, *Bloody Sunday*, pp.86–7.

14. BMH WS 834: Michael Knightly. See also Foy, Michael T., *Michael Collins's Intelligence War*, (Sutton Publishing, Gloucestershire, 2006), pp. 111–12.

15. BMH WS 834: Michael Knightly.

16. Ibid.

17. Ibid. Knightly did not name the journalist, although he claimed to know who he was. See also BMH WS 835: Michael Knightly for his story of

the capture of Kevin Barry.

18. *II*, 22/Oct/1919.

19. See the *II* for the last week of July.

20. *II*, 22/Nov/1919.

21. *II*, 20/Dec/1919.

22. Ibid.

23. *II*, 22/Dec/1919: The amount of damage must have been extensive as, the following February, the *Irish Independent* was awarded £15,000 damages by the Recorder of Dublin City Sessions – MG 19/Feb/1920.

24. Breen, *Freedom*, p. 94. See also BMH WS 835: Michael Knightly. Some of the Volunteers apparently wanted to shoot the editor, but Clancy decided to destroy the machinery instead.

25. Ibid.

26. *II*, 02/Feb/1920,

27. *II*, 23/Feb/1920,

28. Ibid.

29. *II*, 11/Feb/1920,

30. *II*, 19/Jan/1920: In these elections Sinn Féin had taken control of 72 out of 127 Urban Councils, 182 out of 206 Rural Councils.

31. *II*, 05/Mar/1920,

32. *II*, 01/Mar/1920,

33. *II*, 30/Mar/1920: Editorial – See also editorial of 11/Mar/1920 – 'Ulster is Safe'.

34. *II*, 28/Jan/1920: See editorial and report for criticism of the Education Bill. The Education Bill which was abandoned a few months later aroused anger from the Catholic Hierarchy who feared that its provisions for a three-man board of control for education in Ireland would see the church lose its influence over education.

35. Ibid.

36. *II*, 02/Feb/1920: Editorial – 'Saturday's Round Up'.

37. *II*, 05/Feb/1920: Report – 'The Tragic Events in Limerick'. See also editions of 04/Feb/1920, 11/Feb/1920 and 13/Feb/1920: The Inquest found the Crown forces guilty of murder after conflicting testimony by members of the RIC.

38. The result of the inquest was a verdict of murder against 'Lloyd George, French, Macpherson, T. J. Smith, DI Clayton, DI Swanzy, and unknown members of the RIC'. Swanzy was later shot dead by the IRA in retaliation as he was rumoured to have lead the raid on MacCurtain's home.

39. *II*, 22/Mar/1920.

40. *II*, 27/Mar/1920: Editorial – 'Ireland's Condition'.

41. Ibid.

42. *II*, 20/Mar/1920.

43. *II*, 12/Apr/1920: Editorial – 'Heartless Government'.

44. *II*, 13/Apr/1920: Editorial – 'Official Inhumanity'.

45. *II*, 15/Apr/1920: Editorial – 'Released'.

46. Ibid.

47. See especially the paper throughout May, following Nevil Macready's arrival as GOC.

48. *II*, 10/May/1920: Editorial 'Inhuman Government'.

49. *II*, 18/May/1920: Editorial – 'The Iron Heel'.

50. Laffan, *Resurrection*, p. 264.

51. During 1920 the *Irish Independent*'s circulation averaged over 130,000 daily copies per month for the year, rising quickly from 114,967 daily averages in January to a high of 141,751 in July. It ended the year with a circulation of 134,117 per day. These are net daily sales and only include editions bought and paid for. The figures are independently formulated and are extremely impressive. They continued to climb slowly through 1921 (see edition of 16/Mar/1921) and seem to have been tens of thousands of copies ahead of its rivals, the *Freeman's Journal* and *The Irish Times*. See also note 10 above.

52. *II*, 11/May/1920 and 16/Jun/1920: Both were reports on the deaths of police in IRA ambushes.

53. *II*, 07/Jun/1920.

54. See Breen, *Freedom*, p. 102.

55. *II*, 24/Jun/1920: Editorial – 'Orange Government'.

56. *II*, 23/Jun/1920: Editorial – 'Government in Derry'. See also following days.

57. See for example the editions of 25/Jun/1920, 24/Jul/1920, 01/Sep/1920 and 15/Sep/1920. The editorial of 14/Sep/1920 claimed that over the previous weeks 'Carsonite Volunteers' 'shot the latter [Catholics] mercilessly; Burned their dwellings wholesale; ejected scores of families from their homes and expelled between 5,000 and 6,000 from their employment'.

58. *II*, 07/Aug/1920: for a study of the violence in the north at this time see Parkinson, Alan, F., *Belfast's Unholy Wars*, (Four Courts Press, Dublin, 2004).

59. See for example the II of 04/Aug/1920.

60. *II*, 03/Aug/1920: Editorial – 'Not Peace but a Sword'.

61. *II*, 25/Aug/1920: Editorial – 'Anarchical Government'. See also editorial

of 17/Aug/1920.

62. *II*, 05/Sep/1920: Editorial – 'Barbarous Conduct'.

63. Ibid.

64. Ibid: See also 10/Sep/1920.

65. *II*, 04/Aug/1920: Editorial – The editorial maintained that the 'act would make a desert' of Ireland.

66. *II*, 25/Aug/1920.

67. See the issue of 30/Sep/1920 and the following few days for reports on the Mallow reprisal.

68. *II*, 22/Sep/1920.

69. *II*, 24/Sep/1920: Editorial – 'Full Inquiry Imperative'. The paper was calling for an enquiry into the reprisal at Balbriggan.

70. *II*, 04/Oct/1920: Editorial – 'A disgrace to England'.

71. *II*, 03/Nov/1920: See also 05/Nov/1920. The *Irish Independent* and many Irish as well as English newspapers were deeply critical of Greenwood's response to the death of Ellen Quinn. In the House of Commons he had defended the Auxiliaries by saying they 'fired in anticipation of an ambush'. Lloyd George said the incident 'was one of those unfortunate accidents that always happens in war'.

72. *II*, 14/Sep/1920: Editorial – 'The Fatal Decision'.

73. *II*, 26/Oct/1920.

74. *II*, 02/Nov/1920.

75. *II*, 22/Nov/1920.

76. *II*, 23/Nov/1920: Editorial – 'The Road to Peace'.

77. Ibid. The paper had made a similar call after the Balbriggan reprisal: see 27/Sep/1920.

78. *II*, 24/Nov/1920.

79. *II*, 14/Dec/1920: Editorial – 'Reckless Incendiarism'.

80. *II*, 04/Jun/1920. See also 07/Dec/1920.

81. *II*, 08/Dec/1920: Archbishop Clune of Perth in Australia was involved as an intermediary at this time. For details on various peace negotiations throughout 1920 and 1921 see Hopkinson, Michael, *The Irish War of Independence*, (Gill & Macmillan, Dublin, 2002), Chapter 19.

82. *II*, 23/Dec/1920.

83. *II*, 14/Dec/1920.

84. *II*, 08/Feb/1921: See for example the report on the Auxiliaries' practice of taking hostages on patrol to safeguard against ambushes.

85. *II*, 08/Mar/1920. See also the *Freeman's Journal*.

86. CO 904 188, 07/Mar/1921, Macready to Anderson: See also Anderson reply of same date. Anderson knew that to follow such a path

(prosecuting the newspapers) just months after the furore over the *Freeman's Journal* would be damaging to the Administration and probably not supported by Lloyd George.

87. *II*, 28/Feb/1921: On 28/Mar/1921 the paper reported that this number of such deaths had risen to 62.
88. *II*, 01/Mar/1921: Editorial – 'The Cork Executions'.
89. *II*, 29/Apr/1921: Editorial – 'Under Military Direction'.
90. *II*, 02/May/1921: Editorial – 'Election Scandal'.
91. *II*, 14/May/1921.
92. Ibid.
93. *II*, 16/May/1921.
94. *II*, 31/May/1921.
95. *II*, 27/May/1921.
96. *II*, 17/Jun/1921.
97. *II*, 30/May/1921. The report had been taken from the *Daily Telegraph*. Perhaps the report was sabre-rattling on behalf of the British Government with a view to influencing the ongoing negotiations.
98. *II*, 26/May/1921.
99. *II*, 11/Jun/1921: Editorial – 'Shadows of Terror'.
100. *II*, 23/June/1921: Editorial – 'The Partition Parliament'.
101. *II*, 27/Jun/1920: The paper carried the news with the banner headline 'Another Political Surprise'.
102. *II*, 09/Jul/1921: Editorial – 'Steps towards Peace'.
103. Ibid.
104. Ibid.
105. *II*, 14/Jul/1921.
106. Ibid.
107. *II*, 12/Jul/1921. The *Irish Independent* also printed a list of casualties over the previous six months of 1,082 dead and 1,516 wounded. These figures tallied very closely with those of the *Freeman's Journal*. These were the only papers to print a list of casualties.

Chapter 5 – The Cork Examiner

1. *CE*, 22/Jan/1919: Editorial – 'Dail Eireann'.
2. *CE*, 04/Apr/1919.
3. For an account of the events see also Abbott, *Police Casualties*, pp. 33–5.
4. *CE*, 08/Apr/1919: Editorial – 'Limerick Rescue Tragedy'.
5. *CE*, 17/May/1919.
6. *CE*, 01/Jul/1919: Editorial – 'Dominion Home Rule'.
7. Ibid.

8. *CE*, 25/Jul/1919. See also the editorial of 28/Jul/1919, which criticised Lloyd George's claim that there existed 'two Irelands'.

9. See, for example, editorial of 18/Jul/1919.

10. *CE*, 13/May/1919.

11. *CE*, 13/Sep/1919.

12. *CE*, 22/Sep/1919.

13. *CE*, 29/Nov/1919: Editorial – 'Coalition Intriguing'.

14. *CE*, 17/Dec/1919.

15. *CE*, 28/Feb/1920: See also the editorial.

16. *CE*, 01/Mar/1920: See also the editorials of 09/Mar/1920 & 10/Mar/1920.

17. *CE*, 18/Mar/1920: Editorial – 'Bishop of Cork's salutary advice'. The early 1880s were a time of great agrarian violence that saw this period termed the Land War. The Chief Secretary, Forster, imprisoned the leaders of the Land League including Parnell in 1881 and helped usher in the most violent period of the Land War.

18. *CE*, 22/Mar/1920: Editorial – 'Murder most Foul'. See also the next day's editorial, which again urged Cork people 'to comply with the discipline required by the moral law'. See also edition of 08/Apr/1920 where that paper dismissed Lord French's claim that Sinn Féin members had murdered the Lord Mayor.

19. *CE*, 17/Apr/1920.

20. Both the *Freeman's Journal* and *Irish Independent* displayed respect towards the statements of Irish Bishops and occasionally called on their readers to pray for Ireland but they generally avoided religious imagery in their editorials.

21. *CE*, 12/May/1920: Editorial – 'Thou Shalt Not Kill'. The paper also carried Dr Cohalan's denunciation. The paper reported him as saying also that 'since the beginning of the trouble of 1916, on the whole, they (RIC and military) have behaved very well towards the city'.

22. *CE*, 18/May/1920: Editorial – 'Rule by Force'.

23. *CE*, 20/May/1920.

24. *CE*, 10/Jul/1920: Editorial – 'British Democracy and Ireland'.

25. See for example the report 'Police run amok' detailing a reprisal in Limerick city on 16/Aug/1920.

26. Later that month the *Cork Examiner* also received a copy of Under Secretary John Anderson's warning to the press that Irish newspapers were running the risk of prosecution.

27. The photographs of the destruction in Mallow appeared in the paper on 30/Sep/1920 & 01/Oct/1920.

28. *CE*, 28/Aug/1920: Editorial – 'Humanity or Law'.

29. *CE*, 20/May/1920.

30. *CE*, 26/Oct/1920: Editorial – 'Reqiescat in Pace'.

31. Ibid.

32. *CE*, 30/Oct/1920.

33. *CE*, 12/Nov/1920: Editorial – 'Thou Shalt not Kill'. For a detailed study of the circumstances surrounding the death of O' Donoghue see Hart, *IRA*, Chapter 1.

34. *CE*, 02/Nov/1920.

35. *CE*, 01/Dec/1920: There were many more such notices during these months.

36. Borgonovo, *Spies*, p. 11.

37. *IT*, 14/Dec/1920: Greenwood was responding to a question from J.M. Kenworthy.

38. For a background to the introduction of Martial Law see Townshend, *Campaign*, pp. 133–9. For a study of the legal aspects of Martial Law see Campbell, Colm, *Emergency Law in Ireland, 1918–1925*, (OUP, Oxford, 1994).

39. *CE*, 13/Dec/1920.

40. Ibid.

41. Ibid. Editorial – 'The Bishop of Cork's Decree'. See also the editorial of the following day. For a wider study of the events surrounding the burning of Cork see White, Gerry & O'Shea, Brendan, *The Burning of Cork*, (Mercier Press, Cork, 2006).

42. *CE*, 28/Dec/1920: Report. On the same day as the IRA attack on the Cork paper a party of Auxiliaries attacked the offices of the *Freeman's Journal*.

43. *CE*, 23/Nov/1920.

44. *CE*, 30/Nov/1920: Editorial – 'The Path to Peace'. See editorials throughout December.

45. *CE*, 28/Dec/1920: Editorial – 'Christmas Eve': the paper commented – 'The case supplies an example of the amount of mischief a few young fellows in possession of revolvers and explosives can accomplish'.

46. *CE*, 17/Jan/1921.

47. *CE*, 17/Feb/1921: Editorial – 'The Strickland Inquiry'.

48. *CE*, 01/Mar/1921: Editorial – 'The Cork Executions'. See also the edition of 15/Mar/1921on the executions of six more IRA Volunteers in Dublin.

49. *CE*, 05/Mar/1921: Report. The report did not mention what type of material had been censored.

50. Townshend, *Campaign*, p. 134. General Jeudwine compiled a list of advantages also including unity of command between police and military as well as restriction of movement. Macready also considered control of the press a benefit of Martial Law.

51. Macready, *Annals*, p. 532.

52. *CE*, 07/May/1921: Report – Mosley, who would later become infamous for his leadership of British fascists, was a member of the British 'Peace with Ireland Council'.

53. *Westminster Gazette*, 29/Apr/1921.

54. *FJ*, 02/May/1921.

55. *DN*, 30/Apr/1921.

56. *MG*, 03/May/1921: See also *The Times* and *Westminster Gazette*.

57. See for example the news reports for 28/Apr/1921.

58. Townshend, *Campaign*, p. 176.

59. *II*, 03/Mar/1921 and 14/April/1921. See also *Freeman's Journal*.

60. *II*, 21/Apr/1921.

61. *II* 03/May/1921: Cecil was another persistent critic of the British Government's actions in Ireland, especially the treatment of the press.

62. Ibid.

63. *CE*, 15/Mar/1921: Editorial – 'The Dublin Executions'.

64. *CE*, 17/Mar/1921: Editorial – 'St. Patrick's Day'.

65. Ibid.

66. *CE*, 19/Apr/1921.

67. *CE*, 28/May/1921.

68. See Chapter 2.

69. *CE*, 24/May/1921.

70. *Cork Examiner*, 07/Jul/1921: Editorial – 'Prospects of Peace' See also editorials of 30/June/1921 and 05/July/1921.

71. Ibid.

72. *CE*, 12/Jul/1921: Editorial – 'Thursday's Peace Conference'. See also 10/Jul/1921.

73. Ibid. See also 14/Jul/1921.

Chapter 6 – The Irish Times

1. *IT*, 23/Jan/1919: Editorial – 'Cloud-Cuckoo Land'. See also the report on the proceedings that appeared on the previous day.

2. Ibid.

3. Ibid.

4. *IT*, 20/Oct/1919: For example see report on the death of Constable Michael Downing of the Dublin Metropolitan Police at the hands of the

IRA. *The Irish Times* called his death 'Cold-Blooded Murder'. The number of police killed by the IRA in 1919, as gathered from newspaper reports, was 15. See also Abbott, *Police Casualties*, p. 48.

5. *IT*, 11/Nov/1919.

6. *IT*, 20/Dec/1919.

7. Ibid.

8. Ibid.

9. *IT*, 09/Jan/1920: Editorial: 'The Peril of Partition'.

10. *IT*, 27/Jan/1920.

11. *IT*, 31/Jan/1920.

12. *IT*, 09/Mar/1920: Editorial – 'Southern Unionists'. The quotation is from *Macbeth*. The Solemn League and Covenant had been signed by hundreds of thousands of unionists in 1912 in Belfast as an act of protest against the third Home Rule Bill.

13. *IT*, 11/Mar/1920: Editorial – 'No Surrender'.

14. *IT*, 11/Feb/1920.

15. *IT*, 09/Mar/1920: Editorial – 'We refuse to believe that the nation which fought for Belgium will deliver a loyal community into the hands of England's enemies'.

16. *IT*, 20/Mar/1920.

17. *IT*, 03/Jan/1920: Editorial – 'The State of Ireland'.

18. *IT*, 28/Jan/1920: Editorial – 'The Bishop' Statement'.

19. *IT*, 26/Jan/1920.

20. *IT*, 28/Jan/1920.

21. *IT*, 13/Mar/1920: Editorial – 'The Irish Executive'. See also *Freeman's Journal*, 15/Mar/1920 which attacked *The Irish Times*. 'The same authority called for the surgeon's knife in May 1916. The weapon was applied and we are still gathering in the results.'

22. *IT*, 13/Mar/1920.

23. Ibid.

24. *IT*, 07/Feb/1920.

25. *IT*, 09/Feb/1920.

26. *IT*, 24/Mar/1920: Editorial. *The Irish Times*, on more than one occasion, accused the nationalist papers of contributing to the unrest in Ireland through those papers' sustained attacks on the Irish Administration and Crown forces.

27. *IT*, 19/April/1920: Editorial 'The Irish Police'. *The Irish Times* termed the conclusions of the inquest 'a novel stoke of Celtic fantasy'.

28. Ibid.

29. *IT*, 10/Jul/1920: Editorial. See also editorial of 08/Jul/1920: 'The

Collapse of Law'. The Dáil courts were a bureaucratic and propaganda challenge to British rule in Ireland. The vacuum left by the absence of the besieged RIC was filled by these courts, the most visible sign of the collapse of Crown rule in many areas. For a study see Kotsonouris, *Dáil Courts*.

30. *IT*, 07/May/1920: Editorial. See also editorial of 25/Mar/1920.
31. *IT*, 25/Jun/1920.
32. *IT*, 14/Jul/1920.
33. *IT*, 30/Jul/1920: Editorial.
34. Ibid.
35. *IT*, 06/Aug/1920: Editorial – 'The Prime Minister and Ireland'.
36. CO 904/188 (483), John Anderson note, undated (the memo can be dated with certainty to the week covering the very last days of July and early days of August by a reference Anderson makes to a *Freeman's Journal* editorial.
37. *IT*, 04/Aug/1920.
38. Hopkinson, *Last Days*, p.16.
39. Ibid. Fforde also acted as prosecuting counsel in the court martial of the *Freeman's Journal* in November 1920. For more on Wylie and the atmosphere within Dublin Castle at this time, see O'Broin, Leon, *W.E. Wylie and the Irish Revolution, 1916–1921*, (Gill & Macmillan, Dublin, 1989), pp. 102–44.
40. *IT*, 14/Aug/1920: Editorial – 'Southern Unionists and Settlement'.
41. *IT*, 30/Oct/1920.
42. *IT*, 23/Dec/1920.
43. *IT*, 24/Dec/1920.
44. Ibid.
45. Ibid. See also edition of 01/Jan/1921.
46. See Chapter 1. While the nationalist dailies deplored these official lists, as did much of the press in England, *The Irish Times* was supportive, arguing that the reports were not propaganda. See *IT*, 08/May/1920: Editorial.
47. *IT*, 02/Jun/1920.
48. *IT*, 05/Nov/1920: Editorial – 'The Campaign of Murder'.
49. *IT*, 25/Nov/1920: Editorial – 'Law and Murder'.
50. Ibid.
51. *IT*, 23/Jul/1920: Editorial – 'Ireland's Peril'.
52. *IT*, 05/Nov/1920: Editorial – 'The Campaign of Crime'.
53. Ibid.
54. *IT*, 14/Dec/1920.
55. For an account of this process see McColgan, *British Policy*.

56. *IT*, 02/Feb/1921: See also the editorial of 16/Feb1921 for *The Irish Times'* criticism of Lloyd George's speech to the House of Commons in which he claimed the condition of Ireland was improving.
57. *The Irish Times*, 22/Feb/1921: Editorial. For a refutation of this argument by a British journalist, Philip Gibbs, see Chapter 1. Herbert Asquith (Liberal MP) had been British Prime Minister during first half of the First World War and was in office during the 1916 Rebellion. During the years of the War of Independence he was a vocal, if belated, critic of British actions in Ireland.
58. Ibid.
59. *IT*, 02/Mar/1921: Editorial– 'Forces of the Crown'.
60. *IT*, 08/Mar/1921: Report. The *Irish Independent* carefully published that 'it is not conceivable that they were killed by Sinn Feiners or by men belonging to any section of their fellow citizens'.
61. *IT*, 02/Mar/1921.
62. *IT*, 14/Dec/1920.
63. *IT*, 14/Dec/1920: Editorial.
64. *IT*, 21/May/1921: de Valera and Craig had just met to discuss the situation in Ireland. Despite *The Irish Times'* hopes the meeting had not ended with any common ground between the leaders.
65. *IT*, 03/June/1921: Editorial – 'The Northern Parliament'.
66. Ibid. *The Irish Times* had a clear message for Dáil Éireann and Sinn Féin: 'The Southern Irishman who refuses to recognise that fact may remain a patriot but cannot pretend to be a statesman.'
67. Ibid.
68. *IT*, 29/Jun/1921: Editorial – 'Mr De Valera's reply'.
69. *FJ*, 07/May/1921.
70. *IT*, 09/July/1921: Editorial – 'Dawn'.
71. Ibid.
72. *IT*, 11/Jul/1921: Editorial – 'The Truce'.
73. *IT*, 09/Jul/1921.
74. *IT*, 13/Jul/1921.

Chapter 7 – The Times

1. TT, *The History of the Times*, (The Times, London, 1952), p. 439.
2. Ibid. p. 553.
3. Ibid.
4. *TT*, 04/April/1919: Editorial – 'The Irish Tangle'.
5. This vote was passed despite Wilson's objections.
6. *TT*, 24/June/1919: Also, the Irish Convention in Philadelphia had recently

sent a delegation to the Peace Conference. For American views of the situation in Ireland over these years see Carroll, F.M., *American Opinion and the Irish Question, 1910–1923*, (Gill & Macmillan, Dublin, 1978).

7. *History of the Times*, p. 556.

8. *History of The Times*: pp. 554–5. *The Times'* historian utilises a memo from Shaw to Steed dated 13/Jun/1919. Maurice Healy, the Irish Correspondent of *The Times* also worked on the articles. After publication in *The Times* the articles were collated into a booklet and published at the end of July 1919.

9. For a wider study of foreign correspondents in Ireland during this time see Walsh, Maurice, 'Foreign Correspondents and the Irish Revolution' (Unpublished PhD Thesis, Goldsmiths College, 2006). Walsh, a professional journalist, concentrates on a handful of English and American correspondents as well as what he calls literary tourists. He uses their work to examine the coverage of the conflict in Ireland but also to study debates within Britain and America about the role and practice of journalism. A recurring theme in his work is the shame felt by many English journalists at how they were effectively spokespersons for the Government during the First World War. Many of them were determined to recover the 'honour' of their profession in the years after.

10. *TT*, 30/Jun/1919: Report – 'Irish Peace – Is it Possible?'

11. *TT*, 02/Jul/1919: Report – 'Irish Peace – The Basis of Settlement.'

12. Ibid.

13. Ibid.

14. *TT*, 05/Jul/1919: Report – 'Irish Peace – Ulster.' *The Times* article on Ulster claimed that Ulster's case for 'self-determination is equally well grounded with that of the rest of Ireland'. However Herbert Shaw the main composer of the articles had expressed his belief that world interest 'should be focussed on Irish bickerings rather than Anglo-Irish relations'. This was probably a strong reason for his conviction that any settlement in Ireland should comprise the whole island.

15. *TT*, 13/Jul/1919: Report – 'Sir Edward Carson Defiant'.

16. *TT*, 14/Jul/1919.

17. *TT*, 23/Jul/1919: Editorial. *The Times* was perhaps emboldened by the praise rendered on their previous series of articles on an 'Irish Peace' by English newspapers, *The Irish Times* and the *Freeman's Journal*.

18. *TT*, 24/Jul/1919: Editorial and Report.

19. Ibid.

20. See the *Freeman's Journal, Irish Independent,* and the *Cork Examiner,* which were all dismissive of the plan due to fears that it would lead to

permanent partition. The *Irish Independent* termed the proposal 'Permanent Carsonism'. The *Cork Examiner* did concede that the proposals were 'an honest beginning' but a long way from an acceptable solution.

21. *IT*, 26/Jul/1919: Editorial – *The Irish Times* welcomed the proposals that have 'set our minds working in a new direction'. The paper however believed that the two legislatures could not work together as the southern legislature would 'be managed by the party which hates England'. This party, Sinn Féin, could not work to win northern unionist confidence, *The Irish Times* continued, and would thus create a permanent partition.
22. *TT*, 15/Sep/1919.
23. See the *History of The Times*, Part II, p. 561.
24. *TT*, 09/Oct/1919.
25. *TT*, 01/Dec/1919: Editorial – 'Irish Peace in Danger'. The article also claimed that the new military measures so derided by the nationalist Press had 'intensified the smouldering fires of disaffection'. 'The British people do not yet realise the futility of the acts carried out in their name but the Cabinet surely realize it'.
26. *TT*, 16/Dec/1919: Report – 'The State of Ireland'.
27. *The Times* had taken little notice of the first Dáil in January and did not link the events at Soloheadbeg in Tipperary to the Dáil.
28. *TT*, 07/Aug/1919: Editorial – The editorial also urged the British Government to make a settlement in Ireland.
29. *TT*, 15/Sep/1919: Report. The Land War was the name given to the massive rise in agrarian violence that occurred between the years 1879–1882 when landlords and agents were attacked and evictions were often violent affairs. The looting in Fermoy followed an IRA attack on an army patrol and has come to be considered the first reprisal of the conflict.
30. Laffan, *Resurrection*, p. 276.
31. *TT*, 27/Nov/1919.
32. *TT*, 10/Dec/1919: Report – 'The State of Ireland – Organised Disorder.'
33. Ibid.
34. *TT*, 20/Dec/1919.
35. *TT*, 23/Dec/1919: Editorial – 'Self-Government for Ireland'.
36. *TT*, 27/Dec/1919: See also *History of the Times Part II*, p. 550.
37. *TT*, 28/Feb/1920: Editorial – 'The Fourth Home Rule Bill'.
38. *TT*, 02/Mar/1920: Editorial – 'The Hour of Ulster'. See also editorial of 23/Feb/1920.
39. *TT*, 11/Mar/1920: Editorial – 'The Decision of Ulster'. Carson had at

this stage openly and strongly criticised the Northcliffe Press especially *The Times* and the *Daily Mail*, accusing Northcliffe of being a 'turn-coat'. See *The Times*, 03/Sep/1919.

40. *Morning Post*, 13/Mar/1920.

41. *TT*, 22/Mar/1920: Editorial – 'The Cork Murders'. For further example see almost any editorial dealing with the Irish Administration over the previous year.

42. *TT*, 24/Mar/1920.

43. *TT*, 27/Mar/1920: Editorial – 'Irish Assassinations'. See also the report on the shooting of Bell, which gave substantial exposure to the *Freeman's Journal* reports on Bell's work. See also the extensive report on the 'Brutal Dublin Murder', 27/Mar/1920.

44. *TT*, 06/April/1920: Editorial – 'The Outbreak in Ireland'. The editorial concluded with a plea to amend the Home Rule Bill 'in spirit and in form'.

45. *TT*, 13/May/1920: Editorial – 'Murder in Ireland'.

46. *TT*, 19/May/1920.

47. *TT*, 07/July/1920: Editorial – 'The Irish Peril'.

48. *TT*, 04/Aug/1920.

49. *History of The Times*, Part II, p. 561.

50. *TT*, 06/Aug/1920.

51. *TT*, 30/Aug/1920: Editorial – 'The Lord Mayor of Cork'.

52. *TT*, 23/Sep/1920: See the detailed report on Balbriggan. See also George Russell's letter to the paper on 23/Aug/1920 in which he detailed Crown attacks on creameries across Ireland. Russell implored the editor 'to use the powerful influence of your paper to draw attention to the operation of a most dangerous policy in Ireland'.

53. *TT*, 28/Sep/1920: Editorial – 'Perilous Silence'.

54. See for example the editorial of 30/Sep/1920 – 'A National Disgrace'. 'The wreckings at Balbriggan, Tuam, Trim and Mallow are but the most flagrant instances of a system deliberately organized'.

55. *TT*, 30/Aug/1920.

56. *TT*, 26/Oct/1920: Editorial – 'The Death of Alderman MacSwiney'.

57. Macready, *Annals*, p. 494. *The Times* printed extracts from the *Irish Bulletin* concerning Sinn Féin claims of forgery in Dublin Castle designed to implicate Sinn Féin members in the death of Tomás MacCurtain. See *The Times*, 14/Sep/1920.

58. Lee Thompson, J., *Northcliffe: Press Baron in Politics, 1865–1922*, (John Murray, London, 2000), p.341. See also Wickham Steed, Henry, *Through Thirty Years 1892–1922*, (William Heinemann, London, 1924), pp. 350–2.

59. *History of The Times*, Part II, p. 563. See also Boyce, *Englishmen*, p. 81. Despite the paper's claims for 'justice' for Ireland it was distrusted by republicans. See Hogan, *Glorious Years*, p. 266. Here Hogan claims that '*The Times* all through the British terror in Ireland played in its news columns an ignoble part'.

60. *TT*, 03/Nov/1920: Editorial – 'Irish Crime and British Reprisals'. See also 08/Nov/1920 which criticises the Black and Tans.

61. *TT*, 08/Nov/1920.

62. *TT*, 22/Nov/1920: Editorial – 'The Dublin Murders'. The editorial briefly mentioned the deaths in Croke Park.

63. *TT*, 22/Nov/1920: Editorial – 'The Dublin Murders'.

64. *TT*, 30/Nov/1920.

65. *TT*, 01/Dec/1920: Editorial – 'Facing the Facts'.

66. *TT*, 13/Dec/1920.

67. Ibid. See also editorial of 14/Dec/1920 which demanded an investigation and also supported Bishop Cohalan's excommunication of those involved in ambushes. It later criticised other Irish Bishops for not issuing similar statements in support of Cohalan – 05/Jan/1921.

68. *TT*, 23/Dec/1920.

69. *TT*, 18/Jan/1921.

70. *TT*, 29/Jan/1921.

71. Ibid. There is no doubt that Lloyd George knew of reprisals and privately supported them. For evidence of this see Townshend, *Campaign*, pp. 100–01 and an essay by George Boyce in Taylor, *Twelve Essays*. It is not unreasonable to assume that Steed would have known this.

72. *TT*, 11/Feb/1921: Editorial – 'The Irish Deadlock'.

73. Ibid. This editorial was highly praised in the following day's *Freeman's Journal*.

74. Churchill Archive Centre, CHAR 2/111/120–124: Steed to Churchill, 28/Dec/1920.

75. *History of the Times*, p. 569.

76. Taylor, S.J., *The Great Outsiders: Northcliffe, Rothermere and the Daily Mail*, (Weidenfeld & Nicolson, London, 1996), p. 197.

77. Ibid,. p. 196.

78. *TT*, 26/Mar/1920.

79. Ibid. Northcliffe had given a similar interview to the French *Journal des débats* in November 1920. His article in April somewhat contradicts the claims made by the historian of *The Times* that Northcliffe was worried about Steed's Irish policy and that, in March 1921, this led to a conflict between the two men but that Steed won the right to continue his

policy. According to the historian, Northcliffe was secretly planning to sell the paper and was worried that the controversy over the paper's Irish policy would adversely affect the sale. See *History of The Times*, pp. 574–5.

80. *History of The Times*, p. 573. See also Macready, *Annals*, pp. 494–5.

81. Ibid.

82. Costello, *Irish Revolution*, p. 216.

83. *American Commission Interim Report*, p. 13. The final report was published in July. It was a far more detailed version than the interim Report, but just as critical of the British Government and the Crown forces.

84. See Carroll, F.M., '"All standards of human conduct": the American Commission on conditions in Ireland' (*Eire–Ireland*, Vol. xvi, No. 4, 1981).

85. *TT*, 23/Mar/1921: Editorial – 'The Madness of Sinn Fein'.

86. *TT*, 06/Apr/1921: Editorial – 'Irish Peace'.

87. *TT*, 14/Apr/1921: Editorial – 'The Irish Elections'. See also 20/Apr/1921.

88. *TT*, 06/May/1921: Editorial – 'An alternative policy'.

89. *History of The Times*, pp. 571–2.

90. Ibid,, p. 575.

91. Smuts was in London for an Imperial Conference. See *History of The Times*, pp. 574–8 and Costello, *Irish Revolution*, pp. 212–21 for an account of the creation of King George's speech.

92. *TT*, 20/Jun/1921.

93. *TT*, 22/Jun/1921: Editorial – 'Foreground and Background'.

94. For full text of the speech see Mitchell, Arthur and O'Snodaigh, Pádraig, *Irish Political Documents: 1916–1949*, (Irish Academic Press, Dublin, 1985), pp. 111–12.

95. *TT*, 23/Jun/1921: Editorial – 'Playing the Game'. See also *History of The Times*, pp. 577–8. On 25 June Stamfordham contacted Steed to say 'he had been commanded by the King to thank the editor for the great help which *The Times* had given'.

96. *TT*, 16/Jul/1921: Editorial – 'The Irish Conference'.

97. *TT*, 04/Jul/1921.

98. *TT*, 12/Jul/1921: Editorial – 'The Path to Peace'.

Conclusions

1. Walsh, *Correspondents*, pp 98–99. Walsh makes a very interesting point about the word 'frightfulness'. This word occurs with regularity across the press in these years, often in tandem with 'Prussianism'. The word had very specific connotations in the post-war world. It was the English translation of the German word 'schrecklichkeit'. Schrecklichkeit had been the openly

proclaimed policy of the Germans in Belgium during the War. This policy involved the murder of civilians, burning of houses and the terrorisation of local populations. So when the word 'frightfulness' was used about British actions in Ireland it was meant as a direct comparison with the actions of the Germans in Belgium.

2. *MG*, 29/Sep/1920.
3. Mazower, Mark, *Dark Continent*, (Penguin, London, 1999), p. 2.
4. Townshend, *Campaign*, p. 118.
5. Wilson, Trevor (Ed), *The Political Diaries of C.P. Scott*, (Collins, London, 1970), p. 377. Harold Spender informed Scott of his meeting with Lloyd George, 23/Aug/1919.
6. CO 904 168 (901), (09/May/1921). Note of meeting.
7. Briollay, *Rebellion*: p. 52.
8. Mitchell, *Government*, p. 203.
9. Boyce, *Englishmen*, p. 95.
10. There has been a lengthy and ongoing debate on the nature of British rule in Ireland and when or whether Ireland was or was not a colony. Readers interested in this debate would do well to begin with Stephen Howe's superb *Ireland and Empire: colonial legacies in Irish History and Culture*, (Oxford University Press, Oxford, 2000).
11. Hopkinson, *Independence*, p. 182.
12. Callwell, *Wilson*, pp. 253–54. Lloyd George, he said, had two options; 'one is to clear out of Ireland and the other is to knock Sinn Fein on the head' (17/Jul/1920).
13. Ibid., p. 263.
14. Sheehan, *British Voices*, p. 151. Letter to Lieutenant General A.C. Percival, 14/Oct/1923.
15. Mockaitis, Thomas, R, *British Counterinsurgency, 1919–1960*, (Macmillan London, 1990) p. 17.
16. Omissi, David, 'Baghdad and British Bombers', (The *Guardian*, 19/Jan/1991). There was disquiet among some of the British army and the Colonial Office at the tactics used against the Iraqis. But that fact that there was no press attention was a contributory factor in the unrestrained aerial bombing of defenceless villages by the RAF.
17. *FJ*, 23/Mar/1921: quotation from the *Liverpool Post* of 22/Mar/1921.
18. Farrar, Front, pp. 219–30. Walsh, *Correspondents*, Chapter 3.

Appendix I

An example of Censorship under DORA in 1919

These were reports prepared by the newspapers and intended for publication. The portions with the brackets were deleted by the Censor.

Report One

At a meeting in connection with the Sinn Fein organisation, at Armagh City Hall, Mr Edward Donnelly, president of the local Sinn Fein Club said:

['They could make life unpleasant for these paid agents of the Government. They should see that retired R.I.C. men got no jobs in their midst, and in the days of the Land League, the people SHOULD BOYCOTT THEM in the church, in the street and make life so unpleasant for these men that they would soon recognise that they were up against a determined people.']

Report Two

At a demonstration for returned prisoners, on St. Patrick's Day, at Drogheda, Mr Walsh said:

['So far from removing physical force or any other mode of agitation we are at one with Mitchell when he said: "If I could grasp the fires of hell in my hands I would hurl them in the face of my country's enemies". We renounce no means of warfare with England. We hold ourselves free to adopt any means of furthering our cause which God places within our reach. As long as England argues the question with the prison and the convict ship, we cannot be expected to confine ourselves to what they may deem constitutional methods. And every means may be made unconstitutional by Act of Parliament. If England will pledge to abstain from brute force, so will I, but if not, I'll not. Stones loose and dogs tied is no bargain, away with the stones and unmuzzle the world Dogs.']

APPENDIX II

Public Information Branch around the time of the Truce – July 1921

Dublin Castle:
Basil Clarke: General supervision of Dublin and London Branches; editing of matter issued to press; interviewing of press correspondents; collection of information for issue to the public.
Captain C.P. Brown: Writings of reports and issue of matter to press. Dealt specially with military information and maintained liaison with GHQ.
DI Stuart Menzies: As above. Dealt solely with Police information and maintained liaison with DMP, RIC and Auxiliary Police.
Mr Stuart Bellhouse: Helped both of the above in the writing of reports; wrote also special political and other notes under Basil Clarke's direction.
Mr Worger: Press photographer.
Miss Hoey: Shorthand typist and secretarial duties for Mr Basil Clarke.
Miss Archer: Shorthand typist to Messrs. Brown, Menzies and Bellhouse.

Army GHQ Dublin:
Percy J. Russell: Wrote articles for press and collected military information for dispatch to and issue by PIB.
Captain J. W. Brooke: Official Military photographer.

Irish Office London:
Major Street: General supervision under direction from Dublin. Interviewed press correspondents, London editors, etc.
Captain Garro-Jones: Assistant to Major Street. Similar duties.
Miss Housby: Shorthand typist.

Others involved in publicity/propaganda (separate from the PIB):
Major R. Marians: Officer in the Army GHQ press office in Dublin.

Captain C. Tower: Assisted Major Marians. Later worked as press liaison in Army GHQ Belfast.

Major C. Foulkes: From April 1921 worked with Marians in Military GHQ.

M. Loughnane: Personal Press Secretary for Chief Secretary, Hamar Greenwood.

C.V. Philips: Worked in Foreign Office in London with brief covering Ireland. Maintained contacts with Major Street.

Captain H. Pollard: Press Officer of the Information Section of the Police Authority.

Captain C. Darling: Secretary of the Information Section of the Police Authority.

APPENDIX III

Dáil Éireann and Sinn Féin Propaganda Structures
January 1919–July 1921:

Dáil Éireann Department of Propaganda (from March 1921 Department of Publicity)

DIRECTOR OF PROPAGANDA:
Laurence Ginnell: January 1919–June 1919 (arrested by Crown forces).
Desmond Fitzgerald: June 1919–February 1921 (arrested by Crown forces).
Erskine Childers: February 1921–August 1921.

DEPARTMENTAL STAFF:
Frank Gallagher: Chief Assistant to the Director of Propaganda 1919–1921 (played a leading role in the daily writing of the *Irish Bulletin*).
Kathleen Napoli McKenna: Compiled and printed daily issues of *Irish Bulletin*.
Art O'Brien: Press Liaison in London.
Cumann na mBan members provided reports and distributed the *Irish Bulletin*.

SINN FÉIN PUBLICITY DIRECTOR:
Robert Brennan: Worked in *Irish Bulletin* until early 1921 (moved to Department of Foreign Affairs).

IRA PUBLICITY DIRECTOR:
Piaras Béaslaí: Edited *An t-Óglach* 1919–1921 (imprisoned March to September 1919).

IMPORTANT FOREIGN REPRESENTATIVES:

Count George Plunkett: Minister for Foreign Affairs.

George Gavan Duffy: Dáil Éireann representative in Paris 1919–September 1920; Roving Ambassador in Europe until spring 1921: Representative in Rome.

Seán T. O'Kelly: Representative in Paris until 1922.

Dr Patrick McCartan: Representative of Irish Republic in America until March 1920: Representative in Russia until 1921.

SOURCES AND BIBLIOGRAPHY

Primary Sources

Cork
CORK CITY AND CORK COUNTY PUBLIC LIBRARIES
Microfilm Newspaper Collections

UNIVERSITY COLLEGE CORK
Houses of the Oireachtas – Parliamentary Debates
Colonial Office Papers:
Censorship Reports (CO 904/167)
Judicial Proceedings, Enquiries and Miscellaneous Records (CO 904/165)
Public Administration files (CO 904/168)
Sinn Féin and Republican Suspects (CO 904/193–216)
Sir John Anderson Papers (CO 904/188)

Dublin
Military Archives : Cathal Brugha Barracks
Mrs Erskine Childers Collection (CD/6)
Monsignor Michael J. Curran Collection (CD/131)
Dorothy McArdle Collection (CD/9)
Bureau of Military History (BMH) Witness Statements (WS):
Piaras Béaslaí WS 261 & WS 675
Máire Ní Bhriain WS 363
Robert Brennan WS 125, 779 & 790 (includes annotated copy of 'Allegiance')
George Gavan Duffy WS 381
Bernard James Golden WS 281
Michael Knightly WS 834 & 835
Kathleen McKenna Napoli WS 643
Vera McDonnell WS 1050

John O'Donovan WS 1649
Desmond Ryan WS 725

NATIONAL ARCHIVES
Dáil Éireann Papers (DE/2)
Department of Foreign Affairs Papers (DFA)
Sinn Féin Papers

NATIONAL LIBRARY OF IRELAND
Art O'Brien Papers (MSS 8,427)
Piaras Béaslaí Papers (MSS 33,911 to MSS 33,987)
Erskine Childers Papers (MSS 15,444)
Frank Gallagher Papers (MSS, 18,346 & MSS 18,388)
Kathleen McKenna Napoli Papers (MSS 22,494 to MSS 22,786)

TRINITY COLLEGE DUBLIN
Erskine Childers Papers (MSS 7808)
Frank Gallagher Papers (MSS 10050)

UNIVERSITY COLLEGE DUBLIN
Ernest Blythe Papers (P24)
Eamon de Valera Papers (P150)
George Gavan Duffy Papers (P152)
Desmond & Mabel Fitzgerald Papers (P80)
Seán Lester Papers (P203)
Richard Mulcahy Papers (P7)
Desmond Ryan Papers (LA10)

London
GOLDSMITHS COLLEGE LIBRARY
Theses Collection

PARLIAMENTARY ARCHIVES
Lloyd George Papers (LG/F15 – LG/F/24)

UK NATIONAL ARCHIVES
Colonial Office Files (As above)

Pamphlets
Childers, Erskine, A Strike-Breaking army at Work, (1919).
– Military Rule in Ireland, (1920).

– Is Ireland a danger to England, (1921).
Dáil Éireann, Adresse aux Représentants des Nations étrangers, (1921).
– Authority of Dáil Éireann (1920).
– The Constructive Work of Dáil Éireann: Nos. 1, 2 and 3, (1921).
– Two years of English atrocities in Ireland, (1920).
Horgan, J. J., *The Grammar of Anarchy*, (1919).
Irish Labour Party, *Who Burnt Cork City?* (1921).
O' Hegarty, P. S., Ulster: A Brief Statement of Fact, (1919).
The Times, Irish Peace – A Test of British Statesmanship: A suggested Solution, (1919).

Reports

American Commission on Conditions in Ireland: Interim Report, (1921).
American Commission on Conditions in Ireland: Final Report, (1921).
Report of the Labour Commission to Ireland, (1921).

Newspapers

An t-Óglach
Cork Examiner
Daily Mail
Daily News
Freeman's Journal
Irish Bulletin
Irish Independent
Manchester Guardian
Morning Post
Nationality
The Irish Times
The Times
Weekly Summary
Westminster Gazette

Journals and articles

Ainsworth, John S., 'Kevin Barry, the incident at Monk's Bakery and the making of an Irish Republican Legend', (*History*, No. 87, 2002).
Benton, Sarah, 'Women Disarmed: the militarization of politics in Ireland 1913–1923', (*Feminist Review*, No. 50, Summer 1995).
Bew, Paul, 'Moderate Nationalism and the Irish Revolution, 1916–1923', (*The Historical Journal*, Vol. 42, No. 3, 1999).
Bielenberg, Andy, 'Entrepreneurship, power and public opinion in Ireland: the

career of William Martin Murphy', (www.ucc.ie/chronicon No. 2, 1998).

Boyce, D. George, 'British Opinion, Ireland, and the War, 1916–1918', (*The Historical Journal*, Vol. 17, No. 3, September 1974).

Brindley, Ronan, Woodrow Wilson, 'Self-Determination and Ireland, 1918–1919: A view from the Irish Newspapers', (*Éire-Ireland*, Vol. xxiii, No. 4, 1988).

Carey, Tim & de Burca, Marcus, 'Bloody Sunday: New Evidence', (*History Ireland*, Vol. 11, No. 2, summer 2003).

Carroll, F.M., '"All Standards of Human conduct" The American Commission on Conditions in Ireland, 1920–1921', (*Éire-Ireland*, Vol. xvi, No. 4, 1981).

– 'The American Committee for Relief in Ireland, 1920–1922', (*Irish Historical Studies*, Vol. xxiii, No.89, May 1982).

Costello, Francis, 'The Republican Courts and the Decline of British Rule in Ireland, 1919–1921', (*Éire-Ireland*, xxv: 2, 1990).

Costigan, Giovanni, 'The Anglo-Irish Conflict, 1919–1922', (*Irish University Review,* Spring, 1968).

Curran, Joseph M., 'Lloyd George and the Irish settlement, 1921–1922', (*Éire-Ireland*, Vol. vii, No. 2, 1972).

Davis, Richard, 'Ulster Protestants and the Sinn Fein Press, 1914–1922', (*Éire-Ireland*, Vol. xv, No. 4, 1980).

Davis Richard, 'The Advocacy of Passive Resistance in Ireland, 1916–1922', (*Anglo-Irish Studies*, No. 3, 1977).

Doherty, M.A., 'Kevin Barry and the Anglo-Irish Propaganda War', (*Irish Historical Studies*, Vol. xxxii, No. 126, November 2000).

English, Richard, '"The Inborn Hate of Things English": Ernie O'Malley and the Irish Revolution 1916–1923', (*Past and Present*, No. 151, 1996).

Farrell, Brian, 'A Note on the Dail Constitution, 1919,' (*The Irish Jurist*, Vol. IV, 1969).

Fitzpatrick, David, 'Strikes in Ireland, 1914–1921', (*Saothar*, No. 6, 1981).

Fox, Seamus, 'The Kilmichael Ambush: a review of background, controversies and effects', (Seamus Fox webpage, www.dcu.ie, 2005).

Glandon, Virginia E., 'Index of Irish newspapers, 1900–1922 (part II)', (*Éire-Ireland*, Vol. xii, No. 1, 1977).

– 'The Irish Press and Revolutionary Irish Nationalism', (*Éire-Ireland*, Vol. xvi, No. 1, 1981).

Hachey, Thomas E., 'The British Foreign Office and New Perspectives on the Irish Issue in Anglo-American Relations 1919–1921', (*Éire-Ireland*, Vol. vii, No. 2, 1972).

Hart, Peter, 'The Geography of Revolution in Ireland 1917–1923', (*Past and Present*, No. 3, 1997).

Sources and Bibliography

Hopkinson, Michael, 'President Woodrow Wilson and the Irish Question', (*Studia Hibernica*, No. 27, 1993).

Inoue, Keiko, 'Dáil Propaganda and the Irish Self-Determination League of Great Britain during the Anglo-Irish War', (*Irish Studies Review*, Vol. 6, No. 1, 1998).

Kavanagh, Seán, 'The Irish Volunteers Intelligence Organisation', (*Capuchin Annual*, 1969).

Larkin, Felix M., '"A Great Daily Organ": the *Freeman's Journal*, 1763–1924', (*History Ireland*, Vol. 14, No. 3 May/June 2006).

Leeson, David, 'Death in the Afternoon: The Croke Park massacre, 21 November 1920', (*Canadian Journal of History*, April 2003).

Lowe, W.J., 'The War against the RIC, 1919–1921', (*Éire-Ireland*, No. xxxii, Fall–Winter 2002).

Kenneally, Ian, 'Reports from a Bleeding Ireland: the *Cork Examiner* during the Irish War of Independence', (*Cork Historical and Archaeological Journal*, 2003).

McKenna, Kathleen, 'The *Irish Bulletin*', (*Capuchin Annual*, 1970).

Murphy, Richard, 'Walter Long and the Making of the Government of Ireland Act, 1919–1920', (*Irish Historical Studies*, Vol. xxv, No. 97, May 1986).

Newsinger, John, '"I bring not Peace but a Sword":The religious motif in the Irish War of Independence', (*Journal of Contemporary History*, Vol. 13, No. 3, Jul. 1978).

O'Fiaich, Tomas, 'The Catholic Clergy and the Independence Movement', (*Capuchin Annual*, 1970).

Russell, Liam, 'Some Activities in Cork City, 1920–21', (*Capuchin Annual*, 1970).

Ryan, Louise, '"Drunken Tans": Representations of Sex and Violence in the Anglo-Irish War, 1919–1921', (*Feminist Review*, No. 66, Autumn 2000).

- '"Furies" and "Die-Hards":Women and Irish Republicanism in the early Twentieth Century', (*Gender and History*, Vol. 11, No. 2, July 1999).

Seedorf, Martin F., 'Defending Reprisals: Sir Hamar Greenwood and "the Troubles", 1920–1921', (*Éire-Ireland*, Vol. xxv, No. 4, 1990).

Snoddy, Oliver, 'Aspects of English Rule in Ireland', (*Capuchin Annual*, 1970).

Stapelton, William J., 'Michael Collins' Squad', (*Capuchin Annual*, 1969).

Sullivan, Dennis M., 'Eamon de Valera and the Forces of Opposition in America, 1919–1920', (*Éire-Ireland*, Vol. xix, No. 2, 1984).

Sweeney, George, 'Irish Hunger Strikers and the Cult of Self Sacrifice', (*Journal of Contemporary History*, Vol. 28, No. 3, July 1993).

Townshend, Charles, 'The Irish Railway Strike of 1920: Industrial action and civil resistance in the struggle for independence', (*Irish Historical Studies*, Vol. 21).

Walker, Graham, "'The Irish Dr Goebbels": Frank Gallagher and Irish Republican Propaganda', (*Journal of Contemporary History*, Vol. 27, No. 1, January 1992).

Books and Theses

Abbott, Richard, *Police Casualties in Ireland 1919–1922*, (Mercier Press, Dublin, 2000).

Augusteijn, Joost (Ed), *The Irish Revolution – 1913–1923*, (Palgrave, London, 2002).

Anderson, David M. & Killingray, David (Eds), *Policing and De-colonisation: Politics, Nationalism and the Police, 1917–1965*, (Manchester University Press, Manchester, 1992).

Andrew, Christopher & Dilks, David (Eds), *The Missing Dimension*, (Macmillan, London, 1984).

Ashe, Brendan, 'The Development of the IRA's concepts of Guerrilla Warfare, 1917–1921', (Unpublished MA Thesis, University College Cork, 1999).

Ayerst, David, *Biography of a Newspaper: the Manchester Guardian*, (Guardian Newspapers, London, 1971).

Barry, Tom, *Guerrilla Days in Ireland*, (Anvil Books, Dublin, 1991).

Bell, J. Bowyer, *The Secret Army: The Irish Republican Army, 1916–1979*, (Poolbeg, Dublin, 1990).

Bennett Richard, *The Black and Tans*, (Barnes & Noble, New York, 1995).

Borgonovo, John, *Spies, Informers and the 'Anti-Sinn Féin Society'*, (Irish Academic Press, Dublin, 2006).

Boyce D.G., *Englishmen and Irish Troubles*, (Jonathan Cape, London, 1972).

– *The Revolution in Ireland, 1879–1923*, (Macmillan, London, 1988).

Boyle, Andrew, *The Riddle of Erskine Childers*, (Hutchinson, London, 1977).

Breen, Dan, *My Fight for Irish Freedom*, (Anvil Books, Dublin, 1981).

Brennan, Robert, *Allegiance*, (Browne & Nolan, Dublin, 1950).

Brewer, John D., *The Royal Irish Constabulary – An oral history*, (Institute of Irish Studies, Belfast, 1990).

Briollay, Sylvain, *Ireland in Rebellion*, (Talbot Press, Dublin, 1922).

Callwell, C.E. (Ed), *Field-Marshal Sir Henry Wilson: His Life and Diaries*, (Cassell, London, 1927).

Campbell, Colm, *Emergency Law in Ireland, 1918–1925*, (Oxford University Press, Oxford, 1994).

Carey, Tim, *Hanged for Ireland – A Documentary History*, (Blackwater Press, Dublin, 2001).

Carroll, Francis, M., *American Opinion and the Irish Question*, 1910–1923, (Gill

& Macmillan, Dublin, 1978).

Carruthers, Susan L., *Winning Hearts and Minds*, (Leicester University Press, London, 1995).

Churchill, Winston, *The World Crisis – The Aftermath*, (Thornton Butterworth, London, 1929).

Coogan, Tim Pat, *Michael Collins*, (Arrow, London, 1991).

– *De Valera, Long Fellow – Long Shadow*, (Hutchinson, London, 1997).

Costello, Francis J., *Enduring the Most*, (Brandon, Dingle 1995).

– *The Irish Revolution and its Aftermath 1916–1923*, (Irish Academic Press, Dublin, 2003).

– *Michael Collins – In his own words*, (Gill & Macmillan, Dublin, 1997).

Cox, Tom, *Damned Englishman*, (Exposition Press, New York, 1975).

Crozier, F.P., *Ireland for Ever*, (Cedric Chivers, London, 1971).

Cullen, L.M., *Eason & Son – A History*, (Eason & Son, Dublin, 1989).

Dangerfield, G., *The Damnable Question*, (Quartet Books, London, 1976).

Davis, Richard, *Arthur Griffith*, (Dundalgan Press, Dundalk, 1976).

Deasy, Liam, *Towards Ireland Free*, (Mercier Press, Cork, 1973).

Doherty, Gabriel & Keogh, Dermot (Eds), *Michael Collins and the Making of the Irish State*, (Mercier Press, Cork, 1998).

Doherty, J.E. & Hickey, D.J., *A Chronology of Irish History since 1500*, (Gill & Macmillan, Dublin, 1989).

Downes, G.T., 'A Consideration and Evaluation of the Anglo-Irish Propaganda War', (Unpublished M.A. Thesis, Keele University, 1985).

Duffy, Seán (Ed), *Atlas of Irish History*, (Gill & Macmillan, Dublin, 2000).

Duggan John, *A History of the Irish Army*, (Gill & Macmillan, Dublin, 1991).

Dwyer, T. Ryle, *Michael Collins – the man who won the war*, (Mercier Press, Cork, 1990).

– *The Squad: the intelligence operations of Michael Collins*, (Mercier Press, Cork, 2005).

– *Tans, Terror and Troubles: Kerry's real fighting story*, (Mercier Press, Cork, 2001).

English, Richard, *Irish Freedom: the history of nationalism in Ireland*, (Macmillan, London, 2006).

English, Richard, & Walker, Graham (Ed), *Unionism in Modern Ireland*, (Gill & Macmillan, Dublin, 1996).

Elliot-Bateman, M., Ellis, J. & Bowden, Tom, *Retreat to Revolution*, (Manchester University Press, Manchester, 1974).

Fanning, R., Kennedy, M., Keogh, D. and O' Halpin, E. (Eds), *Documents on Irish Foreign Policy; volume 1, 1919–1922*, (Royal Irish Academy, Dublin, 1998).

Fanning, Ronan, *Independent Ireland,* (Gill & Macmillan, Dublin, 1987).

Farrar, Martin J., *News from the Front: War correspondents on the Western Front 1914–1918*, (Sutton, Gloucestershire, 1999).

Farrell, Brian (Ed), *Communications and Community in Ireland*, (Mercier Press, Cork, 1984).

– *The Creation of the Dail*, (Blackwater Press, Dublin, 1984).

Ferriter, Diarmaid, *The Transformation of Ireland 1900–2000*, (Profile Books, London, 2005).

Figgis, Darrell, *Recollections of the Irish War*, (Ernest Benn Ltd., London, 1927).

Fitzpatrick, David (Ed), *Revolution? Ireland 1917–1923*, (Trinity History Workshop, Dublin, 1990).

– *Politics and Irish Life, 1913–1921*, (Cork University Press, Cork, 1998).

Foster, Roy, *Modern Ireland: 1600 – 1972*, (Penguin, London, 1989).

Foy, Michael T., *Michael Collins's Intelligence War*, (Sutton, Gloucestershire, 2006).

Garvin, Tom, *The Evolution of Irish Nationalist Politics*, (Gill & Macmillan, Dublin, 1981).

– *1922: The birth of Irish Democracy*, (Gill & Macmillan, Dublin, 1996).

Glandon, Virginia E., *Arthur Griffith and the Advanced Nationalist Press, 1900 – 1922*, (Peter Lang, New York, 1985).

Gleeson, James, *Bloody Sunday*, (Peter Davies, London, 1962).

Griffiths, Denis, *Fleet Street: five hundred years of the press*, (British Library, London, 2006).

Harnett, Mossie, *Victory and Woe*, (University College Dublin Press, Dublin, 2002).

Hart, Peter, *The IRA and its Enemies*, (Oxford University Press, Oxford, 1998).

– *The IRA at War: 1916–1923*, (OUP, Oxford, 2005).

– *Mick: the real Michael Collins*, (OUP, Oxford, 2005).

Hart, Peter (Ed), *Narratives: British Intelligence in Ireland*, (Cork University Press, Cork, 2002).

Hogan, David (pseudonym of Frank Gallagher), *The Four Glorious Years*, (Irish Press, Dublin, 1953).

Hopkinson, Michael, *The War of Independence*, (Gill & Macmillan, Dublin, 2004).

Hopkinson, Michael (Ed), *The Last Days of Dublin Castle*, Irish Academic Press, Dublin, 1999).

Houses of the Oireachtas, *Parliamentary Debates: 1919–2002*, DVD database, (Houses of the Oireachtas, Dublin, 2002). These are also available online.

Howe, Stephen, *Ireland and Empire: colonial legacies in Irish history and culture*, (Oxford University Press, Oxford, 2000).

Inoue, Keiko, 'Sinn Féin and Dáil Propaganda', (Unpublished MPhil Thesis, University College Dublin, 1995).

I.O. (pseudonym of C.J.C. Street), *The Administration of Ireland*, 1920, (Phillip Allan, London, 1921).

Jackson, Alvin, *Sir Edward Carson*, (Historical Association of Ireland, Dublin 1993).

James, Lawrence, *The Rise and Fall of the British Empire*, (Little Brown, London, 1995).

Jones, Thomas, *Whitehall Diary*, Volume 3: Ireland 1918–1925, (Oxford University Press, Oxford, 1971).

Joy, Sinead, *The IRA in Kerry 1916–1921*, (The Collins Press, Cork, 2004).

Jeffery, Keith, *The British Army and the Crisis of Empire, 1918–1922*, (Manchester University Press, Manchester, 1984).

Kee, Robert, *The Green Flag, Volume 3: Ourselves Alone*, (London, 1976).

Keogh, Dermot, *Ireland & Europe: 1919–1948*, (Gill & Macmillan, Dublin, 1988).

– *The Vatican, the Bishops and Irish Politics, 1919–1939*, (Cambridge University Press, Cambridge, 1986).

Kotsonouris, Mary, *Retreat from Revolution: the Dail Courts, 1920–1924*, (Irish Academic Press, Dublin, 1994).

Laffan, Michael, *The Resurrection of Ireland*, (Cambridge University Press, Cambridge, 1999).

Lee, J.J., *Ireland – 1912–1985*, (Cambridge University Press, Cambridge, 1989).

Lee Thompson, J., *Northcliffe: Press Baron in Politics 1865–1922*, (John Murray, London, 2000).

Legg, Marie-Louise, *Newspapers and Nationalism: The Irish Provincial Press, 1850–1892*, (Four Courts Press, Dublin, 1999).

Lester, D., *A Guide to Collections in North America, Ireland and Britain*, (Greenwood Press, Connecticut, 1987).

Macardle, Dorothy, *The Irish Republic*, (Wolfhound Press, Dublin, 2005).

Macready, Nevil, *Annals of an Active Life*, (Hutchinson, London, 1924).

Mansergh, Nicholas, *The Unresolved Question*, (Yale University Press, London, 1991).

Martin, Hugh, *Ireland in Insurrection*, (Daniel O' Connor, London, 1921).

Maye, Brian, *Arthur Griffith*, (Griffith College Publications, Dublin, 1997).

McBride, Lawrence W., *The Greening of Dublin Castle*, (Catholic University of America Press, Washington, 1991).

McCarthy, Cal, *Cumann na mBan and the Irish Revolution*, (The Collins Press, Cork, 2007).

McColgan, James, *British Policy and the Irish Administration, 1920–1922*, (Allen and Unwin, London, 1983).

McDowell, R. B., *The Church of Ireland: 1869–1969*, (Routledge, London, 1975).

Mitchell, Arthur, *Revolutionary Government in Ireland*, (Gill & Macmillan, Dublin, 1995).

Mitchell, Arthur & O'Snodaigh, Padraig, *Irish Political Documents: 1916–1949*, (Irish Academic Press, Dublin, 1985).

Mockaitis, Thomas R., *British Counterinsurgency, 1919–1960*, (Macmillan, London, 1990).

Mowat, Charles L., *Britain between the Wars: 1919–1940*, (Methuen, London, 1955).

Morrisey, Thomas, *William Martin Murphy*, (Historical Association of Ireland, Dublin, 1997).

Murphy Brian P., *The Origins & Organisation of British Propaganda in Ireland 1920*, (Aubane Historical Society, Cork, 2006).

O'Broin, Leon, *W.E. Wylie and the Irish Revolution*, (Gill & Macmillan, Dublin, 1989).

O'Connor, Ulick, *The Troubles*, (Mandarin Books, London, 1996).

O'Donovan, Donal, *Kevin Barry and his Time*, (Glendale, Dublin, 1989).

O'Farrell, Padraic, *Who's Who in the Irish war of Independence and Civil War, 1916–1923*, (Lilliput Press, Dublin, 1997).

O'Halpin, Eunan, *The Decline of the Union, British Government in Ireland 1892 – 1920*, (Gill & Macmillan, Dublin, 1987).

O'Leary, Cornelius and Maume, Patrick, *Controversial Issues in Anglo-Irish Relations, 1910–1921*, (Four Courts Press, Dublin 2004).

O'Malley, Ernie, *On Another Man's Wound*, (Anvil Books, Dublin, 1979).

– *Raids and Rallies*, (Anvil Books, Dublin, 1982).

Oram, Hugh, *The Newspaper Book*, (MO Books, Dublin, 1983).

Parkinson, Alan F., *Belfast's Unholy War*, (Four Courts Press, Dublin, 2004).

Phillips, W. Allison, *The Revolution in Ireland, 1906–1923*, (Longman, London, 1923).

Philpin, C.H.E. (Ed), *Nationalism and Popular Protest in Ireland*, (Cambridge University Press, Cambridge, 1987).

Piper, Leonard, *Dangerous Waters: The life and death of Erskine Childers*, (Hambledon & London, London, 2003).

Pollard, H.B.C., *The Secret Societies of Ireland: their rise and progress*, (Philip Allan & Co., London, 1922).

Rees, Russell, *Ireland 1905–1925 – Volume 1*, (Colourpoint Books, Newtownards, 1998).

Ryan, Desmond, *Remembering Sion*, (Arthur Barker, London, 1934).

– *Seán Treacy and the Third Tipperary Brigade IRA*, (Anvil Books, Tralee, 1945).

Ryan, Meda, *Tom Barry – IRA Freedom Fighter*, (Mercier Press, Cork, 2006).

Sheehan, William, *British Voices from the Irish War of Independence*, 1918–1921, (The Collins Press, Cork, 2005).

South Gate Books, *The Burning of Cork City*, (South Gate Books, Cork, 1978).

Stewart, Ian & Carruthers, Susan L., *War, Culture and the Media*, (Flicks Books, London, 1996).

Street, C.J.C., *Ireland in 1921*, (Philip Allan, London, 1922).

Taylor, A.J.P. (Ed), *Lloyd George, Twelve Essays*, (Hamish Hamilton, London, 1971).

Taylor, S.J., *The Great Outsiders: Northcliffe, Rothermere and the Daily Mail*, (Weidenfeld & Nicolson, London, 1996).

Times, The, *The History of The Times*, (The office of *The Times*, London, 1952).

Townshend, Charles, *The British Campaign in Ireland, 1919–1921*, (Oxford University Press, Oxford, 1975).

– *Britain's Civil Wars*, (Faber and Faber, London, 1986).

– *Political Violence in Ireland*, (Oxford University Press, Oxford, 1983).

Travers, Pauric, *Settlements and Divisions: Ireland 1870–1922*, (Helicon, Dublin, 1988).

Valiulis, Maryann, *Portrait of a Revolutionary*, (Irish Academic Press, Dublin, 1992).

Vaughan, W.E., & Fitzpatrick, A.J., *Irish Historical Statistics*, (Royal Irish Academy, Dublin, 1978).

Walsh, Maurice, 'Foreign Correspondents and the Irish Revolution', (Unpublished PhD Thesis, Goldsmiths College, 2006).

Wheeler-Bennett, *John Anderson, Viscount Waverley*, (Macmillan, New York, 1962).

White, Gerry & O'Shea, Brendan, *The Burning of Cork*, (Mercier Press, Cork, 2006).

Wickham Steed, Henry, *Through Thirty Years*, 1892–1922, (William Heinemann, London, 1924).

Wilkinson, Burke, *Zeal of the Convert*, (Colin Smythe Ltd, Gerard's Cross, 1976).

Wilson, Trevor (Ed), *The Political Diaries of C.P. Scott*, (Collins, London, 1970).

INDEX

236

Index

Bloody Sunday, 1920, 18, 38, 40–1,
   113, 126, 141
  in *Freeman's Journal*, 92–3
  funerals, 64
  in *Times*, 158
Blythe, Ernest, 50
Bolshevism, 63–4
Bonar Law, Andrew, 89, 97, 111,
   167
Borgonovo, John, 68
Boyce, D. George, 1, 22, 37, 89
boycotts, 6
Boyd, Donald, 74
Boyd, Mr, 74
Breen, Dan, 66–7, 76–7, 105, 110
Brennan, Robert, 44, 46, 48
Briollay, Sylvain, 7, 45–6, 69, 70,
   169
Britain, 35, 72, 98, 177
  Barry execution, 66
  and France, 45, 46
  journalists from, 69, 70
  press and government, 167–8
  propaganda by, 43–4
  reactions to coercion, 62, 96,
     128, 142, 147, 154, 171–2,
     176–8
  relations with USA, 148–9, 158,
     160–1, 162, 165, 172
  SF propaganda in, 54, 56, 64, 74
British Army, 19. *see also* reprisals
  ambushes, 65–6, 80
  assault claims, 50
  comparisons with IRA, 168
  criticisms of, 174–5
  deaths, 96, 102, 140
  fish-barrel raid, 36–7
  intimidation of newspapers,
     9–10, 16–19
  murders by, 97
  and PIB, 26–30, 41–2, 168
  Quirke allegations, 93–4
  republican propaganda against,

   43–75
British Government, 1, 3, 43
  Bolshevism fears, 63–4
  criticisms of, 15, 42, 105,
    110–12, 119, 121, 126–7,
    131, 142, 151–3, 164
  and propaganda, 2, 37–8
  Truce talks, 71, 99–100, 130,
    139
Brixton Prison, 32, 124, 158
Brown, Captain C.P., 27
Broy, Ned, 59
Brugha, Cathal, 6, 55–6, 62, 63, 102
Bureau of Military History, 104
Burke, Edmund, 83
Burton, Mr, 100
Butt, Isaac, 119
Buttevant, County Cork, 14
Byrne, Dr Louis, 94
Byrne, Seán, 120

Canada, 94
Carroll, Kitty, 61, 62
Carson, Edward, 81, 97, 121, 140
  criticisms of, 124
  and partition, 106, 111, 134,
    146, 173
  and *Times*, 150–1, 152, 155
Casey, Patrick, 129
Cashel, Archbishop of, 69
Catholic Herald, 10
Catholic Hierarchy, 77, 106, 125,
   135, 141
Cecil, Lord, 129
censorship, 3, 42, 43, 57, 91, 103,
   166, 174, 178
  DORA, 5–12
  and *Freeman's Journal*, 77
  Martial Law, 127, 128–9
  ROIA, 12–14
Childers, Erskine, 61, 62
  and de Valera, 72
  funds, 63

237

Index